EGYPT
BEYOND
TAHRIR SQUARE

EGYPT
BEYOND
TAHRIR SQUARE

Edited by
Bessma Momani
and **Eid Mohamed**

INDIANA UNIVERSITY PRESS
Bloomington and Indianapolis

This book is a publication of

Indiana University Press
Office of Scholarly Publishing
Herman B Wells Library 350
1320 East 10th Street
Bloomington, Indiana 47405 USA

iupress.indiana.edu

Manufactured in the United States of America

Library of Congress Cataloging-in-Publication Data

Names: Momani, Bessma, editor. | Mohamed, Eid, editor.
Title: Egypt beyond Tahrir Square / edited by Bessma Momani
    and Eid Mohamed.
Description: Bloomington : Indiana University Press, 2016. |
    Includes bibliographical references and index.
Identifiers: LCCN 2016024307 (print) | LCCN 2016040104 (ebook) |
    ISBN 9780253022837 (cloth : alk. paper) | ISBN 9780253023100
    (pbk. : alk. paper) | ISBN 9780253023315 (ebook)
Subjects: LCSH: Arab Spring, 2010- | Egypt—History—Protests,
    2011- | Revolutions—Egypt—History—21st century. |
    Egypt—History.
Classification: LCC DT107.88 .E346 2016 (print) | LCC DT107.88
    (ebook) | DDC 962.05/6—dc23
LC record available at https://lccn.loc.gov/2016024307

1   2   3   4   5   21   20   19   18   17   16

Contents

Acknowledgments

THERE ARE SEVERAL people whom we would like to thank for their work, time, and hospitality. Thanks to the Balsillie School of International Affairs (BSIA) in Waterloo, Ontario, where they hosted our book workshop on May 5 and 6, 2014. We would like to thank the BSIA, especially Tiffany Bradley, John Ravenhill, and Joanne Weston, for providing us with the facilities to hold this workshop and to eventually complete this book with additional funding.

We extend our appreciation to all those who participated in this workshop, our contributing authors as well as participants and discussants, including Mohamed Arafa, David Dewitt, Timothy Donais, Nathan Funk, Hannah R. Gerber, Jasmin Habib, Wael Haddara, Amr Hamzawy, Paul Kingston, Waleed Mahdi, Andrew Thompson, and Renee Worringer.

We would like to thank Indiana University Press, and especially Rebecca Tolen for guiding us through the publication process and for providing us with such helpful feedback throughout the process. Thanks as well to Dee Mortensen and Paige Rasmussen of Indiana University Press.

A special thank you to Elnaz Borandeh and Amanda Sadowski for their work in organizing the book workshop and assisting in preparing chapters. We also thank Busra Hacioglu, Tanzeel Hakak, Reshem Khan, Anna Klimbovskaia, Nick McEwan, and Nadine Thibeh for their assistance. Many thanks to Anton Malkin for his copyediting.

This book has been published with the help of a grant from the International Development Research Council, which was essential to the success of bringing Egyptian scholars together in one room to discuss the book project. Dr. Momani would also like to thank the BSIA for partial funding of book preparation and copyediting.

Drs. Momani and Mohamed would like to thank their respective Egyptian families for their love, support, and patience. The people of Egypt deserve a great nation and this book was written with love for all Egyptians.

EGYPT
BEYOND
TAHRIR SQUARE

Introduction

Bessma Momani and Eid Mohamed

O<small>N JANUARY</small> 25, 2011, the world's eyes were on Egypt's Tahrir Square as millions of people poured into Cairo's city center, demanding "freedom, bread, social justice and human dignity" and defiantly calling for then president Hosni Mubarak to step down. After a successful overthrow of Tunisian longtime autocratic president Zine El Abidine Ben Ali, it seemed as though the entire Arab region would be reshaped by a domino effect of falling Arab dictators. The Egyptian people also felt empowered like never before and believed this would be the moment for real revolutionary change. After camping out in the square for weeks, most Egyptians hoped that through a sheer determination to bring about change, they could uproot and address Egypt's ailing socioeconomic conditions and political institutions. The uprisings in Tahrir soon spread nationwide to cities across Egypt. Mubarak and his notorious police responded violently, with tear gas, batons, and arrests of peaceful demonstrators. On January 28, 2011, the embattled police force collapsed, and army tanks entered the scene to play the role of the popular savior of a revolution. On February 11, 2011, Mubarak relinquished all powers to the military, which, two days later, dissolved parliament and suspended the constitution. In fewer than twenty days, it seemed the authoritarian regime under Mubarak had come to an end. The military's Supreme Council of the Armed Forces (SCAF) rode into power on a wave of popular support as it appeared to usher in a transition toward democracy.

Welcomed by the masses as a caretaker government, the SCAF managed to supervise successful parliamentary and presidential elections. On March 19, 2011, and in the first post-Mubarak vote, Egyptians cast ballots on constitutional amendments sponsored by the military, setting the framework for the transition to democracy, including scheduling the first parliamentary and presidential elections. Islamists backed the amendments as they were eager to hold elections and take advantage of their widespread grassroots support built during the years of repression under Mubarak and his predecessors; in contrast, smaller and newly founded parties had less time to prepare for elections and cried for more time. Many liberal revolutionaries pushed for a "no" vote on the military-written constitutional amendments and argued that a constitution should be written from the bottom up and not rushed. Despite liberals' objections, the constitutional amendments were overwhelmingly approved as people anxiously waited for presidential and parliamentary elections.

In the meantime, the ruling SCAF made plenty of enemies along the way. After churches were sacked and burned in Upper Egypt, peaceful Egyptian protesters, mostly Coptic Christians, called for the dissolution of the SCAF, the resignation of Chairman Field Marshal Mohamed Tantawi, and the dismissal of the governor of Aswan Province. On October 9, 2011, the mainly Coptic protesters were attacked outside the state news and radio building, known as Maspero, by military police that killed dozens. Under pressure from the Coptic protesters and the continued nationwide demonstrations against what was called the "Maspero massacre," the military announced parliamentary elections. Parliamentary elections were held in stages from November 28, 2011, to February 15, 2012, and lead to the victory of Islamist parties. The Muslim Brotherhood, which ran under the banner of the Freedom and Justice Party, won the majority of seats while Salafists, under the banner of the Nour Party, took another quarter of the parliamentary seats. The remaining parliamentary seats went to liberals, leftists, independents, and secular forces. In the Shura Council (consultative council), few voters bothered to cast their ballots, ushering in an Islamist takeover of nearly 90 percent of the seats. The disappointed military, Egypt's SCAF, eventually handed power to the democratically elected Islamist government of the Muslim Brotherhood, and plans for the presidential election were set in motion. On May 23–24, 2012, Egypt witnessed the first round of voting in the presidential elections, with a field of thirteen candidates. The Muslim Brotherhood's Mohammed Morsi and Ahmed Shafiq, the last prime minister under Mubarak, emerged as the top two contenders and would face each other in a runoff. On June 14, 2012, a few days before the second round of voting in the presidential elections, the Supreme Constitutional Court ordered the dissolution of the Islamist-dominated People's Assembly on grounds that a third of its members were elected illegally. The military swiftly closed down the parliament while the presidential elections continued. On June 16–17, 2012, Egyptians voted in the presidential runoff between Morsi and Shafiq. The military issued a "constitutional declaration" giving the SCAF sweeping authority and limiting the powers of the next president. Morsi won the presidential runoff, with 51.7 percent of the vote, and took his oath of office before the Supreme Constitutional Court a day after reading a symbolic oath in Cairo's Tahrir Square, the birthplace of the revolution.

Under Morsi, no new economic or political ideas were brought to the political table. Yet, the Egyptian "deep state" of Mubarak-era cronies prevented change, particularly in the judiciary and elements of the public sector. To make matters worse, Islamists had no real solution to the everyday problems of Egyptians, such as traffic, garbage, lack of effective policing and crime prevention, unemployment, and the sheer chaos that characterized the lives people have long led. Like his predecessors, Morsi tried to court foreign capital, international donors, and international creditors such as the International Monetary Fund. In essence, Morsi's economic policies were business as usual. Undoubtedly Morsi inherited an economic mess and a system rife with corruption that would take more than a year to weed out. Moreover, in the early years after the January 25 protests, Egypt saw its economy tumble, a depreciating exchange rate, a decline in tourism revenue, a growing population with increased demands, and rising debt burdens.

In a bold move, newly elected President Morsi ordered the retirement of the top Mubarak-era leadership of the military SCAF and canceled the military's last constitutional decree, taking back the presidential powers that the generals had granted themselves. The move was seen as a way to curb the military's role in political affairs, but it also gave Morsi the power to legislate unilaterally in the absence of a sitting parliament. Meanwhile, a one-hundred-member constituent assembly, previously created by the dissolved parliament and tasked with writing the postrevolutionary constitution, had continued to work until the members belonging to liberal parties and representatives of Egypt's churches withdrew in late 2012. Those who withdrew from the constituent assembly protested the Islamist-dominated body and voiced their suspicions that Islamists would impose their will on Egyptian society through the constitutional draft. The Mubarak-era appointed judiciary entered the national debate and opposed President Morsi's monopoly on power and authority over the drafting of the new constitution. The stage was now set for a conflict between the presidency and the judiciary, which still held elements of support for the previous regime.

Following the decrees enacted by Morsi, some opposition and revolutionary figures began to characterize him, as well as the brotherhood at large, not just as flawed democrats but as militants, terrorists, and fascists—the old stereotypes of political Islam. Opposition and revolutionary forces were reenergized to protest against the monopolization of power under Morsi and the Islamist-dominated constituent assembly. The constituent assembly approved the 2012 constitution, and it went to a national referendum. Despite liberals and secularists protesting the referendum on the constitution, it was approved amid low voter turnout and increased political apathy.

The military, now lead by General Abdul Fatah el-Sisi, had continued to claim that Morsi and the Islamists were pushing the country toward a civil war. While in power, the Muslim Brotherhood appeared to falter along the way with controversial policies while it also continued to cry foul, claiming that the deep state of the military generals thwarted their efforts to implementing real change every step of the way. Morsi and the brotherhood claimed that there were a number of conspiracies laid out against them. It had become routine for the group's officials to insinuate that an opposition figure had been bought, held bias, or had a "foreign agenda." The visceral debate in Egypt over hidden agendas was at an all-time high as protests against the Morsi government took on a new life. In the summer of 2013, the people returned to Tahrir Square to call for the military's return to power and to end the Muslim Brotherhood's rule under President Morsi. General Sisi claimed that millions came to Tahrir Square to call for the overthrow of Morsi and that he was responding to the desire of the people for political transformation. The technical term for the military's intervention is a *coup*, but for many Egyptians in Tahrir Square this was an attempt to "reset the revolution." After the repression of the Muslim Brotherhood in Rabaa Square, in the middle of Cairo, which led to the death of hundreds and perhaps thousands, Sisi and the military cemented their power over the political organs of the state once more and the SCAF was back in charge of Egypt. As one of its first political moves, the military rewrote the constitution in January 2014 to block religious parties from participating in politics and to strengthen the military's budget and powers.

In May 2014, a highly controversial election was held that saw that General Sisi was sworn in as a "civilian president." Meanwhile, the military and Sisi continued to vilify the Muslim Brotherhood and all those who supported it and the deposed president Morsi. The brotherhood refused to accept the outcome of the June 30 protests, organized by Tamarod (Rebellion) against then-president Morsi, denouncing all those who marched against their leader. The Egyptian military was riding on a high of populism and hypernationalist fervor that Egypt had not seen in decades. Since the 2013 coup, the Egyptian airwaves have been filled with anti-brotherhood rhetoric. In the name of protecting the integrity of the Egyptian state, the army promised to "clean the streets" of the brotherhood. Draped in nationalist symbolism and comparing the brotherhood to rodents, the Sisi government has painted all Islamists as an internal security threat with global tentacles that feed off connections and money coming from Turkey, Qatar, and even the United States. It is these fears, created by media, that have been used by some Egyptians to justify the massacre committed against the pro-brotherhood Egyptians during the security force's dispersal of their Rabaa sit-in. Meanwhile, the rise of the Islamic State (ISIS) since 2014 in Sinai has been used by the military to paint all Islamists with one brush. As the military conveniently calls for the destruction of terrorists in Sinai, the Muslim Brotherhood is caught up in the same antiterrorist rhetoric. Throughout the summer of 2015, low-grade violence between the military and Islamist forces overtook Cairo. While the brotherhood cried its innocence, the military effectively tarred violent Islamist forces and the brotherhood with one brush. Morsi and hundreds of members of the brotherhood were convicted of terrorism charges and sentenced to prison and death by the military-backed judiciary.

Egyptians are internalizing contrasting versions of what has happened to their country since Mubarak fell. And with each impassioned telling, reconciliation recedes further into the distance. Islamists and liberals alike attempted to use democratic participation as a means to secure political gains. Meanwhile, detractors of each camp pointed to ways in which the other is in fact "undemocratic." For many analysts and academics, Egypt appears to be on an unpredictable path. Ardent supporters of the military suggest that the Egyptian revolution is continuing and momentum is being built toward democratic change; in contrast, critics, activists, and opposition movements suggest that Egypt has returned to its autocratic path under a new quasi-military-led regime. How do we assess these past few years of rapid and unpredictable change in revolutionary Egypt? Who were the key stakeholders in Egypt's revolutionary moment(s), and what explains their actions and reactions to the tumultuous post-2011 years?

When canvassing the many books written about the Egyptian revolution, we noticed a striking theme: complete disagreement on many aspects of the events, from who the lead protagonists were to what was (not) achieved after several tumultuous years had passed. That, combined with the reality that Egyptian scholars and analysts alike could have such varied perspectives on the future trajectory of their beloved homeland, prompted us to gather an interdisciplinary group of academics and analysts with direct links to Egypt to discuss, share, and articulate the philosophical, political, and legal perspectives on the volatile years after Egypt's January 25 Revolution. To filter out the noise of external analysis coming from Western and Eastern capitals that have strong geostrategic and political interests in the future of Egypt, we sought to gather authors who perceive themselves to be Egyptian.

The contributors to this volume have an "inside" perspective on Egyptian events, with friends and family in Egypt and personal connections to the country; and yet, they all have an "outside" perspective as well, as academics with ties to the transnational world of scholarly debates and communities. A key goal of this book was to get as close as possible to a bottom-up Egyptian reflection—while recognizing the epistemological differences we professionally hold—on how and why the post–January 25, 2011, events discussed in this volume have unfolded. Despite the contributors' common ties to Egypt, we achieved little in the way of a common interpretation of the 2011 "revolution." Indeed, one of the great strengths of this collection of authors is the diversity of their perspectives on Egypt. Our disciplinary boundaries and our different readings of events shape some of these differences of opinion and perspective. We highlight these differences throughout the collection, not just to showcase the variety of views that are held in Egypt itself, but to acknowledge that many of the authors' views on Egypt are deemed to be very personal.

We do not shy away from the reality that for many of the volume's contributors, there are still open wounds, at times emotional and at times intellectual, when speaking about the changes that Egypt has undergone in the few years since the Tahrir Square uprisings. We did not want our contributors to disregard their particular perspectives, which are also being shaped by their professional paradigms. Instead, we see this collection as a conversation among Egyptian scholars and do not pretend that a common narrative is necessary. This of course poses a natural challenge to devising any edited collection. But the scale of the challenge should not prevent us from presenting the wide range of scholarly views that define Egypt's intellectual landscape.

Taking advantage of the opportunity to physically meet in the same room for several days in Waterloo, Canada, in May 2014, the authors of this book had heated debates about some of the most pressing issues facing Egypt today. For instance, our contributors could not (nor should they be forced to) agree on whether Egypt had undergone a revolution, a rebellion, an uprising, or simply a brief democratic moment. These are not just semantics, but rather have powerful connotations about the depth of (potential) change in Egypt. Prior to the fall of communism, academic theory had privileged the notion of armed conflict as a precursor to revolution.[1] Many theorists heralded the relatively nonviolent crumbling of the Soviet empire as a contemporary revolution. Taking this cue, academics may argue that Egypt experienced a contemporary revolution that did not necessitate an armed struggle. If we take Mehran Kamrava's insight[2] that the various groups that usurp the political order to acquire power and authority can lead a revolution, then perhaps Egypt experienced a revolution. This insight is buoyed by the work of Ted Gurr and Jack Goldstone,[3] who have argued that a revolution may not need to be defined by the violent overthrow of an existing regime. Again, theorists taking cues from the relatively nonviolent overthrow of the communist regimes in Eastern Europe point out that these may have not been revolutions per se, but rather elite forms of negotiation and cooperation in the transferring of power from one regime to another.[4]

While the theoretical literature is mixed on whether violence is a necessary component in the definition of a movement as a revolution, there is a relative consensus that the social structure must change in reaction to the movement in order for it to be labeled a revolution. Hence, the ultimate return (or continued stay) of the political order under the Mubarak-era regime leaves further doubts as to whether the events of January 25, 2011, sparked a genuine revolution. Structural transformations can be class based,[5] values based,[6] or involve deep social reforms,[7] but all are equally important precursors to identifying a revolution. The role of the military can be revolutionary, as was the case in the 1952 Free Officers revolt against the Egyptian monarch, but if the military simply assumes power for itself without effecting regime change, it comes to resemble a coup d'état. Theorists who have traced revolutions to forms of mass psychological grievances[8] have often been criticized by fellow political theorists, and yet many Egyptians have self-identified their struggles precisely as such. At the very least, then, we must recognize such explanations as being theoretically valuable in Egypt.

Varied Disciplines, Perspectives, and Narratives

We gathered academic scholars from fields as diverse as law, cultural studies, literature, media studies, political science, and migration studies. We brought together journalists, historians, and education specialists to also join in the discussion. We tried to gather Egyptians who have lived inside the country, as well as those from the growing ranks of the Egyptian diasporas, which constitute an enormous Egyptian brain drain—those who are both living and working in the West. It must be noted that meeting in Canada, as opposed to in Egypt, was mandatory at the time of our workshop to have the kind of fruitful and frank discussions, on such sensitive issues that are reflected in the chapters of this volume. For some of our contributors, discussing these topics in Egypt in 2014 would be an unacceptable risk to them and their families. The political and security climate in Egypt was not conducive to having the kinds of conversations we held as a group, which is itself worthy of note.

In the first 3 chapters, we explore the key issue of whether Egypt truly experienced a revolution. Did the events in Tahrir Square represent the birth of a revolution or were they simply a moment in time, a gathering of millions of people with no clear path to real change? We begin the book with three chapters that take three very different perspectives: literary-historical, philosophical, and political-economic. In chapter 1, Belal Fadl and Maissaa Almustafa revive historical and literary memories of events that have taken place in several societies that have witnessed political revolutions. This chapter compares the development of historical revolutions, including the French and American revolutions, to the revolution of January 25, 2011, in Egypt. While some Egyptians have begun to see the revolution itself as the cause of their suffering, and others have even blamed the January 25 revolutionaries for the destruction of their sense of national stability, Fadl and Almustafa contend that these critics have misplaced their anger, situating it in the moment of turmoil rather than seeing the revolution as part of the usual ebbs and flows of Egypt's political and historical circumstances. Not surprisingly, Fadl and Almustafa hold that the failure of the Muslim Brotherhood to ensure stability and order in the aftermath of the revolution "has even created a kind of nostalgia among many Egyptians for the days of relative calm under Mubarak." The authors find similar themes, views, and arguments across past Egyptian revolutions, including the view that external and conspiracy forces were always at play. They suggest that when analyzing Egypt's January 25 Revolution, we need to privilege the view of the *longue durée* and search for structural changes rather than focusing on particular events.

In chapter 2, Mohammad Fadel also reflects on the literary history of Egypt and compares the January 25 Revolution to successful transitions outside Egypt. He also asks why Egypt's revolution failed to materialize into a full and true democratic consolidation under Morsi and beyond. By putting revolutionaries into three broad categories, Fadel suggests that idealistic revolutionaries held demands that were too pure and argues that they wanted nothing less than a complete transition to an ideal democracy. Their lack of pragmatism ended the revolutionary course of events and ushered in a coup. The revolutionaries made strategic mistakes because they did not pay enough attention to Egypt's institutional, economic, political, and social circumstances. These idealists were generally politically liberal and did not want to compromise. Pitting the military forces against the Islamist-led government, the idealists were able to sway public opinion against the Islamists and force the downfall of the Morsi government. However, Fadel argues that the liberal idealists were unreasonable in their expectations of what could be achieved in the short period of time under Morsi's rule.

In chapter 3, Sahar Aziz concurs with many of the same observations made by Fadel, particularly regarding the judicial, legal, and, most importantly, institutional limitations imposed on Morsi's time in office to achieve substantive changes. Both Aziz and Fadel are most critical about whether Egypt experienced a political revolution in the first place. Aziz reaches beyond the philosophical questions posed by Fadel and argues further that the Morsi government failed to enact any substantive socioeconomic changes because he was stymied by the entrenched political interests that formed the Mubarak regime—namely, Mubarak's deeply rooted patronage network—and because the military effectively used the revolutionary moment to seize power for itself. Both Aziz and Fadel suggest that the military had its own grievances with the Mubarak regime, especially for consolidating too much power in the hands of the presidency and for shifting economic and business interests to the private, neoliberal sector. Aziz examines Egyptians' continued grievances with the unequal distribution of wealth and power and suggests that as these political-economic grievances continue to grow under the firm grip of military rule by President Sisi, Egypt is bound to experience another revolutionary moment. Here Aziz shares some of the views of Fadl and Almustafa, who beseech us to take the *longue durée* view of Egypt's history.

In chapters 4 through 6 we examine the dynamics of political identity and key protagonists of Egypt's revolution. After decades of political repression marked the political sanction and control of political parties and professional syndicates, juxtaposed against social movements that were not co-opted by the autocratic Mubarak regime, the January 25 Revolution unleashed new dynamics of political identity. The role of the Egyptian intellectual, media, religious leaders, youth, elites and state officials were thrust into the limelight. Having unseated the regime, the ways in which these actors negotiated with new political powers and the ways they portrayed their "struggle" or "narrative" in the context of the revolution(s) to the Egyptian people were in constant flux.

In chapter 4, Shereen Abouelnaga challenges readers to appreciate the role of cultural intellectuals in Egypt's tumultuous years. She argues for a reconsideration of the very definition of the intellectual in Egypt in light of the disrupted and disruptive intersectionality between regime complicity and revolutionary politics. It is in that space between the two that Abouelnaga examines the decline of the intellectual in Egypt, particularly under the decades-long regime of Mubarak. According to Abouelnaga, the precipitous fall in the production of academic research in a country in which fear, repression, and complicity had blunted all real attempts at critical scholarly work leads her to conclude that "none of the definitions of the intellectual advanced by philosophers, critics, or politicians are applicable to the intellectuals who 'ruled' the cultural scene in Egypt prior to the revolution." Echoing the view of other authors in this volume, Abouelnaga argues that it is the interplay between religion and culture that has become a potential site of conflict in identity politics in Egypt. This leads her to call for a reconsideration of the very definition of the intellectual as it is understood in the Egyptian case.

Abouelnega, like Fadl and Almustafa of chapter 1, also uses a historical and literary approach to show how the goals of justice, freedom, and dignity have inspired people to break out into the streets, protesting against those in power and demanding rights for themselves. Abouelnaga, like many other contributors, argues that the path of revolution is not always easy and that revolution is best understood as a process that comes in waves, not through a single, radical—or final—break with the past. Moreover, Abouelnaga agrees with Fadl and Almustafa that the root causes of the social and political crises in Egypt remain present. Indeed, most contributors agree that many of the same conditions that precipitated the revolution on January 25, 2011, were further exacerbated by the Brotherhood's blatant attempts to manipulate the political process, and have contributed markedly to the political and social turmoil in Egypt under the Muslim Brotherhood.

Both chapters 5 and 6 examine the institutional relationship between organized religious movements and the Egyptian state during the years of political revolution and upheaval. Dalia Fahmy's exploration of the Muslim Brotherhood and Mai Mogib Mosad's examination of the Coptic Church both take an institutional approach to understanding the groups' successes and failures in negotiating with the regime and the larger Egyptian society. In both cases, the authors show how these groups, which each pursued the politics of identity in its own way, quietly worked within regime structures to carve out pockets of political power and legal rights within the regime's monopolization of political, legislative, and judicial power. Both chapters trace the rise and fall of religious identity politics in the face of revolutionary upheaval.

In chapter 5, Fahmy illustrates how even with Mubarak's ouster and Morsi's election, a repressive state still managed to absorb the Muslim Brotherhood into its corrupt institutional machinations. She does not excuse the Muslim Brotherhood for its own repressive tactics and tendencies. Rather, she underscores the extent to which the rise of the Muslim Brotherhood has been due to its ability to adapt to the changes brought on by the fall of Mubarak's regime, the political space afforded them by the transitional military rule under the SCAF, and then finally the democratically elected Islamist government of Morsi. Fahmy also shows how the brotherhood's ability to leverage its various ties to the state helped it rise to power, and how, in the end, it managed to overplay its own hand and precipitate its downfall.

Fahmy points out that in Egypt, social movements with set ideological positions, long perceived to be the agents of social and political change, failed to bring about the revolution that they had envisioned, a point that concurs with that of Fadel in chapter 2 regarding the role of liberal idealists. Fahmy breaks down the role of the Muslim Brotherhood in the political dynamics of revolutionary Egypt and, like both Fadel and Aziz, she finds elements of the deep state at work against the Muslim Brotherhood. Fahmy, echoing Aziz's political economy arguments, compares Egyptian society's high expectations of economic revival and reforms with the reality of entrenched business and military elites who continued to thwart the brotherhood's efforts. Fahmy, like Fadel, argues that the rise and fall of the Muslim Brotherhood's power was unpredictable under the circumstances of contemporary Egypt.

Fahmy responds to some of the critiques leveled by Abouelnaga and by Fadl and Almustafa about the complicit failure of the brotherhood to take the reins of power. Fahmy traces the changes and adaptations made by the brotherhood during key political moments, and argues that contrary to the views of others in the book, the brotherhood used ideological moderation as well as a political strategy of inclusion through limited electoral participation to gain political power. Fahmy notes that the Muslim Brotherhood, overextending its reach, ultimately failed because it abandoned some of its traditional political strategies, such as seeking only limited political influence, and thus upset entrenched power interests. This stands in contrast with Fadl and Almustafa's argument that the military's coup resulted from Egyptians' nostalgia for social and political stability.

In chapter 6, Mosad examines the political participation of the Christian community and the Coptic Church prior to and after the Egyptian revolution. Using an approach similar to that of Fahmy, Mosad traces the historical institutional ties formed between the Coptic Church and the autocratic Mubarak regime. The Coptic Church and its pope were treated as a homogeneous Christian bloc, which empowered the Coptic Church under Mubarak's rule. Nevertheless, Christian participation in the revolution that overthrew Mubarak in Tahrir Square was visible and created a striking moment of Egyptian unity. After successfully deposing Mubarak, many Christian Egyptians continued their revolutionary position, but new identity politics influenced the position of many Copts: the rise of political Islamic tendencies and frequent sectarian attacks against Copts destroyed their sense of security and discredited the church as a broker between them under the ruling regime. As the church's political brokerage role no longer ensures their security, Copts have increasingly taken to independent political organization. Mosad takes up the question of the interrelated and complicated rapport between religion and politics in contemporary Egypt. Like Fahmy and other authors in this volume, Mosad undertakes a historical overview in order to contextualize the current events in the modern Egyptian state. Unlike the other contributors, however, Mosad speaks directly to the failure of the Egyptian state to continuously protect Coptic Christians.

Mosad details how unspoken arrangements between the state and the church, in which the Mubarak regime held up the claims of Copts as victims of "religious (Islamic) violence," and which led to the Mubarak regime offering a certain degree of autonomy to church leaders—notably to Pope Shenouda III—can be seen as an outcome of Egypt's long-entrenched and endemically corrupt authoritarian regimes. However, Mosad also points out that the events leading up to and following January 25 have encouraged a nascent political awakening among Coptic youth in that "the unity expressed in overthrowing Mubarak gave Copts a new sense of participation in the rebuilding of Egypt." Moreover, the SCAF's continued lack of interest in the violence perpetrated against Copts by the police and by the Muslim Brotherhood eventually led many Copt youth to challenge existing power structures. Like Fahmy, Mosad argues that the tumultuous years before and after the events in Tahrir Square have reshaped religious identity politics. New narratives of victimization and repression at the hands of the regime in power and the limited societal support for the military's heavy-handed approach to returning stability and order will continue to shape and alter the identity politics of both the Muslim Brotherhood and the Coptic Church. Both Mosad and Aziz indicate that Egypt's youth are still not satisfied with the current Sisi regime, which hints at the possibility for continued calls for change on the part of these groups.

In witnessing and chronicling the Egyptian revolution, Mohamad Hamas Elmasry and Mohammed El-Nawawy examine the political role of Egypt's media in chapter 7. While the chapters on the Muslim Brotherhood and the Coptic Church examine these groups' attempts to preserve or gain privilege within the established political structure, Elmasry and El-Nawawy look at the long-term failures of the media in shaping its own voice. Much like Abouelnaga in chapter 4, the authors of chapter 7 discuss a lack of professionalism in Egypt's media and among its journalists. Whereas both Fahmy and Mosad contextualize events by unearthing the institutional structures of authoritarianism that shaped the political dynamics and interactions of the Muslim Brotherhood and of the Coptic Church with the regime, Elmasry and El-Nawawy see a complicit failure of the Egyptian media to create a professional and oppositional role to authoritarian powers. Whereas Abouelnaga shows more sympathy for the intellectual, Elmasry and El-Nawawy argue that even during periods of relative freedom from the dictates of the authoritarian regime, the press has shown itself unready for the burdens of responsible and impartial reporting, choosing instead to employ practices that the authors at one point call "biased."

Through their comparative analysis of the performances of the Egyptian press during the rule of Mubarak, the SCAF transitional period, and the brief Morsi period, Elmasry and El-Nawawy argue that standards in journalistic practice and education remain sorely absent in Egypt. Journalists in Egyptian media have not cultivated an identity as a fourth estate—an oppositional critic to the powers that be—even during times of a relative freedom of the press. Elmasry and El-Nawawy make their point very clear: in order to pave the way for a full transition to democracy, Egypt's press must be granted a significant degree of independence from the state. This includes independence from media owners whose close ties to various government institutions continue to hamper journalistic professionalism in Egypt.

The final chapters examine the relationship between the Egyptian state and its judiciary, police, and military. The rule of law, or the lack thereof, in Egypt's turbulent transition to democracy both before and after the historic January 25 Revolution is examined in this final section. There has been a great deal of external scholarly focus on constitutional matters, including the independence of the judiciary, freedom of expression, women's and minority rights, freedom of the press, and the separation of powers among the branches of Egypt's government. Our final chapters consider some of the questions and broader concerns raised earlier by both Aziz and Fadel.

In chapter 8, Dina Rashed looks at the relationship between the Egyptian military and the presidency over forty years of republican rule. Using a comparative historical approach, Rashed finds a common pattern of growing presidential frustration with the encroaching power of the military. Like Aziz, Rashed points out that Mubarak shifted economic power away from the military to civilian cronies of his inner political and financial circle. Rashed explains that the Egyptian military supported the eventual overthrow of Mubarak because of the fiscal cuts to its budget. Whereas Aziz argues that the military supported the revolution because the neoliberal cronies surrounding Mubarak were taking economic wealth from the military's industrial complex, Rashed suggests it was the simpler cuts to military expenditures that unearthed the military's resentment of Mubarak. Rashed proposes that Morsi's failures stemmed from not according more economic discretion to the military and from long-standing military suspicions of the Muslim Brotherhood's loyalty to the Egyptian state.

Rashed, unlike others in the volume, suggests that historical experience shows that the Egyptian military does not want to intervene in civil affairs and was quite happy to transfer power to the presidency. The rift between Mubarak and the military had motivated the military to intervene on behalf of the people's demands for a regime overthrow in Tahrir Square. Echoing the findings of Fadel, Rashed explains that the military favored a minimalist or cosmetic overthrow of the regime by removing Mubarak from office while insulating the entire institutional structure that underpinned his regime from the protesters' demands for change. Unlike Fahmy, who emphasizes the interventionist role of the military in the Morsi period of rule, Rashed argues that history shows that Egypt's military prefers minimal intervention in dealing with domestic matters; it prefers to leave those matters for the hated police, which is discussed in the subsequent chapter.

In chapter 9, Hesham Genidy and Justine Salam tackle the role of the police in Egypt's revolution. They note the pervasive use of brutality and rampant corruption in the police force and discuss some of the root causes behind the failure of the institution. The police, subsumed under the hated Ministry of Interior (MoI), came to symbolize everything that was wrong with the Mubarak regime, to the point that officers who simply acted in self-defense were overzealously victimized. Like Aziz, who traces the consolidation of power and authority under the MoI and the police, Genidy and Salam show how the police further securitized prerevolutionary Egypt for Mubarak's gain. The call for the fall of Mubarak often included a call for the police, as an institution, to follow suit. Taking advantage of Genidy's unique position as a former employee of the MoI, the authors challenges the idea that legal reforms could fix Egypt's broken judicial and policing system. They suggest that there is a need for more tangible reforms in the daily procedures and methods of policing.

Police corruption and brutality are an undeniable reality in Egypt, and Genidy and Salam's chapter parallels the descriptions by both Mosad and Fahmy of how state-sanctioned violence incited Egyptians to protest against the country's authoritarian regime. However, as Genidy and Salam demonstrate through descriptions of Genidy's own experiences and through their interviews with former police officers, Egyptian police forces have always been in the difficult and precarious position of upholding the regime's legitimacy, which, as many officers have been cognizant of all along, was simultaneously undermined by the brutal and arbitrary acts they were ordered or incentivized to commit against civilians. It will be difficult, as it was even before Egypt's 2011 revolution, to reform what many Egyptians see as the police's execution of "selective justice" on behalf of Egypt's corrupt leaders, and while they in no way deny this, Genidy and Salam outline various practical initial steps toward effective police reform. Mubarak's rule relied on maintaining a ruthless police state capable of crushing political or social challenges to the regime's power. But by January 28, 2011, the police were defeated across the country and had rapidly retreated. Evidently, army leaders were prepared to sacrifice Mubarak to save the country, but the police had no such luxury of simply switching allegiances, as the institutional underpinnings of the MoI rested with the Mubarak government itself.

Throughout this book, the authors unpack the complicated and multilayered interactions between the people, the state, and entrenched institutions prior to and in the aftermath of the revolution. Ismail Alexandrani and Isaac Friesen wrote our conclusion chapter with these themes in mind. Friesen, as an inside/outside academic with ties to Egypt, spent years in the small town of Beni Suef in Egypt to learn Arabic and teach English, and Alexandrani is a freelance journalist and researcher from Alexandria. Together, they offer important outsider perspectives on the revolution in Tahrir Square. They provide a glimpse into important dynamics that have, true to this volume's title, taken place beyond Tahrir Square.

Friesen and Alexandrani reflect on the book's findings, but also add to them in important ways. The authors conclude the volume by bringing our attention to some of the most important dynamics in Egyptian politics that are often ignored by the international media and even in academic discussions: the role of Egypt's ethnic minorities and of autonomous protest movements in regions and cities beyond Cairo and Tahrir Square. The authors survey environmental activism in the city of Aswan, radicalization in Egypt's North Sinai region, and the significant gains made by the long-marginalized ethnic Nubians—the Fadjiicka and the Matocka (the Kenuz) peoples. The Sinai and Nubian activism serve as important counternarratives to the Tahrir Square story that we often hear. Providing an important juxtaposition to the image of a victorious military leadership in Aziz's chapter, Friesen and Alexandrani's description of the deteriorating security situation in the North Sinai region shows weaknesses in the military's reconsolidation of power after the ouster of President Mubarak. The narrow focus of Nubian activists on securing nationality rights, rather than joining the January 25 movement in demanding systemic change, demonstrates that not all significant political constellations in Egypt were pushing for change.

The book provides a wide range of views on the extraordinary events in Egypt that caught the world's attention. It gives us myriad ways of looking at the causes and outcomes of the mass protests that exploded on January 25, 2011. True to the various authors' intentions, the volume shows us how the daunting complexity of Egyptian politics eluded not only international observers but also the very Egyptians who fought for change in the streets. Our contributors reflected honestly on the nationwide moment of transformation that was embodied by the

Egyptian revolution; naturally, there were both great disagreements and shared views on the way that the post–January 25 events have unfolded. Our goal was to bring their voices to the world in an English-language academic collection and to let them tell their stories from their own perspectives. The book's diversity of views and approaches is a testament to the diversity of Egypt today.

Notes

1. April Carter, *People Power and Political Change: Key Issues and Concepts* (Abingdon, Oxon, UK: Routledge, 2010).
2. Mehran Kamrava, "Causes and Leaders of Revolutions," *Journal of Social, Political, and Economic Studies* 15 (2010): 79–89.
3. Jack A. Goldstone and Ted R. Gurr, *Revolutions of the Late Twentieth Century* (Boulder, CO: Westview, 1991).
4. See Timothy Garton Ash, "1989!," *New York Review of Books*, November 5, 2009.
5. Theda Skocpol, *States and Social Revolutions* (Cambridge: Cambridge University Press, 1979).
6. Samuel Huntington, *Political Order in Changing Societies* (New Haven, CT: Yale University Press, 1968).
7. Anthony Giddens, *Sociology* (Cambridge: Polity, 1989).
8. Goldstone and Gurr, *Revolutions of the Late Twentieth Century*.

1 Egypt's Revolutionary Spirit across Time

Belal Fadl and Maissaa Almustafa

All roads led into the mire in my time.
My tongue betrayed me to the butchers.
There was little I could do. But those in power
Sat safer without me: that was my hope.
So passed my time

Which had been given to me on earth
Our forces were slight. Our goal
Lay far in the distance
It was clearly visible, though I myself
Was unlikely to reach it.
So passed my time
Which had been given to me on earth. . . .

—Bertolt Brecht (1898–1956)

THROUGHOUT MODERN EGYPTIAN history, the goals of justice, freedom, and dignity have inspired people to break out into the streets, protesting against those in power and demanding recognition of their own rights. The path to revolution is not always an easy one. However, with the goal of a better future in mind, many people have been able to continue their fight against repressive regimes. This chapter is an attempt to revive our memories of historical circumstances that have taken place in several societies that have witnessed political revolutions. It then compares the development of these revolutions to the revolution of January 25, 2011, in Egypt. An examination of the political, economic, and social crises in Egyptian history will also demonstrate that the Egyptian population currently faces similar challenges, and that the root causes of these crises remain the same.

Egyptian History Repeats Itself

Even before the emergence of the modern Arab state, the great Arab, Tunisian, and North African philosophical work of Ibn Khaldun in his book the *Muqad-*

dimah ("Introduction or Prolegomena"), written in the fourteenth century, presented concepts that can help to illuminate some of the contemporary political, economic, and social crises in Middle Eastern societies today. According to Ibn Khaldun, "A ruler can achieve power only with the help of his own people. They are his group and his helpers in his enterprise. . . . With the approach of the second stage, the ruler shows himself independent of his people, claims the glory for himself."[1] Ibn Khaldun also explains how rulers can either acquire people's trust or generate anger: "Exaggerated harshness is harmful to royal authority and in most cases causes its destruction. . . . If the ruler continues to keep forceful grip on his subjects, group feeling will be destroyed. If the ruler is mild and overlooking the bad sides of his subject, they will trust him and take refuge with him. They love him heartily and are willing to die for him in battle against his enemies. Everything is then in order in the state."[2] According to Ibn Khaldun, "Injustice brings about the ruin of civilization."[3] He notes how people lose their interest in production when they become subjects of injustice: "Attacks on people's property remove the incentive to acquire and gain property. . . . When people no longer do business in order to make a living, and when they cease all gainful activity, the business of civilization slumps and everything decays."[4] Ibn Khaldun's explanation of the "dynasty's senility" as the last stage of a state's life is still valid and applies to contemporary political experiences. This phase attributes the split of a dynasty to its ruler's arrogance and willingness to maintain his absolute individual authority:

> When royal authority comes into its own and achieves the utmost luxury . . . and when the ruler controls all the glory and has it all for himself, he is too proud to let anyone share in it. . . . He eliminates all claims in this direction by destroying those of his relatives who are possible candidates for his position and whom he suspects. Those who participate with the ruler in this (activity) often fear for their own (safety) and take refuge in remote parts of the realm. . . . The refugee related (to the dynasty) gains control. His power grows continually, while the authority of the dynasty shrinks.[5]

Ibn Khaldun then confirms that when the stage of senility occurs, nothing can stop it: "Senility is a chronic disease that cannot be cured or made to disappear because it is something natural." He interestingly adds, "At the end of a dynasty, there often also appears some power that gives the impression that senility of the dynasty has been made to disappear. It lights up brilliantly just before it is extinguished."[6] Considering the current upheavals in the Middle East, Ibn Khaldun's words are relevant for many of Egypt's past and current politicians, who face political unrest within their respective borders.

Modern Egyptian history witnessed several social and political crises, many of which were linked to state corruption and repression. Many of those crises involved social uprisings and riots. Critical analysis of these uprisings shows that most of their leaders lacked revolutionary vision and the movements failed to result in the improvement of the living conditions among Egyptian people. This section surveys Egyptian analysis of modern revolts to demonstrate how the themes of duplicity and failed leadership predicted revolutionary failure in the past. In his work *The Social Crises in Egypt in the Seventeenth Century*, Naser Ahmad Ibrahim draws a tragic picture of daily life in Egypt from 1678 to 1703. He examines the relationship between malnutrition and epidemic diseases and the economic crises caused by rapid price increases during the period. According to Ibrahim, such crises were not caused by food scarcity throughout Egypt, but rather by pricing policies and market monopolies imposed by wealthy merchants. At the same time, Egyptian rulers did not interfere or assist their people during the hardships of repeated starvation. In fact, research shows that the crises were the result of political and administrative policies adopted by Egyptian rulers, rather than disease or exogenous factors. For example, the illegal multiple taxes imposed on the people by the corrupt governors were high enough to absorb Egyptian farmers' entire annual incomes, leaving them in a severe state of destitution and further damaging their already decaying agricultural infrastructure.[7]

Due to these devastating conditions, four public uprisings occurred when people broke out into the streets of Cairo to protest against inflation. Angry groups attacked shops, looted, and burned warehouses of grain. In studying the nature of the seventeenth-century uprisings and the reasons why they failed to improve the living conditions of average Egyptian people, Ibrahim notes that the main participants were temporary workers, peddlers, beggars, and porters. They were the most marginalized groups in Egyptian society, and the first to become victims in any crisis. Farmers, however, did not join the seventeenth-century riots, as they were engaged in domestic conflicts over water rations. At the time, scholars and religious figures—the educated class in Egypt—were used by the regime to mitigate people's anger and to encourage the mob (as they were considered to be) to obey their rulers as good citizens and good Muslims. Instead of leading the uprisings, the educated were therefore used by authorities to control the people through religious teachings and social customs.[8]

For centuries, the continued lack of vision and the absence of inspired revolutionary leadership were behind the failure of many social uprisings in Egypt. The spirit of the Orabi Revolt (1879–1882) has been an inspiring symbol of success for many generations of Egyptians. However, in his book *Orabi Revolt and the English Occupation*, historian Abdul Rahman Al Rafie claims that the great charismatic leader Ahmed Orabi was defeated by his own arrogance and political inefficiency. Orabi, who was able to attract different classes of Egyptians to his revolutionary cause and gain their trust, was not politically qualified to be the supreme leader of a revolution. He refused to consult his qualified comrades to assist him in leading the country toward victory. In October 1901, Orabi even supported the British occupation in order to return from his exile.[9] Historian Ahmad Amin presents a different perspective of the Orabi Revolt in his book *Reform Leaders in the Modern Era*, in which he talks about the well-known Egyptian reformer Mohamad Abdou (1849–1905). Abdou, who had an ambitious project of reforming Egypt, opposed Orabi's revolution. He believed that Orabi would destroy the reform movement in Egypt and refused to join the revolution, until he realized that it was proving to be an attractive movement for many Egyptians. At that moment, he felt it was not a conflict between parties or leaders; rather, it was a battle between Egypt as a nation and the British-led occupation. He joined the revolution at a later stage, and was eventually imprisoned and exiled.[10]

The Egyptian Revolution of 1919, which was led by the revolutionary figure Saad Zaghlul and other members of the Wafd Party against the British occupation, is another inspiring revolutionary experience in Egyptian history, as it forced British authorities to recognize Egyptian independence in 1922. However, a careful reading of history will show that internal conflicts between revolutionary leaders actually damaged Egyptian national unity, thus allowing British authorities to maintain their forces in the strategic Suez Canal.

In his book The Events of May 1922: *Unknown Chapter of 1919 History*, historian Hamada Mahmoud Ismail discusses how two of the main figures of the revolution, Zaghlul and Adli Yakan, went from being close friends to enemies as they failed to unify the Egyptian people against the British occupational authorities. They both sought to maintain Egyptian unity, but their actions were in opposition to one another. The situation deteriorated as each figure accused and faulted the other in their public speeches, destroying what they had both worked hard to accomplish from the outset of the revolution. British authorities fueled the disagreement between the two leaders so that Egyptians would be perceived as incapable of governing themselves and protecting their own interests.[11]

This 1919 conflict led to a political deadlock, followed by waves of violence among Egyptians. Many national figures attempted to prevent the violence from spreading across the country. For example, Prince Omar Tousan issued a statement reminding Egyptians of their goals of independence and freedom. He argued that they should adopt the principles of civil coexistence, in which parties respect one another and avoid public marginalization and exclusion. Unfortunately, no one listened to Tousan's call for calm, and the conflict between Zaghlul and Yakan continued to divide the nation, creating an environment of tremendous civil unrest. Waves of severe political and economic chaos followed, (mis)leading millions of Egyptians to believe that their struggles were the result of the revolution. In later years, they were ready to accept the abolishment of their parliament and political parties, and were cheering for a military ruler who seemed capable of resolving the turbulent security situation in the country. The people were willing to surrender their freedom for a certain degree of economic and political stability in Egypt.

Western Revolutions: Were There Any Changes?

Egyptian revolutions shared similar characteristics with Western revolutionary movements in places where chaos and unrest were common features. People often lose their confidence or appetite for change due to the economic and political disorders that accompany revolution, becoming disappointed once they realize that changes leading to a better life will not occur overnight. This was the case for many Egyptians who claimed that the January 25 Revolution did not bear fruit to produce a new Egypt. But has there ever been a revolution that was able to produce an entirely new society in a short span of time? History shows that many revolutions were in fact a series of revolutionary movements rather than a single radical step in the direction of change. For example, the French Revolution was a series of revolutionary waves that happened over a long period of time. In his book *Anatomy of Revolution*, Crane Brinton presents an analytical study of the life cycle of a revolution: "We shall regard revolutions . . . as a kind of fever. . . . In the society and during the generation or so before the outbreak of revolution, in the old regime, there will be found signs of the coming disturbance. Rigorously, these sings are not quite symptoms since when the symptoms are fully enough developed, the disease is already present. . . . Then comes a time when the full symptoms disclose themselves, and when we can say the fever of revolution."[12]

Brinton explains that a revolution will subsequently witness a "Reign of Terror" but concludes that, "once the fever is over, and the patient is himself again, [he will] actually be strengthened by the experience, but certainly not wholly made over into a new man." Brinton argues that such processes take place in the social sphere as well, a "parallel [that] goes through to the end, for the societies that undergo the full cycle of revolution are perhaps in some respect the stronger for it, but they [are] by no means entirely remade."[13]

In his book, The Psychology of Revolution, Le Bon notes that during the French Revolution, the revolutionaries were preoccupied with executing the old regime's figures through revolutionary courts controlled by fanatics, while crime prevailed in society in the absence of state institutions. The majority of the French Revolution's leaders were neutral moderates who did not dare to challenge the radicals. Le Bon explains that the determined but narrow-minded radical minority dominated the majority of neutral moderates. He claims that the moderates damaged the revolution alongside the radicals. In fact, the radicals' strength was derived from the moderates' weakness. Le Bon also mentions a third group that was interested in participating in the revolution: an opportunistic group of unemployed lawyers, failed doctors, and retired priests who supported the radicals. Additionally, by examining the fatal conflict between two of the main figures of the French Revolution—Georges Danton and Maximilien Robespierre—Le Bon demonstrates how the damaging revolutionary fanaticism dragged France into chaos and instability. By the end, the French were ready to accept a tyrant like Napoleon as their savior, and he was said to at least have brought prosperity back to France.[14]

The eighteenth-century American Revolution gives another example of the gradual nature of the world's major political revolutions. In his book *Unruly Americans and the Origins of the Constitution*, historian Woody Holton explains how the American people were disappointed by the creators of the Constitution, who were supposed to utilize America's Revolutionary War against the British Empire to create a democracy but did not. Average Americans believed the Constitution was manufactured in order to take power away from states and the people.[15] American historian Howard Zinn describes the bitterness American people felt after their revolution in his book *A People's History of the United States*. Zinn uses the expression "sort of revolution" to describe the events that took place in the United States in the revolutionary period, referring to the long struggle that people went through to achieve rights for the marginalized classes within American society.[16] However, Richard B. Morris also indicates that, at the time, people felt oppressed because the Constitution's statement, "We the people of the United States of America," only referred to white males and therefore excluded natives, African Americans, women, and other marginalized groups. In fact, it is worth noting that during the American Revolution, the slave trade dramatically increased. Politicians and officials worked hard to strengthen policies that led to widespread poverty, as only the elites benefited from the economic gains that followed independence from the British.[17] The elite class also used laws and legal institutions to suppress those who dared to challenge established authorities. Such practices pushed authors like Henry David Thoreau, decades later, to write works of civil disobedience. In his seminal book, *Civil Disobedience*, Thoreau asserted, "It is not desirable to cultivate a respect for the law, so much as for the right. The only obligation which I have a right to assume is to do at any time what I think right. It is truly enough said that a corporation has no conscience; but a corporation of conscientious men is a corporation *with* a conscience. Law never made men a whit more just; and, by means of their respect for it, even the well-disposed are daily made the agents of injustice."[18]

Yet, the American people continued their struggle toward a version of the Constitution that would serve them well as citizens of the United States. Even the great American leader Thomas Jefferson has been quoted as saying, "I hold that a little rebellion now and then is a good thing, and as necessary in the political world as storms in the physical."[19]

Indeed, while revolutions need time to reach their goals and to change people's lives, they can eventually lead to stronger societies Brinton argues that a revolution's ability to produce a stronger society depends on the intensity of the conflict between the moderate and radical revolutionaries. In fact, the result of this internal conflict determines the success or failure of any potential revolution. Brinton examines the four major political revolutions in the Western world: the English Revolution of 1640, the French Revolution, the American Revolution, and the Russian Revolution of 1917. Brinton notes that although not all revolutions are identical, they all go through a similar cycle. At the beginning, revolutionaries act as one organized and united group, but as they gain more support and influence, internal dissent grows, betraying the lack of cohesive vision. The brief "honeymoon" period follows the fall of the old regime and lasts until the "contradictory elements" among the victorious revolutionaries surface. The first stage of revolution produces a "legal" government of moderates who compete against a radical "illegal" power, thus creating what Brinton refers to as "dual sovereignty." The revolutions discussed by Brinton demonstrate how radicals attacked moderates by accusing them of attempting to bring about an end to the revolution. Moderates became weaker as they lost the people's trust and, rather than focusing on their duties as a new government, they defended their position. They were thus dragged into a fatal but inevitable conflict.[20]

With the exception of the American Revolution, in Brinton's examples of revolutions, radical groups, who were usually aided by a fanatical group of followers devoted to their cause, defeated moderates. Moreover, the small numbers of radicals gave them "the ability to move swiftly, to make clear and final decisions, to push through to a goal without regard for injured human dispositions." Radicals then governed through authoritarian rule, dissociated themselves from the people, and devised slogans against the previous regime.[21]

In order to preserve the continuity of any revolution, it is essential to refresh people's memories about the injustices that spurred the revolution in the first place. Successful revolutions are those that channel people's anger toward change. If the anger becomes the end rather than the means, however, revolutionaries will lose their vision and will fail to determine the priorities of the revolution. To mitigate this risk, everyone, including leaders, must act responsibly and ensure the development of the revolution's distinct cause, remembering that overthrowing a dictator does not mean defeating the regime. As Gene Sharp explains in his book *From Dictatorship to Democracy,*

> Since 1980 dictatorships have collapsed before the predominantly nonviolent defiance of people in Estonia, Latvia, and Lithuania, Poland, East Germany, Czechoslovakia and Slovenia, Madagascar, Mali, Bolivia, and the Philippines. . . . The collapse of dictatorships in the above named countries certainly has not erased all other problems in those societies: poverty, crime, bureaucratic in-

efficiency, and environmental destruction are often the legacy of brutal regimes. However, the downfall of these dictatorships has minimally lifted much of the suffering of the victims of oppression, and has opened the way for the rebuilding of these societies with greater political democracy, personal liberties, and social justice.[22]

The January 25 Revolution in Egypt

The January 25 Revolution in Egypt encountered many of the dilemmas that other revolutionary movements had experienced. After successfully overthrowing the old regime in 2011, revolutionaries attempted to produce a new leadership that could lead Egypt toward achieving the peaceful exchange of power; building a functional, democratic parliament; and abolishing the absolute authority of an authoritarian ruler. The young leaders of the revolution faced the challenge of stepping into the realm of politics for the first time and had to act as professional politicians immediately after overthrowing Hosni Mubarak. They were in a race against time to gain the trust of the people.

Many Egyptians claim that the January 25 Revolution was an external conspiracy against Egyptian national security and economic stability. However, throughout history Egyptian revolutions have typically been the subject of conspiracy theories. In his memoirs, the Azharite scholar Abdul Wahab Al Najjar describes how British occupation authorities claimed that the Egyptian Revolution of 1919 was a German conspiracy against Britain.[23] They falsely accused Germany and the Turkish Union of funding and supporting the revolutionaries. Western revolutions have also been accused of being conspiracies of a small group of elites to usurp power. Brinton explains how the French Revolution was called the "Masonic Conspiracy," while many Russians still believe that the Russian Revolution of 1917 was arranged by a ruthless minority of Bolsheviks to achieve their own political gains. A popular British conspiracy also surfaced following the American Revolution to discredit its aims.[24]

While many Egyptians believed in the idea of "constitution first," many claimed that the January 25 Revolution failed, as it did not lead to the drafting of a new constitution after the overthrow of Mubarak. However, given the political and social unrest that emerged in Egypt after the events of January 25, and which is in fact still present, no constitution can credibly promise success. At this critical phase, new leaders should prioritize their goals in a way that can lead to building the social foundations for democracy and freedom. After overthrowing the Mubarak regime, Egyptians struggled with a new kind of oppression: that created by the Muslim Brotherhood. From the beginning of the January 25 revolution, the brotherhood did not share the dreams of the people for social justice and human dignity. The brotherhood joined the revolution at a later stage, with aims of replacing the old, corrupt regime. In spite of the fact that the January 25 revolution offered it the chance to operate naturally in Egyptian society, the Muslim Brotherhood proved that it was only interested in seizing power. The brotherhood failed to lead Egypt through its postrevolutionary turmoil and refused to cooperate with other political parties. It destroyed all possibilities for collaborative work with other national elements of Egyptian society and ignored the fact that its legitimacy as an elected authority could only be protected if it represented the interests of all Egyptians.

According to Sharp, "Authority is perceived as legitimacy."[25] Authority allows a person or institution to be accepted as superior in one way or another. Individuals or institutions with authority are seen to have the right to command and be obeyed or followed. Governments cannot successfully continue to hold power without acquiring people's consent or approval. If such consent is lost, immediate and radical reforms should be adopted by the regime to regain its legitimacy. The Muslim Brotherhood leaders, including its elected president Mohammed Morsi, could have saved Egypt from the political and social turmoil that followed the ouster of Mubarak. It was possible, at the time, to call for early presidential elections, followed by parliamentary elections under the supervision of a transnational but neutral government—a process that would have required the brotherhood to be held accountable for its actions. But Morsi and his followers were obsessed with attaining political power and opted to sacrifice Egyptian security in the pursuit of it.

Still, the mistakes made by the Muslim Brotherhood, either when they were in power or before, do not justify the current actions being taken against it. The systematic repression of the party and the attempts to incriminate all its members will only repeat the mistakes of the past. In fact, such practices threaten national unity. Mahmoud Al Nukrashi had tried to outlaw the Muslim Brotherhood in 1948, seizing its assets and incarcerating its members, yet this did not end the movement; the brotherhood merely continued to operate as an illegal underground organization. The long years of prohibition did not weaken the group. In fact, if Al Nukrashi had chosen to bring the members of the Muslim Brotherhood to a fair trial—to expose their crimes to the public—he could have saved his life and the lives of countless other Egyptians. Instead, he was assassinated by the brotherhood after the ban was implemented.

Muslim Brotherhood leaders should be prosecuted for their crimes through fair trials that guarantee their legal rights. Such trials will assist in restoring the reputation of the Egyptian legal institutions and help rebuild the credibility of the state. Egyptians, who refused the old regime for its dictatorial practices, should not adopt those practices against other Egyptians in order to maintain peace and security. The revolution is not a cleansing movement; rather, it is a step toward a free and democratic Egypt, where people accept each other regardless of their beliefs by working together to achieve the goals of justice, freedom, and dignity.

The Muslim Brotherhood's failure to ensure peace and order has even created a kind of nostalgia among many Egyptians for the days of relative calm under Mubarak. Some have gone even further by accusing the revolutionaries of destroying national peace. Such groups are misled by the belief that their suffering is the product of the revolution. Unfortunately, far too many were ready to surrender their freedom and civil rights, even welcoming acts of repression against other Egyptians, in exchange for an end to the chaos and unrest that is currently a fact of life in Egypt. Simply put, people are unaware of the fact that they are just forcing history to repeat itself.

Where Are We Now?

Today, millions of Egyptians have become hostages of an open conflict between a blind and bloody terrorism that is consolidating and legalizing tyranny and an incompetent, reckless government that is deepening the roots of terrorism by killing the political process and oppressing freedom while using media informants to depict humans as exasperating beasts. President Abdul Fatah el-Sisi's efforts in promoting himself to the Western world as a leader of the Egyptian enlightenment and of religious reform are farcical. The repetitive Mubarak logic of "It's either me or terrorism" has become unsatisfactory for Sisi. A new model of governance with exciting headlines that is being presented to a Western audience abroad obscures the reality of unlawful detention and beheadings. Sisi's rule is transforming Egypt into a police state based on the rule of God and his messenger, the Prophet Muhammad. This is being reflected in the religious overtones of his speeches, and in the use of Al-Azhar and the Salafists to legalize the killing and oppression of his opponents. Sisi continues to refuse to make freedom of religion a legal and constitutional reality. What Sisi and his government do not realize is that social fear and hysteria cannot be transformed into a positive vision of a new society. Hysteria produces distorted human tendencies that resemble fire: it will consume itself if it cannot find anything else to consume. It also provides strong hysterical justification to its victims, especially when left with nothing else to lose, and society enters a bloody cycle in which the language of logic and the mind are no longer feasible. Time reveals that it is impossible to resolve political differences with violence and oppression; society will eventually come to realize that it has paid the ultimate price that it has lost time and blood and produced countless victims, persuaded by emotional speeches filled with lies. Egyptian society needs anything but hysteria to dig itself out of this mess.

Religious terrorism leads to explosions of anger among regular civilians; anger is spread by the failure of authorities to stem it. In this context, anger begets violence, causing more bloodshed as people forget that the conditions that provide solidarity no longer exist. Sisi's jurisdiction, security and the media, should bravely carry the responsibility of the sins committed. Sisi should do this not only for the sake of saving the country, but also for the sake of saving himself from a fate that will marginalize everyone.

Freedom of thought and doctrine is linked to a general freedom of speech within an open political environment where people realize their own faults by experience rather than by killing opponents and oppressing and persecuting those who carry unpopular thoughts and doctrines. If one contemplates the disastrous conditions of our region, one can understand the emergent extremism and the multilayered roots and causes of its existence and fast spread. In a place where the oppression and suppression of basic freedoms are practiced with repetitive "national interest" rhetoric, many Egyptians are in agreement, motivated by hatred toward the Muslim Brotherhood and all thoughts and behavior that accompany it. Others become seduced by power and perpetuate a rhetoric no less oppressive and violent than the one espoused by the religious extremism that they adamantly oppose. As a result, a deepened and frightening social gap emerges and increases. However, one must realize that ignoring the fact that such armed forces will never be able to wipe out existing thoughts, no matter how much hatred one carries for such thoughts, and ignoring political conflicts that perpetuate such tyranny, is only going to produce a stronger and more idiotic terrorism that will ensure increasing blood and tears.

Notes

1. Ibn Khaldun, *The Muqaddimah: An Introduction to History*, Bollingen Series (Princeton, NJ: Princeton University Press, 1967), 146.

2. Ibid., 153.

3. Ibid., 238.

4. Ibid.

5. Ibid., 336.

6. Ibid., 245.

7. Naser Ahmad Ibrahim, *The Social Crises in Egypt in the Seventeenth Century* (Cairo: Dar Al Affaq Al Arabia, 1998).

8. Ibid.

9. Abdul Rahman Al Rafie, *Orabi Revolt and the English Occupation*, 4th ed. (Cairo: Dar Al Maaref, 1984).

10. Ahmad Amin, *Reform Leaders in the Modern Era* (Cairo: Dar Al Koutoub Al Elmieh, 2012).

11. Hamada Mahmoud Ahmad Ismail, *The Event of May 1922: Unknown Chapter in 1919 Revolution* (Cairo: The General Egyptian Establishment for Books, 1994).

12. Crane Brinton, *Anatomy of Revolution* (New York: Prentice Hall, 1965), 16.

13. Ibid.

14. Gustave Le Bon, *The Psychology of Revolution* (New York: Dover Publications, 1913).

15. Woody Holton, *Unruly Americans and the Origins of the Constitution* (New York: Hill and Wang, 2008).

16. Howard Zinn et al., *A People's History of American Empire* (New York: Metropolitan Books, 2008).

17. Richard B. Morris, *The American Revolution: An Anvil Original* (New York: Van Nostrand, 1956); *The American Revolution Reconsidered* (New York: Harper and Row, 1966).

18. Henry David Thoreau, *Civil Disobedience: Resistance to Civil Government*, part 1 of 3 (1849; repr., Thoreau Reader, 1999), http://www.thoreau.eserver.org/civil.

19. Thomas Jefferson, letter to James Madison. Paris, January 30, 1787, American History, http://www.let.rug.nl/usa/presidents/thomas-jefferson/letters-of-thomas-jefferson/jefl53.php.

20. Crane Brinton, *The Anatomy of Revolution* (New York: W. W. Norton, 1938).

21. Ibid.

22. Gene Sharp, *From Dictatorship to Democracy: A Conceptual Framework for Liberation* (Boston: The Albert Einstein Institution, 2010), 2.

23. Ahmad Zakria Al shalaq, *The Red Days: Memoir of Skeikh Abdul Wahab Al Najjar on 1919 Revolution* (Cairo: Books and National Document Press, 2010).

24. Crane Brinton, *Anatomy of Revolution* (New York: Prentice Hall, 1965).

25. Sharp, *Sharp's Dictionary of Power and Struggle: Language of Civil Resistance in Conflicts* (New York: Oxford University Press, 4).

2 Egyptian Revolutionaries' Unrealistic Expectations

Mohammad Fadel

AFTER EIGHTEEN DAYS of protests, Hosni Mubarak resigned as president of Egypt. Less than three years later, the Egyptian security state apparatus appeared to have reestablished political control of the country. Why did the democratic transition fail? Answers range widely. Some blame the poorly designed transition process, which made trust among different political groups unachievable. Others point to a lack of leadership within Egypt's political organizations, particularly the Muslim Brotherhood. Still others focus on a devastating economic crisis that post-Mubarak governments could never address given the political divisions within the country.

These explanations are plausible and not mutually exclusive. But they all miss something important: the January 25 revolution was also a striking failure of political theory. More precisely, it was a failure of the theories embraced by the most idealistic revolutionaries. Their demands were too pure; they refused to accord any legitimacy to a flawed transition (and what transition is not flawed?), which could only yield a flawed democracy. They made strategic mistakes because they did not pay enough attention to Egypt's institutional, economic, political, and social circumstances. These idealists, generally, were politically liberal. But the problem does not lie in liberalism itself. The problem lies in a faulty understanding of the implications of political liberalism in the Egyptian context—an insufficient appreciation of factors that limited what could reasonably be achieved in the short term. This chapter argues that a more sophisticated liberalism would have accounted for these realities.

Three Revolutionary Forces

Although the masses in Tahrir Square appeared unified on the day Mubarak was ousted, in actuality there were three broad groups vying for power. The first, associated with the military, took a minimalist view: the revolution was simply about removing Mubarak and his cronies from power and ensuring that his son Gamal Mubarak did not succeed him to the presidency. Given this group's desire to preserve as much as possible of Mubarak's order (without Mubarak), it was able to reconcile with old-regime elements. Moreover, although this first group originally lacked a distinctive ideology, it eventually adopted a nationalist, sometimes even xenophobic, posture that distinguished it from the cosmopolitanism of Islamist, liberal, and socialist revolutionaries.

According to the second group, the revolution aimed at broad reforms of the Egyptian state without uprooting it entirely. For this reformist group, the crisis stemmed from corruption. Mubarak, they argued, had undermined the state's integrity by usurping its institutions to fulfill his and his allies' personal and political ends. The revolution needed to reform the state's institutions so that they would meet the formal requirements of a legal order and be accountable to the public will. Formal democracy was a crucial demand of this group because it was seen as the only way to ensure that the state would not again be hijacked in order to further the interests of a narrow group of Egyptian elites. The Muslim Brotherhood and its allies belonged to this second group.

The third group, composed largely of young Egyptians, understood the revolution as an attempt to fundamentally restructure state and society. The revolution provided an opportunity to create a virtuous state. Doing so would, however, require a complete rupture with the ancien régime. This radical group had an ambivalent relationship with formal democracy. Thus, although elections were desirable, the most important goal was the substantive transformation of the state and society: "revolutionary legitimacy" trumped whatever legitimacy formal representative democracy could provide.

The degree of public support enjoyed by each of these three groups remains uncertain. No one disputes that the youth, the third group, served as the revolutionary vanguard, having planned and executed the antiregime demonstrations on January 25. The Muslim Brotherhood joined later, and the military, for obvious reasons, was the last to take up the banner.

Egypt's most idealistic revolutionaries did not understand the implications of political liberalism. Still, one should not exclude the military from the revolutionary coalition. The protesters at Tahrir welcomed the military, which they believed to be more sympathetic to their cause than the detested police. Demonstrators treated the military as a legitimate authority.[1] For example, when protesters caught agent provocateurs working for the regime, the latter were turned over to the military.

Other actions also underscored the willingness of Tahrir revolutionaries to recognize the continued legitimacy of at least some parts of the old order. For example, prominent liberal lawyers within the revolutionary camp continued to abide by the constitution that Mubarak had put in place in the waning years of his presidency. This constitution included a series of amendments, adopted in

spite of gross procedural irregularities that were intended to ensure his son's succession. During the revolution, one liberal lawyer even published an appeal to
Mubarak in the *Washington Post* demanding that he perform the formal steps
required for a legal transition.[2]

More restrained interpretations of the revolution continue to have strong
support among Egyptians even after Mubarak's resignation. Subsequent elections
have confirmed this. In the March 19 referendum, voters favored a quick transition and rejected radicals' appeals to complete a draft constitution before selecting
a new government. In the subsequent parliamentary elections, Islamist-affiliated
parties won almost 70 percent of the seats, while postrevolutionary liberal parties took only 10 percent. And in the presidential elections of 2012, with Mohamed ElBaradei withdrawn from the race, the liberals could not even field a
candidate. The top two vote-getters in the first round, Ahmed Shafiq, Mubarak's
last prime minister, and Mohammed Morsi, of the Muslim Brotherhood, were affiliated, respectively, with the minimalist and reformist camps.

Whatever else can be said about the political preferences of Egyptians as revealed by their postrevolutionary voting patterns, elections demonstrated that a
successful and peaceful democratic transition would require a coalition of mini-
malists, reformists, and radicals. In other words, each of the three groups would
have to accommodate the other two.

The Challenge of Pluralism

Accommodations are hardly unusual in societies emerging from a long period
of authoritarian rule. Consider Chile, where General Augusto Pinochet was
granted immunity in the aftermath of his bloody regime. All over Latin America, citizens accepted a substantial continuing role for free market economics,
even though it had been a commonplace feature of dictatorships in the region.[3]
Successful democratic transition inevitably requires some degree of compromise with old ways.

The challenge Egyptians faced throughout the transition was to build an inclusive polity in the face of their deep divisions. They could resolve these divisions
either by suppressing disagreements through a forceful exercise of state power, or
by competing at the ballot box. The first strategy requires massive state violence
in the short term and almost always leads to suspension of formal democracy,
without any guarantee of a return to democracy in the medium or long term.[4] The
second strategy involves less force, establishes at least the formal elements of
democratic rule, and preserves the possibility of additional democratic gains in the
future, even if it requires concessions to undemocratic or illiberal political groups
in the present and is marked occasionally by episodes of political violence.[5]

Both liberal and Islamic political theories endorse the second option. Traditional Islamic political theory prioritizes social peace in circumstances where achieving a more ideal polity would require widespread violence. Preserving social peace is also a crucial moral value of such political thinkers as Thomas Hobbes and John Rawls.[6] These theories applied in Egypt: a formally democratic regime that allowed for fair and nonviolent competition over political office was the only means of including all three of Egypt's political forces, and thus the most likely way to preserve social peace. Any attempt to suppress one of the three groups, on the other hand, would contradict this fundamental moral precept and would launch the country into civil war, or else result in the imposition of emergency law. Both outcomes would preclude meaningful politics.

From a Rawlsian perspective, Egypt's divisions meant that social peace could only be achieved through a constitution that established a temporary agreement among the parties. Such a constitution could do no more than guarantee formally democratic procedures of governance. It could not satisfy the requirements of justice, since it would be grounded in a particular balance of social power rather than an overlapping consensus on a shared conception of justice. Nevertheless, such a constitution, in Rawls's view, is usually a necessary step toward the establishment of a just, well-ordered society.[7]

The fourteenth-century Arab Muslim political thinker Ibn Khaldun's tripartite typology of regimes—natural, rational, and Islamic—is consistent, in broad terms, with Rawls's analysis.[8] Natural states are based on relations of domination between the ruler and the ruled, restrained only by the limitations of the ruler's actual power. Rational and Islamic states, by contrast, impose moral restraints on the exercise of political power. According to Ibn Khaldun, rational and Islamic regimes transcend the relations of the domination characteristic of natural regimes and establish overlapping conceptions of the common secular good. Ibn Khaldun's rational and Islamic regimes can both foster the convergence in political morality that, like Rawls's overlapping consensus, characterizes a just constitution. Critically, this convergence or consensus must occur organically. Ibn Khaldun argued that coerced adherence to Islamic law fails to produce virtuous subjects. Likewise, coerced imposition of even a just constitution cannot produce an effective system of justice if large numbers of citizens are incapable of freely adhering to its terms.[9]

Although procedural democracy by itself did not promise the Egyptian radicals the substantive changes they hoped for in the short term, it did offer the possibility of social peace and an opportunity to generate, over time, a broader consensus on the fundamental questions of how to establish a just and effective state worthy of citizens' voluntary allegiance. It also offered the foundation of a more liberal political order.

Morsi's Constitutional Declaration

The most powerful postrevolutionary political actors in Egypt accepted a pragmatic option: they rejected radicalism and endorsed procedural democracy. In November 2012, when Morsi moved to insulate his decisions and the content of the 2012 constitution from judicial review, he was following the pragmatic course. Proponents of a liberal constitution objected, but their aims were not achievable without further political strife.

Most commentary points to Morsi's November 2012 declaration as the final blow to the Muslim Brotherhood's relationship with the liberal and radical revolutionaries, effectively setting in motion the events that led to the July 2013 coup. Morsi was hardly the first Egyptian politician to issue such a decree. The military had used constitutional declarations regularly throughout the transition process in order to ensure that a formal legal order would remain in place. Morsi's goal was not outlandish either. He intended to prevent the judiciary from interfering with the constitutional drafting process so that a text could be completed in accordance with the provisions of the transitional road map, which had been approved by the March 2011 referendum. The radicals, however, interpreted Morsi's decree as an intolerable assault on democracy, which confirmed their suspicions that Morsi and the Muslim Brotherhood were attempting to create a new kind of authoritarian state.[10]

Yet, the real issue was the makeup of the constituent assembly and the substance of the constitution it would draft. The parties eventually arrived at a deal, including the semi-presidential structure of the state (with executive power shared by a prime minister and a popularly elected president), but the role of religion remained a point of contention. Because parliament had selected the members of the constituent assembly, and because Islamists had won the majority of seats in parliament, Islamists dominated the constituent assembly. Liberals argued, not unreasonably, that those parliamentary elections exaggerated Islamists' long-term political strength. Liberals also thought that the draft sacrificed or limited too many personal rights and freedoms in the name of religion, morality, and family values. They argued that the constitution would not be legitimate unless it was a consensual document capable of gaining acceptance by all significant social groups in Egypt.[11]

The individual-rights provisions of the constitution were clearly deficient from the perspective of international human rights law. In particular, the attempt to limit personal rights in the name of respect for traditional religious values does not comport with wider commitments to liberty. Liberal dissidents, however, never faced up to the reality that Egypt is divided on these personal rights. Should the state underwrite freedom of expression even if that enables blasphemy and apostasy? Should gender equality override religious rules, Christian or Muslim, particularly in the context of family law? Given that so many Egyptians disagree with the liberal position on these matters, it is difficult to understand what the demand for a consensual constitution recognizing personal rights could have meant in practical terms. The argument that the constituent assembly unreasonably exaggerated the strength of Islamist parties was plausible, but even granting this point, any democratic process would have placed a significant block of Islamists in the constituent assembly. As a result, there was no democratic path for liberals to establish a constitution that secured the personal rights and freedoms they sought.

By the time Morsi issued his November 2012 declaration, constitutional deliberations had effectively ground to a halt. From Morsi's perspective, the declaration was the only means available to prevent the Supreme Constitutional Court from dissolving the constituent assembly. He had reasonable grounds to worry that the court was prepared to intervene. A case demanding dissolution was pending, and the court had already issued two rulings that interfered in the democratic transition: the first disbanding Egypt's first freely elected parliament since 1952, the second overturning a law that attempted to bar old-regime elements, such as Shafiq, from running for the presidency. The dissidents' boycott of the constituent assembly's deliberations was a not-so-subtle sign to the court that, as far as they were concerned, its intervention would be welcome. In light of the court's opposition and the fast-approaching deadline for completion of the draft constitution, Morsi felt he had no choice but to cut the court out.

There is little doubt that Morsi, as the democratically elected president, was the more legitimate arbiter of this dispute. The court is not democratically accountable, and the draft constitution could not come into effect unless it won approval in a popular referendum. While one might disagree with Morsi's methods, it is reasonable to conclude that he acted in accordance with his responsibilities as the only democratically accountable official in the country. To describe his actions as a "naked power grab," as ElBaradei suggested at the time,[12] requires a presumption of bad faith inconsistent with democratic commitments. The radicals' violent opposition to the November declaration would only have been justified if the constitution Morsi acted to protect failed to promote a pluralistic and inclusive political system. This was not the case: the 2012 constitution provided a more open political system than had prevailed prior to the revolution. It increased formal political rights, reduced the power of the president, and increased the power of the prime minister and parliament.[13]

These were meaningful changes. For the first time, anyone could form a political party or publish in print without the prospect of government censorship. By contrast, during the Mubarak era, the formation of political parties required the state's approval, thereby ensuring that no party capable of challenging the ruling National Democratic Party could develop. Under the new constitution, the president would also be limited to serving two terms, would face stricter rules on declaring states of emergency, and would no longer be able to dismiss the prime minister. Parliament was newly empowered to withdraw confidence from the government, and the president would be required to select the prime minister from the largest party in parliament.

The new constitution also boosted the capacity of the political branches by leaving open the content of many rights. Limitations on personal rights could only become operational upon the passage of positive law. The same was true of the provision contemplating military trials for civilians: Egypt's future governments had the power to reduce the jurisdiction of military courts or to eliminate it through legislation. And though the constitution did not recognize a universal right to religious exercise—protection is limited to followers of the three Abrahamic religions—it did not prevent the state from doing so in the future by statute.

This structure reduced the influence of the courts—in particular the Supreme Constitutional Court—by vesting the power to define rights in the political branches. This was a reasonable constitutional strategy in a society characterized by sharp division on fundamental personal rights. Indeed, from a Rawlsian perspective, we would expect such a society to adopt a constitution that guarantees only those political rights necessary for democratic participation in lawmaking. The 2012 constitution appeared to accomplish that, leaving the more contentious issues of individual rights to future deliberation. Unlike constitutions of nearby states, such as Morocco, the 2012 constitution did not entrench any provisions, including those on the role of Islam, as supra-constitutional norms impervious to amendment.[14] Nor did it place any substantive, ideological limitations on the formation of secular political parties, provided that they were not organized on a discriminatory basis. It did not impose religious piety or a theological test as condition for public office. This ensured that the constitution would not privilege the Muslim Brotherhood, other Islamist parties, or even the role of Islam itself above other provisions of the constitution.

Democratic Faith

Even in a well-ordered, just society, Rawls argued, a polity may in some cases legitimately restrict the liberty of conscience of the intolerant, but only when there is a "reasonable expectation that not doing so will damage the public order which the government should maintain."[15] While Egypt is not a well-ordered society in Rawls's sense, his principle casts light on how liberals should have reacted to the prospect of a military-led coup against an illiberal elected president and his illiberal political party. Extrapolating from Rawls's treatment of restrictions on liberty of conscience, we might say that preservation of the constitutional order is the only justification for such an intervention. Furthermore, we could conclude that this claim is only legitimate when it is based on objective evidence, widely accessible, demonstrating that the threat to the lawful public order is not "merely possible or in certain cases even probable, but reasonably certain or imminent."[16]

It is hard to conclude that Morsi's conduct as president, however disappointing, crossed this threshold. Many radical revolutionaries justified their support for Morsi's removal not on the grounds that his actions represented an imminent threat to the political order, but rather on the grounds that Morsi did not confront the military and the police with sufficient vigor.[17] In their eyes he thus betrayed the revolution.

It is not clear, however, that Morsi had the power to transform these instruments of oppression in the year he was in office. The security forces were largely immune to Morsi's influence. They refused to protect the offices of the Muslim Brotherhood and its political party, the Freedom and Justice Party. Even businesses affiliated, or thought to be affiliated, with the Muslim Brotherhood could not rely on police or military protection. When the presidential palace was attacked during demonstrations in the wake of Morsi's constitutional decree, the security services were nowhere to be found. For Morsi's opponents, however, his failure to reform the security services was taken not as a sign of his weakness, but as evidence that he and the Muslim Brotherhood were conspiring with the military and police to destroy the liberal and radical opposition.[18]

Even less plausible than fears of a secret alliance between the Muslim Brotherhood and the security services was Egyptian liberals' belief that, in acting against Morsi, the military would promote democracy rather than restore the security state.[19] Even if liberals were right about Morsi's and the Muslim Brotherhood's intentions, the only rational democratic strategy would have been to insist on parliamentary elections. There were at least three routes to such an outcome. If the opposition were able to win a two-thirds majority in upcoming parliamentary elections—which should have been easy if its claims about the universal unpopularity of the Muslim Brotherhood were true—it could have impeached Morsi. If Morsi were found guilty at trial, he would have been removed from office. Even if unsuccessful in removing Morsi, such a strategy would have strengthened the cause of Egyptian democracy. A less dramatic step would have been to use parliament's powers to withdraw confidence and appoint a new government. The final lawful option would have been to defeat Morsi or another Muslim Brotherhood candidate in the 2016 presidential elections.

Instead, the opposition, including radical revolutionaries, demanded early presidential elections. But there were no legal grounds for hastening the election schedule. Military intervention, a strategy that discredited political parties as the representatives of the Egyptian people in favor of the military, police, and other state institutions, was left as the only means to oust Morsi. Thus, Egypt's most ardent democrats, under the banner of "The Revolution Continues," passed on constitutional options in favor of methods that would only advance authoritarianism.

The idealists who halted the democratic experiment failed to understand what democratic theorists have long recognized: that the very conditions that produce democracy—namely, liberty and equality—also produce factionalism, instability, and violence. If clashes are not mediated through some acceptable institutional arrangement, they are likely to be resolved through despotism. This risk was especially palpable in Egypt, given the dominant role that the military and security services have played since 1952.

Citizens in a democracy must accept compromise with political adversaries, meaning that ideologues of every stripe will be disappointed (indeed, strident Islamists criticized Morsi and the Muslim Brotherhood for making too many compromises with secular democrats). The failure to achieve all of one's political goals is the price of democratic politics. The refusal to accept this price may lead to the kind of political disaster we are now witnessing in Egypt. Democracy, though grounded in the values of equality and liberty, is never born in societies perfectly reflecting these values. If these values are realized, it is through the patient practice of democratic politics, even when its substantive outcomes conflict with one's political ideals. A successful democracy emerges gradually, inspired by the fierce, even fanatical, faith in the ability of democracy to improve the people's political virtue over time. Ironically, Egypt's most radical democrats did not have this faith.

Liberal and radical critics of the Muslim Brotherhood failed to realize that the real choice in Egypt was not between an Islamic state and a civil state, but between a state based on some conception of the public good—religious or nonreligious—and one based on pure domination. In accordance with Ibn Khaldun's argument about the relationship between the religious conception of the state and the rational one, there should have been plenty of scope for agreement between religious and secular democratic forces. Tragically, liberals underestimated the people's desire for security and their willingness to submit even to arbitrary and predatory power in order to achieve it. Their extralegal strategies—protests, boycotts, and, finally, military intervention—gravely undermined the prospects that the emerging government would provide this crucial public good, thus opening the door for the return of the security state.

Egypt remains burdened by years of mismanagement and ill-conceived policies that have been destructive for the common good, promoted corruption, and enfeebled the state's nonsecurity functions. Egypt cannot have a stable democracy if it does not overcome this legacy. Repression of the Muslim Brotherhood—the country's most organized political group and one that, at least in principle, supports democratic practices—only puts off the day when Egypt can begin these needed reforms. By advocating military intervention in the political process and, in too many cases, backing a coup against the legitimate government, the liberal and radical opposition have for the time being ruined the conditions for democracy. If the military-installed regime fails to establish political stability, which is a real possibility, Egypt faces the prospect of political chaos and even state failure. This is the price of dogmatism in politics.

After the Coup

This essay, when first written at the start of the 2013 coup, predicted a bleak future for Egypt. Because it is so rare that the prognostications of academics turn out to be correct, they are usually happy to be vindicated when reality squares with their predictions. That is not the case here, however. I would have been delighted had Egypt, contrary to my pessimistic outlook in 2013, proven me wrong and continued on its march toward the democratic future that the January 25 revolution promised. If anything, however, early conclusions were not sufficiently pessimistic. One could not have imagined a scenario in which a former military officer with no significant accomplishment other than leading a military coup and slaughtering hundreds, if not thousands, of his countrymen, would be elected president without facing any meaningful opposition a mere three years after Mubarak had resigned. Nor could one have imagined that the Egyptian judiciary would hand out mass death sentences with a casualness appropriate perhaps for a traffic court proceeding, but certainly not for charges implicating the death penalty. Political repression has gone beyond expectations of this author as well. Unsurprisingly, there have been mass arrests of Muslim Brotherhood members, or those accused of being members of the Muslim Brotherhood. More surprising, however, has been the vigor with which the reconstituted Egyptian security state has pursued non-Islamist political activists such as Ahmad Maher, the leader of the April 6 Movement, who was imprisoned, along with countless others, for violating Egypt's post–June 30 protest law.

Other than the "election" of President Abdul Fatah el-Sisi and the referendum approving amendments to the controversial 2012 constitution, self-government has come to a halt in Egypt. As of mid-2015, Egypt still lacks a parliament, ostensibly because the government has been unable to draft an elections law that satisfies constitutional requirements. The consistent failure to adopt a constitutionally satisfactory elections law, however, in circumstances where the president has a monopoly of lawmaking power, suggests that indifference is at work here, not principled differences on what an adequate system of representation would look like. This suspicion is also confirmed by the seeming complete absence of public demands for parliamentary elections. As suggested in the original essay on which this chapter is based, the June 30 counterrevolution, far from heralding a deepening of Egyptian democracy, has heralded the death of democratic politics and the surrender of the Egyptian people to despotism in the irrational hope that an all-powerful despot could solve the problems that they had shown themselves to be so incapable of dealing with during the short, fifteen-month democratic experiment that drew to an end with the June 30 coup.

One of the commonly heard justifications for the coup was that Egypt was on the cusp of a civil war, and, but for the military intervention, Egypt would have descended into the same kind of internecine war of all against all that has come to plague Syria and Iraq. While it is impossible to know what would have happened to Egypt in the absence of the coup, it is indisputable that armed violence against the state has escalated sharply in the wake of the coup. North Sinai is in the throes of an all-out insurgency, and Sinai-based militants have openly pledged fealty to the self-declared caliphate of the Islamic State (ISIS). The increasing intensity of the Sinai insurgency has cost scores of Egyptian soldiers and police their lives, culminating in the 2015 bold attack on the Sinai town of Shaykh Zuwaid in which countless Egyptian soldiers and police were killed. Sinai-based insurgents have also claimed credit for a myriad of bombings in the Nile valley that have claimed the lives of dozens of security personnel. In a brazen bombing in Cairo, militants successfully detonated a bomb targeting the motorcade of Egypt's prosecutor general, Hisham Barakat, killing him. While it is unlikely that this insurgency would succeed in toppling the Sisi regime, it undermines the regime's claim to legitimacy by highlighting its failure to stop these attacks. The attacks not only risk sapping the morale of security services but also, perhaps more crucially, risk undermining the confidence of investors, reducing the attractiveness of Egypt as an investment destination.

Another justification given for the necessity of the coup was that the Egyptian economy was on the verge of collapse. This, we can say with some certainty, was clearly an exaggeration. While the economy certainly stagnated in the wake of the January 25 revolution, the economy continued to grow throughout the transition period till June 30, albeit at an anemic pace. Whether this growth is sustainable is highly questionable, but there is no doubt that economic growth accelerated sharply during Sisi's first year in office. Unprecedented support from the Gulf States, as well as the $8.5 billion expansion of the Suez Canal, undoubtedly injected massive stimulus into the Egyptian economy, with growth in the third quarter of 2014 reaching 6.8 percent. The rate of growth, however, has already begun to decline as the effects of this massive one-time stimulus dissipate, and now, with the completion of the canal's expansion, little is left to spend on other badly needed infrastructure projects. The Sisi regime, however, deserves credit for beginning to reduce the unsustainable energy subsidies that have crippled Egypt's public finances. However, despite this important measure, and despite the 2015 collapse in global energy prices, Egypt's current account deficit continues to increase, and its budget deficit is still in excess of 10 percent of its GDP. It is no surprise, then, that the Egyptian pound has depreciated significantly in 2014 and 2015, and will need to depreciate even further before it reflects the fundamentals of Egypt's economy, even if this comes at the risk of increasing Egypt's already elevated rate of inflation.

In short, no dramatic improvements have been achieved on the economic front that suggest that the coup produced an economic outcome for Egypt that is materially superior to that which would have been achieved had Egypt continued along its democratic path. The Egyptian economy continues to be on life support, dependent on outside assistance from the Gulf. Should this assistance disappear, it could have dramatically negative consequences for the stability of the Egyptian economy.

Despite the dramatic security and economic failures of the Sisi regime, it is unlikely that Egypt can now simply turn its back on the coup and renew a march toward democracy. The coalition that made the January 25 revolution possible has been completely shattered. Non-Islamist revolutionaries, with the exception of a few, are unwilling to question their participation in the June 30 coup or to consider reconciliation with the Muslim Brotherhood or its rehabilitation from its newly designated status as public enemy number one. The Muslim Brotherhood, battered by the arrest of the top three tiers of its leadership, has effectively lost control over its rank-and-file followers. If even a small percentage of them fall into the arms of ISIS, there is a real risk that the insurgency in Sinai could expand in scope and intensity in the Nile valley. This risk will only increase once the Egyptian government carries out the numerous death penalties that have been issued against members of the Muslim Brotherhood, including former president Morsi and the entire senior leadership of the brotherhood. The Egyptian state, moreover, has gone "all in" behind Sisi, making it inconceivable that significant portions of the civilian bureaucratic elite could ally itself with revolutionary groups within civil society.

What this essentially means is that unless Sisi succeeds in radically restructuring the Egyptian state, either it will eventually implode under the weight of its own incompetence and inefficiency, or some kind of revolutionary action will overwhelm it again. Sadly, the prospects of a peaceful transition to a better future for Egypt are even more remote today than they were eighteen months ago when this chapter was first published. And since there is no evidence that Sisi is succeeding in creating a new governing coalition capable of facing Egypt's challenges, Egypt's future looks grim. The only point of dispute is how grim that future will be.

Notes

This chapter originally appeared on the two-year anniversary of the January 25 revolution under the title "What Killed Egyptian Democracy?," *Boston Review*, January 21, 2014, https://bostonreview.net/forum/mohammad-fadel-what-killed-egyptian-democracy.

1. Shadi Hamid, "Egypt: The Prize," in Kenneth M. Pollack et al., *The Arab Awakening: America and the Transformation of the Middle East* (Washington, DC: Brookings Institution Press, 2011).

2. Hossam Bahgat and Soha Abdelaty, "What Mubarak Must Do before He Resigns," *Washington Post*, February 5, 2011, http://www.washingtonpost.com/wp-dyn/content/article /2011/02/04/AR2011020404123.html.

3. Roberto Patricio Korzeniewicz, "Democracy and Dictatorship in Continental Latin America during the Interwar Period," *Studies in Comparative International Development* 35, no. 1 (2000): 41–72.

4. F. Gregory Gause III, "Why Middle East Studies Missed the Arab Spring: The Myth of Authoritarian Stability," *Foreign Affairs* 90 (2011): 81.

5. Gene Sharp, *From Dictatorship to Democracy: A Conceptual Framework for Liberation* (London: Profile Books, 2011).

6. John Rawls, "The Law of Peoples," *Critical Inquiry* 20, no. 1 (1993): 36–68.

7. Ibid.

8. Ibn Khaldun, *The Muqadimmah: An Introduction to History*, 3 vols., trans. Franz Rosenthal [from Arabic] (London: Routledge and Kegan Paul, 1969).

9. Michael Blake, "Economic Justice, Coercion, and Foreign Policy," in *Justice and Foreign Policy* (Oxford: Oxford University Press, 2013).

10. Benjamin Isakhan, "Democratising Governance after the Arab Revolutions: The People, the Muslim Brotherhood and the Governance Networks of Egypt," in *Democracy and Crisis: Democratising Governance in the Twenty-First Century*, ed. Benjamin Isakhan and Steven Slaughter (London: Palgrave Macmillan, 2014).

11. Ahmed Mustafa, "Egyptian Liberals Unite to Test Muslim Brotherhood at Polls," *Al Monitor*, September 26, 2012, http://www.al-monitor.com/pulse/politics/2012/09/egypt-liberals -meet-to-form-alliance-capable-of-competing-with-brotherhood.html.

12. Sam Dagher, "Egypt Opposition Pushes Back," *Wall Street Journal*, November 26, 2012.

13. For an English text of the declaration, see "English Text of Morsi's Constitutional Declaration," *Ahram Online*, November 22, 2012, http://english.ahram.org.eg/News/58947.aspx.

14. Daniela Pioppi, "Playing with Fire: The Muslim Brotherhood and the Egyptian Leviathan," *International Spectator* 48, no. 4 (2013): 51–68.

15. John Rawls, *A Theory of Justice* (Cambridge, MA: Harvard University Press, 1971), 187.

16. Ibid., 215.

17. Taha Özhan, "New Egypt versus the Felool: Struggle for Democracy," *Insight Turkey* 15, no. 1 (2013): 13–24.

18. Charles D. Smith, "Democracy or Authoritarianism? Army or Anarchy? First Takes and Later Reflections on the Arab Spring," *Middle East Journal* 67, no. 4 (2013): 633–643.

19. Jeff Martini and Julie Taylor, "Commanding Democracy in Egypt: The Military's Attempt to Manage the Future," *Foreign Affairs* 90, no. 5 (2011): 127–137, http://www.foreignaffairs .com/articles/68218/jeff-martini-and-julie-taylor/commanding-democracy-in-egypt.

3   Egypt's Revolutionary Moment Turned Uprising

Sahar Aziz

O<small>N</small> JANUARY 25, 2011, the world watched as millions of Egyptians filled the streets demanding political and economic justice and an end to the Hosni Mubarak regime. After decades of suppression, political sentiments among Egyptians could no longer be contained. For eighteen gut-wrenching days, Egyptians surprised the world with their resolve to bring down a dictator. The protesters in the streets were not simply looking to topple Mubarak, but rather sought to create a new political system that served the people.[1] The message was loud and clear: Egyptians demanded and deserved democracy and they were willing to fight for it.

What followed, however, was not a new democracy, but a military-run regime with the Supreme Council of the Armed Forces (SCAF) at its helm. Political scientists who had long studied the regime were quick to catch on to the fact that this turn of events was fatal for the revolution.[2] But it would be months before most Egyptians came to this realization. Indeed, even today many Egyptians still harbor the belief that the events of January 25, 2011, triggered a revolution, despite clear indications to the contrary.

Accordingly, this chapter examines the failure of the January 25, 2011, revolution to bring about an open and democratic political system in Egypt. I argue that despite indications of political contestation at the margins, and a short hiatus from authoritarianism, Egypt's government has largely defaulted back to repressive state practices under the firm grip of the military-security apparatus. I propose that by acknowledging the failure of the revolution to achieve democratic outcomes, we can begin a candid discussion on whether a real revolution is imminent.[3]

Moving beyond Semantics

Labeling the eighteen days between January 25 and February 11, 2011, as an uprising is more than merely an exercise in semantics. To the contrary, admitting that Egypt did not experience a revolution has profound implications for our understanding of the nature of the Abdul Fatah el-Sisi regime—that is, the similarities and differences between it and the previous Mubarak government—and, in turn,

Egypt's social and political future. In assessing the outcome of the January 25 uprising, I use three specific criteria to measure the extent of revolutionary change: (1)
a sudden, radical, or complete political, social, or economic change;[4] (2) a fundamental change in political organization; and (3) the overthrow of a ruler or government. Based on these criteria, this chapter argues that Egypt experienced neither a political nor a socioeconomic revolution. Wealth and power alike continue
to be concentrated in the hands of the pre–January 25 elite but for a reshuffling of
the elite hierarchy.[5] The military now sits at the helm, followed by the domestic intelligence and police, and the economic elite just below them. While the country
underwent a revolutionary moment[6] that contributed to the country's present state
of political uncertainty, the long-term impact of this revolutionary moment turned
uprising remains unknown. As such, I ask the following question: Did the events of
January 25 trigger long-term political change that will eventually lead to popular
sovereignty and representation, or were the past four years a temporary period of
instability within a long history of authoritarianism? At the writing of this chapter, the latter appears to be the case.

The moment the Egyptian military declared it would not follow Mubarak's
orders to shoot demonstrators in Tahrir Square and elsewhere, the days of the
Mubarak regime were numbered. But as soon as General Mohamed Tantawi became the chief executive of the state, supported by a council of generals, it became
clear that the outcome—at least the initial outcome—of the mass protests was
merely a return to the status quo. Though the unpopular head of state was deposed, the military establishment that brought him to power and remained the
source of his elite coalition's strength and legitimacy remained in place.[7]

For more than half a century, the military was the bastion of power and political legitimacy for Egypt's successive authoritarian regimes—a defining feature
of Egypt's postcolonial state. But the institution's grip on power, which peaked
during General Gamal Abdel Nasser's presidency, was gradually reduced by both
Anwar Sadat and Mubarak. Sadat began eroding the military's power by reshuffling elite coalitions to offset the questionable loyalties of military officials from
the late Nasser's regime. Mubarak continued the demilitarization of politics by
replacing military elites with domestic security forces housed in the Ministry of
Interior. By 2010, only 8 percent of Mubarak's ministerial appointments came
from the military's ranks.[8] An aggressive economic liberalization program that
reduced the role of the state in Egypt's economy further eroded the military's role
in it as well. For example, defense expenditures decreased from 19.5 percent of the
GDP in 1980 to 2.2 percent in 2010.[9]

This redistribution of power from the military ranks to other members of the
country's elite created tensions between Mubarak and the military, with the latter seizing the moment on January 25 to reassert its control over the country. Not
surprisingly, some scholars have described January 25 as a soft coup[10]—an assess-

ment corroborated by the military-friendly 2014 constitution, not to mention the events that led up to the country's revolutionary moment and the those that followed.[11]

January 25 was a moment filled with tremendous optimism, not only for many Egyptians but also for a large number of political analysts who believed—naively as it turned out—that the SCAF's assumption of power was a temporary and transitional necessity.[12] But the SCAF wasted no time in amending the constitution and issuing executive decrees that aimed to reverse the decades-long erosion of their power and in turn guarantee their long-term political dominance.[13] The military's efforts were ultimately successful, culminating in the overthrow of the democratically elected Mohammed Morsi government in July 2013, followed by General Sisi's ascension to the presidency in June 2014. With the benefit of hindsight, it is now clear that Egypt has entered a new phase of authoritarianism controlled by the military.[14] The question remains, however, as to whether Egyptians who experienced political freedom, even if only for a brief historical moment, will accept another decades-long dictatorship. That the same factors leading to the 2011 uprisings still exist does not bode well for Egypt's long-term political stability.

The Impetus behind the Uprising

The Egyptian uprising was motivated by chronic grievances that came to a boiling point on January 25, 2011. Mounting mass discontent arising from extreme wealth disparities, rising unemployment, unchecked systemic corruption, a deteriorating infrastructure, and a political system that left little room for citizens to determine their political fate all contributed to the mass uprisings that deposed President Mubarak. Few Egyptians expected a quick fix to the vast array of problems facing the country. Instead, demonstrators fought for a regime that would guarantee basic human and civil rights and empower them to create a more accountable, less corrupt government. Motivated by economic grievances as much as political ones, Egyptians sought more equitable wealth redistribution, equal opportunities for employment (especially among educated youth), and wage increases after decades of stagnation.

Long-standing prohibitions on public protests facilitated the proliferation of the use of social media and the internet for airing grievances and organizing opposition to the status quo. Digital activism would transform, rather than replace, collective resistance to the regime as well as create avenues for organizing resistance that authorities were ill prepared to suppress. The resistance to Mubarak crossed class lines, as middle-class youth mobilization dovetailed with working-class labor unrest. In outright defiance of laws prohibiting labor strikes, workers refused to work until they received desperately needed pay increases. These developments coincided with increasing discontent among the military elite, who has been pushed further down the power hierarchy by Mubarak's latest round of elite reshuffling aimed at grooming his civilian son to succeed him.

Economic Inequality and the Fall of the Middle Class

The economic decline of the middle class was arguably the most significant impetus for the populist uprising of January 25. Declining average wages were inadequate to support even the most basic needs for food, clothing, shelter, transportation, and education. As the government ratcheted up economic liberalization and privatization policies, subsidy reduction resulted in a 30 percent increase in gasoline prices in the summer of 2006.[15] Skyrocketing food prices on the international market also increased the cost of food.[16] From 2005 to 2008, the cost of staples such as milk, cheese, eggs, and beans increased by 100 to 150 percent.[17] The prices of vegetables and cooking-gas cylinders also rose, disproportionately hurting the lower middle class and the poor.[18] In mid-2010, the price of rice went up by 50 percent, meat prices rose by 40 percent and poultry by 25 percent. The increases could not be absorbed by state subsidies, leaving many Egyptians in a state of food insecurity.[19] Meanwhile, the widening wealth gap between the common people and the elite was compounded by the rising cost of supporting a family among blue- and white-collar workers alike. In 2010, even households with two working-class incomes lived below the poverty line,[20] as the average monthly wage of a typical textile worker stood at $45–$107 per month.[21]

At the time of the uprising, most Egyptians' real wages had diminished to the extent that approximately 20 percent of the country fell below the poverty line, while another 25 percent subsisted just above it.[22] This stood in stark contrast to the fortunes of the country's business elites, who used their privileged position in the National Democratic Party (NDP) to pass laws that channeled public wealth into their personal businesses. Beginning in the 1990s, when Egypt undertook a series of market-oriented reforms and enacted large-scale privatization, Egypt's superrich became even richer as privatization schemes placed valuable state assets into their hands.[23] Egypt's burgeoning poor lived in slums while the economic elite lived in exclusive gated communities on the outskirts of Cairo and vacationed in expensive beach homes on the Mediterranean and Red Sea.[24] And while wealthy Egyptians drew on the state's treasury to pad their own pockets, over half of Egyptians could barely make ends meet.[25]

Large-scale labor migration into Cairo that began as early as the 1970s[26] had turned the city into a teeming metropolis with over seventeen million inhabitants, many of whom lived in informal shantytowns. Poor Egyptians scraped together the little resources they had to build houses without regard for safety standards. To light their homes and access water, they tapped the state's electrical grid and water pipelines without government approval.[27] Meanwhile, over 10.6 million more apartments than households lay vacant in 2006, compared to only 1.5 million more dwellings than households in 1976.[28]

Further compounding economic grievances was the chronic police harassment of the public, particularly the poor. Officers demanded bribes from shopkeepers and minivan drivers, extorted street vendors and restaurants, and detained anyone unable to pay the bribes.[29] Low-income Egyptians were frequently beaten, tortured to give false confessions, and pressured to become police informants.[30] By the end of 2010, the police became the most loathed public institution in the country. Thus, it was no surprise that the January 25 uprising included violence against police officers and the burning of police stations.[31] Indeed, such events were a testament to the extent of public anger toward the police as a state institution.

Not all socioeconomic conditions declined during Mubarak's thirty-year rule, however. Literacy rose significantly, from 40 percent in 1990 to 64 percent in 2010.[32] School enrollment, as a result, reached its highest levels. By the time Mubarak was deposed, 94 percent of children were enrolled in primary school, 88 percent were enrolled at the secondary level, and 35 percent were enrolled in high school.[33] Despite the rise in school enrollment, investment in public education was declining. As a result, overcrowding in schools and overworked and underpaid teachers produced low-quality public education.[34] That the protests of 2011 were instigated by the youth thus was not surprising. Egypt's newly educated youth had expectations that their education would lead to a higher quality of life than that afforded to their parents—expectations that ran up against the harsh realities of Egypt's lack of employment opportunities.

By 2010, more than 850,000 people entered the labor force every year.[35] Approximately 75 percent of new entrants had to wait an average of five years to find their first job, with college-educated youth experiencing the highest rates of unemployment.[36] Ninety-five percent of the jobless youth were college educated in 2006, up from 87 percent in 1998.[37] In addition to slow growth, the privatization of state-owned enterprises contributed to high youth unemployment rates, as the government was no longer the primary source of employment for college-educated labor-market entrants.[38] Employment in the public sector was halved from 1.08 million to under five hundred thousand between 1998 and 2004, with the formal private sector unable to absorb the growing number of new labor entrants.[39] Instead, over 75 percent of new labor-force entrants were pushed into the informal sector. By 2006, the informal sector constituted 61 percent of actual employment and produced one-third to one-half of the officially measured GDP.[40]

Despite these troubling trends, proponents of economic liberalization touted Egypt's official decrease in unemployment from 11.7 percent in 1998 to 8.3 percent in 2006. Many economists, however, pointed out that the benefits of reduced unemployment were outweighed by the declining quality of employment and stagnant wages. In 2003, Egyptian lawmakers amended the country's labor law to allow employers to hire workers on short-term contracts without medical or social insurance benefits.[41] The law also stripped employees of labor rights by failing to provide guidelines on contract lengths, salary levels, hours at work, overtime compensation, vacation, and lunch breaks.[42] Nor were employers required to provide health and injury insurance to their employees.[43] In order to evade the new law's already minimal employee protections, employers forced new hires to sign contracts that allowed the employer to fire them without warning, cause, or severance pay.[44] Meanwhile, the monthly minimum wage had not been raised since 1984, which was the equivalent of twenty-five US dollars.[45] Were it not for remittances sent from approximately 2.3 million Egyptians working abroad as of 2009, millions more Egyptians would have found themselves under the poverty line.[46]

With more than half of Egypt's population under the age of thirty, and a third between the ages of fifteen and twenty-four, the economic insecurities perpetuated by Egypt's economic liberalization programs and new labor law reached new heights.[47] Youth-led movements such as the April 6 Kefaya movement and the Youth for Change leveraged the discontent to mobilize for political change.[48] They sought what their peers in Western countries possessed: human rights, economic rights, democracy, and social justice.[49] Youth activists rejected the government's top-down-oriented initiatives aimed at gradual reform, and instead demanded a radical break from the existing regime, which they saw as fundamentally irredeemable.[50]

High youth unemployment also led many Egyptian youth to delay getting married and starting households.[51] In a socially conservative Muslim country, this produced social problems such as increased sexual harassment of women in the streets, secret customary "orfy" marriages, and prolonged financial dependence on parents. As socioeconomic pressures mounted, more youth joined the ranks of an increasingly well-organized civil society. Political resistance to the Mubarak regime became markedly more aggressive than in the past in openly challenging the government and leveraging international media to shed light on their abusive practices.

A Burgeoning Civil Society

In contrast to other Arab countries, Egyptian civil society has a long history of social engagement. It is composed primarily of nongovernment professional associations, charities, universities, and community betterment groups.[52] Hence, the bulk of its organizations have not been concerned with politics. Instead, they focused on filling the gaps left by the state's inadequate provision of social services by providing (among other services) free health clinics, orphanages, education services, and food for the poor. The high need for social services caused the government to tolerate NGOs, including those operated by the Muslim Brotherhood. Only a handful of organizations historically focused on human rights, political freedoms, or economic justice—all issues that could land a person in jail.

Starting in the 1990s, more overtly political advocacy groups began to champion human rights and women's rights and even call for the democratization of Egyptian politics. Although their reach was limited to the Egyptian intelligentsia and international NGOs, advocacy groups such as the Hisham Mubarak Legal Center, the Egyptian Organization for Human Rights, the Arab Network for Human Rights Initiative, the Cairo Institute for Human Rights Studies, and Al Nadeem set the foundation for the proliferation of civil rights groups in the 2000s.[53] Organizations such as the Egyptian Initiative for Personal Rights, the Association for Freedom of Thought and Expression, and the New Woman's Foundation took on more politically sensitive issues such as rural and urban poverty, deteriorating environmental conditions, the harassment of women, restrictions on the press, policy coercion, and fraudulent elections.[54] By 2007, over twenty-four thousand civil society organizations operated in Egypt, dozens of which advocated openly for political and economic rights.[55]

Despite the regime's efforts to enforce draconian laws aimed at reining in civil society, the new youth-based groups proved difficult to control. No longer relying on street protests or organizing secret meetings, youth groups openly organized and mobilized support through new media channels.[56] Youth activists also engaged in boycotts, protest art, and cyber-activism to elude security forces' attempts to silence them.[57] For example, the April 6 Movement mobilized over seventy thousand mostly educated youth using Facebook. They demanded free speech, economic welfare, and an end to corruption.[58] Their efforts culminated in a wildly successful general strike on April 6, 2008, of over 1.7 million demonstrators in support of striking textile workers.[59]

The internet also provided new channels for established political advocacy organizations to directly communicate their findings on civil rights suppression and worker abuses to the general public, bypassing traditional media channels that were either controlled by the government or susceptible to censorship and harassment by it.[60] As a result, the decade leading up to the January 25 uprising included political dissent and advocacy on an unprecedented scale. But the expression of dissent was not limited to social media. From the protest movements against the wars on Iraq in 2003 and Gaza in 2008 to the labor protests spreading throughout the country, Egyptians were also increasingly turning to the streets to express their grievances.[61] The latter was particularly consequential: had it not been for the rise of the labor movement, it is unlikely that Mubarak could have been deposed in as little as eighteen days.

The Labor Movement Shakes Egypt

Since the 1950s, the state-sponsored Egyptian Trade Union Federation held a monopoly over approving and organizing labor action.[62] Laborers were thus disarmed and had few legal means of challenging employers. Nonetheless, in the mid-1980s and early 1990s, Egypt's state-owned sector saw numerous instances of strike action.[63] State-owned enterprises were sold to private investors, causing managers to cut labor costs to make the companies more attractive to investors.[64] Mass layoffs, forced early retirements, and pension reductions became commonplace, making the economic future of workers all the more precarious.[65] As the government ramped up privatization, labor actions increased and reached an average of one hundred per year from 1998 to 2003.[66] Private investors purchased eighty state-owned companies in four years, amounting to 27 percent of the total state companies sold since 1991.[67] The consequent labor cuts doubled the number of strikes from 2004 to 2006 to approximately two hundred per year.[68]

Growing discontent culminated in 2006 when twenty thousand textile workers in the city of Mahalla went on strike for three days after the municipal government reneged on its promise to give them a two-month bonus.[69] Workers saw these bonuses as essential to their subsistence, as real wages had not increased since 1984.[70] And although Egypt's real GDP had grown by 7 percent for three consecutive years, from 2006 to 2008, few economic benefits trickled down to the workers.[71] Quite the opposite: strong macroeconomic growth produced declining work conditions for Egyptian workers, as they were forced to make concessions to an economic climate that was welcoming to wealthy investors seeking flexible labor markets and weak labor laws.[72]

With Egypt's new private-sector owners increasingly relying on short-term contracts, inadequate pay, and minimal benefits, the number of strikes increased exponentially.[73] Indeed, after 2006, Egypt experienced "the longest and strongest wave of worker protest since the end of World War II."[74] Labor conditions were so bad that historically complacent government employees joined blue-collar workers in protests.[75] Over 2,100 strikes and other labor actions took place from 2006 to 2009. A string of successful labor protests emboldened workers to mobilize further.[76] In total, over three million workers participated in 3,500–4,000 collective actions in the twelve years preceding January 25, 2011.[77] Despite draconian laws restricting labor action and a lack of legal means for organizing outside the government-controlled union, laborers became increasingly apt at extracting concessions from the government.[78]

While the labor movement represented far more Egyptians than the political advocacy groups, the former's agenda was narrowly focused on improving labor conditions and wresting union leadership from government control.[79] Glaringly absent from the labor movement's list of demands was a call for an end to civil rights abuses and political corruption.[80] Nevertheless, the narrow labor agenda produced over a decade of strikes, sit-ins, and demonstrations that ultimately set the stage for the January 25 uprising. Perhaps more importantly, when over a million workers went on strike and joined the demonstrations on February 8, 2011, the country's economy effectively ground to a halt, giving the military pretext to abandon Mubarak.

The removal of a dictator did not bring an end to the dictatorship; instead, it simply removed Mubarak and his NDP allies and reinstated military generals as the new governors. The youth movement, defined by its participants' outsider status and their lack of political experience, was doomed to be pushed to the margins of the country's new political arrangement. The Muslim Brotherhood, despite being well organized, was defined by exclusionary politics that made it all the more vulnerable to the political traps set by the military-security apparatus.

The 2010 Parliamentary Elections: Losing the Elite Coalition

Authoritarians do not rule alone, and Mubarak was no exception.[81] To stay in power for three decades, Mubarak relied on a patron-client network of economic elites who were granted access to economic resources in exchange for loyalty to the regime and a willingness to abandon fellow elites who ceased to adhere to the regime's interests. Mubarak's NDP served as the primary vehicle through which elites hoarded state resources. Thus, nomination to run for parliament became a means of rewarding past loyalty as well as securing future allegiance.

However, in the centralized political structure controlled by the presidency, the NDP was a weak and depoliticized institution. Few members were actually loyal to the party, but rather sought to employ it as a means of membership in the elite coalition. Doing so led to plum political appointments, access to government contracts, and other forms of self-enrichment.[82] Electoral contestation boiled down to a contest among various elites competing for power within the ruling party. Thus, the People's Assembly, far from serving as a check on executive authority, instead was an extension of the executive that served to perpetuate a patron-client relationship that maintained Mubarak's grip on power.[83]

Most Egyptians grew to accept this arrangement as an inevitable political reality, and thus did not bother to vote.[84] To ensure that the public would not use the ballot box to challenge their power, NDP candidates deployed armed thugs to intimidate opposition supporters.[85] Likewise, security forces fraudulently engineered electoral outcomes in favor of the NDP, creating inaccurate voter registration lists and destroying ballots cast for opposition candidates. In districts with a strong opposition following, central security forces used tear gas, rubber bullets, and live ammunition to prevent citizens from voting.[86] Leaders of the Muslim Brotherhood, for example, were regularly targeted during elections and routinely detained and imprisoned during preelection raids.[87] NDP candidates did not shy away from directly intervening in the electoral process to ensure their success. This included stuffing ballot boxes and committing other types of electoral fraud.[88] To maintain the facade of democratic politics, opposition parties and civil society leaders were permitted limited participation in elections—so long as they did not win enough seats to effect change and alter the status quo.[89]

By most accounts, the 2010 elections were the most farcical in Egypt's history.[90] Established political opposition groups, including the Muslim Brotherhood and the Wafd Party, were nearly shut out from parliament, as 97 percent of parliamentary seats went to the NDP. Street battles occurred in dozens of districts across the country as police attacked voters and opposition leaders.[91] The crackdown extended to the media, university students, and cultural expression. For instance, private businessmen who owned media outlets were pressured by the regime to dismiss outspoken editors, opinion writers, and talk-show hosts who criticized the government.[92]

The crackdown on the opposition was so severe that it eroded the regime's elite patronage networks. Not only were these elections rigged—there was nothing unusual about that—but the results also removed members of the old political elite from power. Since 2002, Gamal Mubarak had become increasingly assertive in his power over the NDP and installed his supporters in powerful positions in the party, the cabinet, and parliament. Consequently, Hosni Mubarak's longtime inner circle of elites became increasingly marginalized. The Mubarak regime may have won control of parliament in 2010, but it failed in its pursuit for indefinite power.[93]

Different Leader, Same Regime

Although the military has been a powerful institution since Egypt's 1952 military coup,[94] Egypt's war against terrorism in the 1990s promoted the Ministry of Interior in the country's political hierarchy.[95] By 2010, Egypt's active military personnel were outnumbered by domestic security services by three to one, with approximately 1.5 million personnel in the Ministry of Interior. Counting the army of plainclothes thugs, agent provocateurs, and informants that constitute the Ministry of Interior's undercover community, security forces may have reached as high as three million.[96] The lower ranks of the police hailed from the expanded paramilitary Central Security Forces (CSF), of whom 60 percent were uneducated and poor.[97] CSF police were effectively indentured policemen receiving two meals a day and four dollars a month who harbored deep class-based resentment against the public.[98]

In Egypt, police not only oversee law enforcement but also are involved in almost every aspect of Egyptians' daily lives.[99] The police keep records on, and issue, virtually all forms of personal identification in the country, including driver's licenses, passports, and birth and death certificates.[100] The hiring of university presidents, deans, and professors is subject to vetting and approval by police authorities.[101] Opaque national security criteria are used to determine the eligibility of graduate students to be hired as teaching assistants, select textbooks, and approve faculty travel abroad.[102] State security can even bar students from running in university elections. Anyone deemed to be affiliated with the Muslim Brotherhood is often vetoed. By 2010, Egypt could accurately be described as a security state.[103]

As the demand for internal security grew, so too did the Ministry of Interior's budget. Some experts estimate that Egypt's total security budget totaled $1.5 billion in 2006, surpassing the nation's health care budget.[104] As state expenditure on internal security grew, the military budget shrank.[105] To offset the decrease, the regime granted the military more financial autonomy and the authority to dabble in a variety of profit-making enterprises, including construction companies and service projects.[106] The military soon became the largest landowner in the country, with extensive business and commercial interests over which there was little or no civilian oversight.[107] The business ventures funded the military's security budget as well as subsidized private hotels, sporting clubs, grocery stores, and other businesses available exclusively or at a discount to military personnel.[108] These economic interests put the military at odds with the January 25 demonstrators' demands for systemic economic and political reforms, including civilian oversight of military private-sector endeavors.[109]

Starting in 2004, when Gamal Mubarak's ally Ahmed Nazif was appointed prime minister, the economy came under the control of a small group of businessmen within Gamal's inner circle.[110] While forty million Egyptians lived at or below the poverty line, macroeconomic policy was increasingly used as a tool to enrich this small group of elites.[111] Gamal and his cronies purchased land at far below market value, enacted privatization schemes that benefited themselves at the expense of the public purse, and effectively monopolized the steel and energy sectors.[112] The military resented Gamal's rise to power. Not only did he lack military credentials, but his economic liberalization schemes were increasingly at odds with the military's business interests,[113] which represented as much as 40 percent of Egypt's economic output. Thus, the military was eager to appease public demands to remove Hosni Mubarak, and as a consequence his son, from power.

In the euphoria that gripped Egypt upon Mubarak's forced departure, few noticed the military's ingenious move to occupy the apex of a deeply entrenched authoritarian political system. The system, composed of depoliticized institutions formed around loyalty to the president as opposed to common ideological or institutional interests, effectively made its head the most powerful state institution.

Having no other institution to turn to, Egyptians welcomed the military's willingness to serve as the caretaker government until democratic elections could be conducted. As a result, Egypt witnessed not a breakthrough for democracy but a reshuffling of the ruling elite and the fundamental perpetuation of the institutions that formed the authoritarian status quo.[114]

The SCAF employed duplicitous legal tactics to legitimize and even expand its rule, all the while obscuring its political objectives from public scrutiny. Exploiting the public's elated state of disbelief that Mubarak was finally gone, the SCAF carefully manipulated a public referendum on the timing of the parliamentary elections to determine whether they should precede or follow the drafting of a new constitution. Despite the referendum's narrow mandate, the SCAF successfully imposed a constitutional declaration on the country that preserved its grip on power. The military's leadership sidelined democratic governance and unilaterally appointed an unrepresentative committee of eight experts to draft the nine articles that would serve as Egypt's interim constitution.[115] For example, the military appointed Tariq Al Bishri, a retired judge with Islamist leanings, to head a committee that included a Muslim Brotherhood leader, Sobhi Saleh, but excluded other opposition parties, women, and leaders of the January 25 uprising.[116] Under the guise of emergency, temporary measures, the SCAF manipulated or entirely ignored public sentiment and the revolutionaries' demands as it secured its grip on power.[117]

The constitutional referendum was ultimately approved by 77 percent of voters on March 19, 2011.[118] Eleven days later, despite a narrow public mandate to amend only nine articles of the 1971 constitution, the SCAF unilaterally abrogated the 1971 constitution altogether and issued a sixty-three-article interim constitutional declaration that superseded the approved constitutional amendments.[119] The SCAF's scheme blatantly mirrored Mubarak's tactics, promulgating unchecked executive power under the guise of the rule of law.[120] Article 189, for example, was amended to effectively allow the presidential election process to be delayed indefinitely without affecting the constitutional drafting process. Coupled with Article 61, which maintained the SCAF's executive privilege until both parliamentary and presidential elections could be completed, any delay in presidential elections translated into prolonged SCAF rule.[121] Moreover, the absence of much of the 1971 constitution's checks on executive power resulted in the SCAF retaining executive prerogative to resolve issues not addressed in the constitutional declaration.[122] The SCAF thus commanded virtually unchecked power until elections were held.[123]

When the SCAF announced its plans in the fall of 2011 to postpone the presidential elections by two years, their ulterior motives became all the more difficult to hide from the public.[124] If any doubt remained that the military was out to secure its economic and political interests, skeptics were convinced by the SCAF's issuance of "supra-constitutional principles" authorizing them to appoint eighty of the one hundred members of the forthcoming constituent assembly tasked with drafting the country's new constitution.[125] This all but guaranteed that the next constitution would protect the military's interests, and any pretense of defending the supposed gains of the 2011 revolution was exposed.[126]

Same Regime, New Leader

For many Egyptians, it was difficult to fathom having sacrificed so much only to be left with a new variation on the same authoritarian system. Not until late 2011 did most Egyptians realize the SCAF's subversion.[127] They returned to the streets in the fall of 2011, calling on the SCAF to go.[128] But as the people's calls for systemic reforms became louder, the SCAF responded through state-sanctioned violence and the criminalization of dissent.

Unaccustomed to public criticism, the military drew a "red line" demarcating the limits on activism and reform efforts.[129] Anyone caught overstepping this arbitrary line was quickly whisked away to a military court. Indeed, in its first six months in power, the SCAF tried more than ten thousand civilians in military trials, thereby surpassing the number of military trials over the course of Mubarak's entire thirty-year rule. Workers, young revolutionaries, and anyone that criticized the SCAF's Mubarak-era tactics faced prosecution in military courts, police raids, or criminal prosecution pursuant to SCAF executive decrees.[130] Female protesters were subjected to humiliating "virginity tests" aimed at deterring their peers from joining subsequent protests.[131] The military parroted Mubarak's rhetoric in justifying their actions under the guise of preserving national unity and preventing public discord.[132]

Meanwhile, with a corrupt federal labor union disinterested in representing laborers' rights remaining in place, workers had no other venue but street protests.[133] Strikes continued as thousands of workers, including airport and public transport workers, ambulance drivers, and even police, joined the protests. Although Mubarak was gone, laborers had yet to see the implementation of their most sought-after demands. These included an increase in the minimum wage to make it livable, the removal of corrupt union leaders, the improvement of working conditions, and the provision of permanent contracts to temporary workers.[134] Instead of negotiating, the SCAF responded with a decree on March 23, 2011, that prohibited worker strikes that disrupted production.[135] But workers were not deterred. Years of strikes in the face of a brutal and unresponsive state left them battle hardened and unafraid to protest loudly and regularly, even in the face of the SCAF's repressive tactics.

When the SCAF announced in November 2011 that the presidential elections would be postponed, Egypt nearly exploded with unrest. Tahrir revolutionaries headed back to the square to salvage their revolution as the media exposed the SCAF's scheme to hold on to power. Facing the prospect of another nationwide revolt, the SCAF was forced to go ahead with elections in June 2012. By then, its post–January 25 political capital had been spent. In early spring 2011, 88 percent of Egyptians believed the military played a positive role and 90 approved of General Tantawi, then chairman of the SCAF.[136] By October 2011, two-fifths of Egyptians believed the SCAF was subverting the gains of the revolution.[137]

Despite the concessions, the revolution had already been hijacked by the military. While Egyptians certainly had more political space to debate, engage in political contestations, and vote in relatively free and fair elections than they had experienced in their lifetime, the military had insulated itself from the public will and enshrined its veto power over the country's political affairs. Subsequent political leaders now have little choice but to protect the military's interests—any significant move to the contrary would effectively be political (if not actual) suicide. Thus was the fate of Egypt's first democratically elected president, Morsi.

On its face, the election of a Muslim Brotherhood candidate to the presidency was revolutionary in Egypt. After decades of state repression, the Muslim Brotherhood won a majority in the 2012 parliamentary election and won the presidency later that year. After decades in hiding, the Muslim Brotherhood established a political party and created new television stations and newspapers. But long before Morsi occupied the presidential palace, his failure was preordained. The military, judiciary, domestic security forces, and media joined forces to prevent meaningful changes in governance, denouncing what they ominously called the "Brotherhoodization" of Egyptian society. These institutions that composed the "deep state" were intent on obstructing any attempts to alter the regime's power structure, regardless of the proponent. In the end, it mattered little whether the challenger hailed from the Muslim Brotherhood, the revolutionary youth, the labor movement, or any other political faction or movement at odds with the deep state's interests. Ultimately, Egypt's centralized, authoritarian political system was so deeply entrenched that eighteen days of nonviolent protests could not possibly uproot it.

Perhaps a real revolution would have been a viable option had the first caretaker government been composed of civilian stakeholders without a vested interest in preserving the status quo. Or perhaps it was naive for Egyptians to think that the regime could be toppled without a protracted conflict between the state and the people. What is clear, however, is that the same economic, social, and political factors that contributed to the January 25 uprising still fester. And thus, the door has yet to close on the prospect of a genuine revolution in the foreseeable future.

A Hunger Revolution May Be Imminent

It will be years before historians can provide an accurate picture of what caused Egypt's revolution to fail. Some of them will argue that the Muslim Brotherhood and former president Morsi shoulder the blame for pushing Egyptians back into the arms of the military. Others will blame the dysfunction of Egypt's secular, liberal groups and their incompetence in effectively campaigning in parliamentary and presidential elections. Still others will revert to Orientalist stereotypes that Egyptians are not ready for democracy and thus incapable of living in a pluralistic society without a strong military man as their leader. Surely, while many interrelated and complex factors contributed to the inability of Egyptians to topple their authoritarian government, Egypt's military had never ceased to control Egypt. When it deposed Mubarak, the military had no intention of succumbing to a civilian government. As such, the military seized a golden opportunity to regain the power it had incrementally lost since the death of former president Nasser.

To the dismay of Egyptians, the authoritarian regime was so deeply entrenched and the wide-reaching networks of elite patronage were so deeply rooted in the state's institutions that the events of January 25, 2011, promising as they may have been, failed to overthrow them. While the system may have been shaken, and the top leadership sacrificed to appease popular discontent, the sources that have perpetuated authoritarian rule in Egypt for decades remain in place. That Egypt successfully held relatively free and fair parliamentary and presidential elections is no small feat. It signifies Egyptians' desire to transform their political system into one that is based on the will of the people, not the arbitrary rule of an entrenched military elite.

Despite such gloomy assessments, it remains to be seen whether Sisi's regime is sustainable in a post–January 25 Egypt. A vast majority of the grievances that led to the January 25 uprising have not been addressed, and in some ways the situation has worsened. Unemployment stood at over 13 percent in 2014, and among youth it was as high as 25 percent—both higher than the rates recorded in 2010.[138] Current wages, especially for unskilled workers, are stuck at 1990s levels, leaving the labor struggle almost exactly in the same place that it was before it joined the 2011 uprising.[139] Annual inflation continues to hover near 10 percent. Egypt's GDP dropped to 2 percent in 2014, down from 5.1 percent in 2010, just before the uprising.[140] Electricity shortages are at unprecedented levels, Egypt's population of ninety million is growing at a rate of 1.7 percent, and 5.6 million housing units are vacant despite an annual housing shortage of 3.5 million.[141]

In addition to increasing economic hardships, Egyptians are also facing an increased suppression of political dissent. Soon after Morsi was deposed from office on July 3, 2013, the police systematically cracked down on the groups that triggered and sustained the January 25 uprising.[142] The Muslim Brotherhood and its supporters were the first targets of what appeared to be an orchestrated vendetta by the police. After killing over one thousand people protesting in Rabaa and Nahda Squares against the deposal of Morsi, the police directed its crackdown at anyone suspected of being a sympathizer of the Muslim Brotherhood.[143] Next in line were those—secularists or Islamists—claiming that the July 3, 2013, overthrow was a military coup. Wiretaps, surveillance of social media, and public statements were leveraged to interrogate, arrest, or detain these dissidents.[144] Then, the military-security apparatus turned its wrath on the revolutionary youth, who had eventually realized that forcibly removing Morsi would lead to more, not less, repression. Using an antiprotest law unilaterally issued by the interim president Adly Mansour, police arrested and charged many prominent youth leaders who had begun protesting against the ensuing regression of individual rights.[145] As of the time of writing this chapter, most of Egypt's opposition leaders have been arrested, prosecuted, and sentenced to jail or death for crimes ranging from terrorism to violating the protest law. Those who remain free have been scared into silence as they witness the high price their colleagues have paid for defending individual rights. It is too early to predict how such regression to oppressive authoritarian practices will affect Egypt's political future.

Although some Egyptians believe Egypt can be stable only under the firm hand of a military general, many Egyptians have now tasted the fruit of freedom. Egypt's youth, in particular, will not so easily accept another era of authoritarianism that suffocates their political expression and sacrifices their future to enrich a handful of elites. They are wired to one another in a world in which citizens now expect and demand democratic political representation. Egyptians broke Mubarak's wall of fear, and they are just as likely to break the new walls currently being built by Egypt's new police state. The military certainly won the battle for authoritarian rule, but it is far from clear whether they have eluded a prospective revolution for a democratic state.

Notes

This chapter was originally published as Sahar F. Aziz, "Bringing Down an Uprising: Egypt's Stillborn Revolution," *Connecticut Journal of International Law* 30 (2014): 1.

1. Jeannie Sowers, "Egypt in Transformation," in *The Journey to Tahrir: Revolution, Protest, and Social Change in Egypt*, ed. Jeannie Sowers and Chris Toensing (London: Verso, 2012), 1, 2.

2. Hend El-Behary, "Hamzawy Interview: 'We Are Returning to the Old Regime,'" *Egypt Independent*, May 25, 2014, http://www.egyptindependent.com//news/hamzawy-interview-%E2%80%98we-are-returning-old-regime.

3. Tamir Moustafa, "Law in the Egyptian Revolt," *Middle East Law and Governance* 3, nos. 1–2 (2011): 181–191.

4. Joel Beinin, "The Working Class and the Popular Movement in Egypt," in Sowers and Toensing, *Journey to Tahrir*, 92–106.

5. Sheila Carapico, "Egypt's Civic Revolution Turns 'Democracy Promotion' on Its Head," in *The Arab Spring in Egypt: Revolution and Beyond*, ed. Bahgat Korany and Rabab El-Mahdi (Cairo: American University in Cairo Press, 2012), 166.

6. Charles Tilly, *From Mobilization to Revolution* (New York: McGraw-Hill, 1978).

7. Jason Brownlee, *Democracy Prevention: The Politics of the US-Egyptian Alliance* (Cambridge: Cambridge University Press, 2012); Holger Albrecht, "Authoritarian Transformation or Transition from Authoritarianism? Insights on Regime Change in Egypt," in Korany and El-Mahdi, *Arab Spring in Egypt*, 251–270.

8. Joshua Stacher, *Adaptable Autocrats: Regime Power in Egypt and Syria* (Stanford, CA: Stanford University Press, 2012).

9. Hazem Kandil, "Back on Horse? The Military between Two Revolutions," in Korany and El-Mahdi, *Arab Spring in Egypt*.

10. Dalia Fikry Fahmy, "This Is Not Mubarak-Lite: The New Face of Authoritarianism," *The Immanent Frame: Secularism, Religion, and the Public Sphere* (blog), May 19, 2014, http://blogs .ssrc.org/tif/2014/05/19/this-is-not-mubarak-lite-the-new-face-of-authoritarianism/; Emad Shahin, "Struggle for Democracy in Egypt," Professor Panel, International Institute of Islamic Thought, February 5, 2014, https://www.youtube.com/watch?v=cLdnFVYHoNs.

11. Dalia Fikry Fahmy, "Muslim Democrats: Moderating Islam, Modifying the State" (PhD diss., Rutgers University, October 2011), http://hdl.rutgers.edu/1782.1/rucore10001600001.ETD .000063401; Dalia Fikry Fahmy, quoted in "Panel with Prof. Emad Shahin and Prof. Dalia Fahmy," International Institute of Islamic Thought, February 5, 2014, http://www.iiit.org/NewsEvents /News/tabid/62/articleType/ArticleView/articleId/349/Default.aspx); Kandil, "Back on Horse?," 193.

12. Brownlee, *Democracy Prevention*, 3 (noting that the events of January 25 arose from grassroots mobilizing rather than intraregime cleavages, thereby failing to eliminate authoritarianism); Kandil, "Back on Horse?," 193 (discussing the scaf's declaration to withdraw from politics after a six-month transition period).

13. Brownlee, *Democracy Prevention*, 152.

14. Ibid., 155 (arguing that the United States supported the Egyptian military's efforts to retain power as a means of preserving US interests in the region).

15. Ibid., 127.

16. Albrecht, "Authoritarian Transformation or Transition from Authoritarianism?," 254.

17. Ibid.

18. Ibid.

19. Beinin, "The Working Class and the Popular Movement in Egypt," 105 (summarizing a World Bank report finding that "nearly 44% of Egyptians are 'extremely poor' [unable to meet minimum food needs], 'poor' [unable to meet basic food needs], or 'near-poor' [able to meet basic food needs, but not much more]").

20. Joel Beinin, "Egyptian Workers Demand a Living Wage," *Foreign Policy*, May 12, 2010, http://mideastafrica.foreignpolicy.com/posts/2010/05/12/egyptian-workers-demand-a-living -wage.

21. Beinin, "The Working Class and the Popular Movement in Egypt," 105.

22. Ahmed Farouk Ghoneim, "Egypt and Subsidies: A Country Living beyond Its Means," Middle East Institute, May 5, 2015, http://www.mei.edu/content/egypt-and-subsidies-country -living-beyond-its-means.

23. Javed Maswood and Usha Natarajan, "Democratization and Constitutional Reform in Egypt and Indonesia: Evaluating the Role of the Military," in Korany and El-Mahdi, *Arab*

Spring in Egypt, 231. Most of these rich individuals and their companies paid minimal taxes to the state, contributing toward a limited 4.4 percent of total tax revenue coming from commercial and industrial profits. Albrecht, "Authoritarian Transformation or Transition from Authoritarianism?," 253–254. Meanwhile, salaried employees who collectively earned much less than private industry contributed 4 percent to the state's total revenues, Samer Soliman, "The Political Economy of Mubarak's Fall," in Korany and El-Mahdi, *Arab Spring in Egypt*, 43, 52.

24. Sowers, "Egypt in Transformation," 11; also see Albrecht, "Authoritarian Transformation or Transition from Authoritarianism?," 259.

25. Eric Denis, "Demographic Surprises Foreshadow Change in Neoliberal Egypt," in Sowers and Toensing, *Journey to Tahrir*, 235, 239; Amina Kheiri, "Egypt's Slums: A Ticking Time Bomb," *Al-Monitor*, November 7, 2013, http://www.al-monitor.com/pulse/politics/2013/11/egypt-slums-ticking-time-bomb.html#.

26. Regina Kipper, "Cairo: A Broader View," in *Cairo's Informal Areas between Urban Challenges and Hidden Potentials*, ed. Regina Kipper and Marion Fischer (Cairo: German Technical Cooperation, 2009), 13, 18.

27. Jessica Winegar, "Taking Out the Trash: Youth Clean Up Egypt after Mubarak," in Sowers and Toensing, *Journey to Tahrir*, 64–65 (noting that the government did not provide clean water, affordable housing, or trash collection the increasing rural poor migrating to urban areas).

28. Denis, "Demographic Surprises Foreshadow Change in Neoliberal Egypt," 239.

29. Ann M. Lesch, "Concentrated Power Breeds Corruption, Repression and Resistance," in Korany and El-Mahdi, *Arab Spring in Egypt*, 19.

30. Ibid.; Stacher, *Adaptable Autocrats*, 146.

31. Soliman, "The Political Economy of Mubarak's Fall," 56.

32. Central Intelligence Agency, "World Factbook," accessed June 2, 2014, https://www.cia.gov/library/publications/the-world-factbook/fields/2103.html.

33. Dina Shehata, "Youth Movements and the 25 January Revolution," in Korany and El-Mahdi, *Arab Spring in Egypt*, 107.

34. Louisa Loveluck, "Education in Egypt: Key Challenges, Address before the Education in Egypt Roundtable," Middle East and North Africa Programme, Chatham House, January 19, 2012, 4, http://www.chathamhouse.org/sites/files/chathamhouse/public/Research/Middle%20East/0312egyptedu_background.pdf.

35. Shehata, "Youth Movements and the 25 January Revolution," 107.

36. Ibid.

37. Ibid.

38. Loveluck, "Education in Egypt," 3.

39. Karen Pfeifer, "Economic Reform and Privatization in Egypt," in Sowers and Toensing, *Journey to Tahrir*, 203, 207–208.

40. Ibid. In 2012, some scholars estimated that Egypt's informal sector composed 40 percent of the GDP. See Taha Kassem, "Formalizing the Informal Economy: A Required State Regulatory and Institutional Approach Egypt as a Case Study," *International Journal of Humanities and Social Sciences* 4, no. 1 (January 2014): 27–48. See also Abdel Qader Ramadan, "Legalising Informal Sector Would Increase Economic Growth and Improve Living Conditions: ECES," *Daily News Egypt*, May 11, 2014, http://www.dailynewsegypt.com/2014/05/11/legalising-informal-sector-increase-economic-growth-improve-living-conditions-eces/.

41. Lesch, "Concentrated Power Breeds Corruption," 17, 26.

42. Ibid.

43. Ibid.

44. Ibid.; Denis, "Demographic Surprises Foreshadow Change in Neoliberal Egypt," 238 (noting that most households today cope with job insecurity, low-wage work, and inflation).

45. Lesch, "Concentrated Power Breeds Corruption," 26.

46. Pfeifer, "Economic Reform and Privatization in Egypt," 207–208 (noting that remittances rose from $3 billion in 2000–2003 to $5 billion in 2004–2005).

47. Shehata, "Youth Movements and the 25 January Revolution," 107.

48. Ibid., 118.

49. Ibid., 117.

50. Ibid., 118.

51. Ted Swedenberg, "Imagine Youths," in Sowers and Toensing, *Journey to Tahrir*, 285, 286.

52. Carapico, "Egypt's Revolution Turns 'Democracy Promotion' on Its Head," 204.

53. Marc Lynch, *The Arab Uprising: The Unfinished Revolutions of the New Middle East* (New York: PublicAffairs, 2012), 44; Hisham Mubarak Legal Center, accessed June 3, 2013, http://hmlc-egy.org/ Egyptian Organization for Human Rights, accessed June 3, 2013, http://en .eohr.org; Arabic Network for Human Rights Initiative, accessed June 3, 2013, http://www.anhri .net/en/; Al Nadeem, accessed June 3, 2013, http://www.alnadeem.com.

54. Bahgat Korany, "Egypt and Beyond: The Arab Spring, the New Pan-Arabism, and the Challenges of Transition," in Korany and El-Mahdi, *Arab Spring in Egypt*, 271, 286; Asef Bayat, "The 'Arab Street,' " in Sowers and Toensing, *Journey to Tahrir*, 73, 78–79.

55. Social Development Division, Social Policy Section, United Nations Economic and Social Commission for Western Asia, *Looking the Other Way: Street Children in Egypt*, policy brief, March 2009, 14, http://www.escwa.un.org/divisions/div_editor/Download.asp?table _name=divisions_other&field_name=ID&FileID=1260.

56. Korany, "Egypt and Beyond," 286.

57. Bayat, "The 'Arab Street,' " 81.

58. Ibid., 83.

59. Ibid.; Lesch, "Concentrated Power Breeds Corruption," 19; Mona El-Ghobashy, "The Praxis of the Egyptian Revolution," in Sowers and Toensing, *Journey to Tahrir*.

60. Lesch, "Concentrated Power Breeds Corruption," 32.

61. Ibid.

62. Beinin, "The Working Class and the Popular Movement in Egypt," 92.

63. Ibid.

64. Brownlee, *Democracy Prevention*, 127; Dina Bishara, "The Power of Workers in Egypt's 2011 Uprising," in Korany and El-Mahdi, *Arab Spring in Egypt*, 83, 85.

65. Brownlee, *Democracy Prevention*, 127.

66. Ibid.

67. Ibid.; Beinin, "The Working Class and the Popular Movement in Egypt," 92.

68. Brownlee, *Democracy Prevention*, 127; Sowers, "Egypt in Transformation," 7.

69. Brownlee, *Democracy Prevention*, 127; Ali Omar, "Mahalla Textile Workers' Strike Enters Eighth Day," *Daily News Egypt*, February 17, 2014, http://www.dailynewsegypt.com/2014 /02/17/mahalla-textile-workers-strike-enters-eighth-day/.

70. In addition to more pay, workers called for independent union leadership rather than the government-controlled General Union of Textile Workers. Despite some compromises on bonuses, the regime held fast to its centralization of labor unions as a means of controlling an increasingly contentious labor section. Brownlee, *Democracy Prevention*, 127.

71. "Egypt Minimum Monthly Wages," Trading Economics, http://www.tradingeconom ics.com/egypt/minimum-wages (accessed July 30, 2016) (showing minimum wage stagnation and increase in the consumer price index from 1984 until 2010; the dynamic graph allows

users to compare the consumer price index with minimum wages to demonstrate that the real minimum wage had not increased since 1984.)

72. Brownlee, *Democracy Prevention*, 127.

73. Beinin, "The Working Class and the Popular Movement in Egypt," 92. Forty percent of protesting workers after 2008 were employed in the private sector. Ibid.

74. Bishara, "The Power of Workers in Egypt's 2011 Uprising," 85.

75. Ibid., 86.

76. Ibid.

77. Beinin, "The Working Class and the Popular Movement in Egypt," 92.

78. Ibid.

79. Brownlee, *Democracy Prevention*, 124.

80. Ibid., 128.

81. Stacher, *Adaptable Autocrats*, 35.

82. Samer S. Shehata, "Political Da'Wa," in *Islamist Politics in the Middle East: Movements and Change*, ed. Samer S. Shehata (London: Routledge, 2012), 120, 125.

83. Ghobashy, "The Praxis of the Egyptian Revolution," 21 (noting that parliament was viewed as merely a "décor" and an empty shell devoid of real power).

84. Mona El-Ghobashy, "The Dynamics of Elections under Mubarak," in Sowers and Toensing, *Journey to Tahrir*, 132, 134; Shehata, "Political Da'wa," 122 (describing the 1995 legislative election as particularly violent, with over fifty deaths and hundreds of injuries, and the 2000 elections as somewhat less violent, with ten casualties and hundreds of injuries); International Institute for Democracy and Electoral Assistance, "Voter Turnout Data for Egypt," accessed June 4, 2014, http://www.idea.int/vt/countryview.cfm?CountryCode=EG (citing that the voter turnout percentage in 2010 was 27.47 percent and in 2012 62.04 percent).

85. Issandr El Amrani, "Controlled Reform in Egypt: Neither Reformist nor Controlled," *Middle East Report* 276 (Fall 2005): 149, 153; Brownlee, *Democracy Prevention*, 84.

86. Shehata, "Political Da'wa," 121; Brownlee, *Democracy Prevention*, 84 (discussing how in the 2005 elections, police cordoned off and blocked polling stations where voters turned out in support for opposition candidates).

87. Shehata, "Political Da'wa," 122.

88. Amrani, "Controlled Reform in Egypt," 153.

89. Ghobashy, "The Praxis of the Egyptian Revolution," 21.

90. Ghobashy, "The Dynamics of Elections under Mubarak," 133.

91. Shehata, "Political Da'wa," 122 (noting that at least thirteen people were killed and hundreds of others were injured during the 2010 elections).

92. Lesch, "Concentrated Power Breeds Corruption," 24.

93. Maswood and Natarajan, "Democratization and Constitutional Reform in Egypt and Indonesia," 238.

94. Stacher, *Adaptable Autocrats*, 4. Indeed, under Mubarak, generals accounted for most presidential appointments as provincial governors.

95. Ibid., 6.

96. Roger Owen, *The Rise and Fall of Arab Presidents for Life* (Cambridge, MA: Harvard University Press, 2012), 47. Nonuniformed employees played an increasing role in breaking up peaceful antigovernment demonstrations, sit-ins, and rallies.

97. Brownlee, *Democracy Prevention*, 53.

98. Ibid.

99. Alaa Al Aswany, *On the State of Egypt: What Made the Revolution Inevitable* (New York: Vintage, 2011), 24.

100. Ghobashy, "The Praxis of the Egyptian Revolution," 24.

101. Lesch, "Concentrated Power Breeds Corruption," 25.

102. Ibid.

103. Stacher, *Adaptable Autocrats*, 7.

104. Owen, *The Rise and Fall of Arab Presidents*, 47.

105. Stacher, *Adaptable Autocrats*, 6.

106. Ibid.

107. Owen, *The Rise and Fall of Arab Presidents*, 45.

108. Stacher, *Adaptable Autocrats*, 5.

109. Kristen Stilt, "The End of 'One Hand': The Egyptian Constitutional Declaration and the Rift between the 'People' and the Supreme Council of the Armed Forces," *Yearbook of Islamic and Middle Eastern Law* 19 (2012).

110. Aswany, *On the State of Egypt*, vii; Stacher, *Adaptable Autocrats*, 6.

111. Aswany, *On the State of Egypt*, vii.

112. Brownlee, *Democracy Prevention*, 156 (describing allegations that Gamal and Alaa Mubarak accepted villas in Sharm El Sheikh in exchange for facilitating underpriced land purchases for their friends); Stacher, *Adaptable Autocrats*, 6 (noting steel magnate Ahmed Ezz's near monopoly over the Egyptian steel industry).

113. Maswood and Natarajan, "Democratization and Constitutional Reform in Egypt and Indonesia," 238.

114. Stacher, *Adaptable Autocrats*, 78, 159–160.

115. Nathalie Bernard-Maugiron, "Egypt's Path to Transition: Democratic Challenges behind the Constitution Reform Process," *Middle East Law and Governance* 3 (2011): 43, 55.

116. Stilt, "The End of 'One Hand,'" 5.

117. Brownlee, *Democracy Prevention*, 158.

118. Michele Dunne and Mara Revkin, "Overview of Egypt's Constitutional Referendum," Carnegie Endowment for Democracy, March 16, 2011, http://carnegieendowment.org/2011/03/16/overview-of-egypt-s-constitutional-referendum/1t6.

119. Ibid.

120. Stilt, "The End of 'One Hand,'" 7.

121. Ibid., 14.

122. Ibid., 12.

123. Bernard-Maugiron, "Egypt's Path to Transition," 45.

124. David Arnold, "SCAF's Pre-election Moves in Egypt Could Upend Revolution," *Middle East Voices*, November 16, 2011, http://middleeastvoices.voanews.com/2011/11/scafs-pre-election-moves-in-egypt-could-upend-revolution/#ixzz33jIfxOtX.

125. Ibid.

126. Bernard-Maugiron, "Egypt's Path to Transition," 48. See also Stilt, "The End of 'One Hand.'"

127. Denis, "Demographic Surprises Foreshadow Change in Neoliberal Egypt," 235, 265.

128. Arnold, "SCAF's Pre-election Moves in Egypt Could Upend Revolution."

129. Ursula Lindsey, "Revolution and Counterrevolution in Egyptian Media," in Sowers and Toensing, *Journey to Tahrir*, 53, 62.

130. Brownlee, *Democracy Prevention*, 158–159.

131. Amnesty International, "Egypt: A Year after 'Virginity Tests,' Women Victims of Army Violence Still Seek Justice," March 13, 2012, http://www.amnesty.org/en/news/egypt-year-after-virginity-tests-women-victims-army-violence-still-seek-justice-2012-03-09.

132. Albrecht, "Authoritarian Transformation or Transition from Authoritarianism?," 267.

133. Beinin, "The Working Class and the Popular Movement in Egypt," 106.

134. Bishara, "The Power of Workers in Egypt's 2011 Uprising," 98.

135. Sowers, "Egypt in Transformation," 7.

136. Ibid., 159.

137. Ibid.

138. Sara Aggour, "Unemployment Rates Reach 13.4% in 3Q 2013," *Daily News Egypt*, November 17, 2013.

139. Motaz Khorshid et al., "Assessing Development Strategies to Achieve the MDGs in the Arab Republic of Egypt," United Nations Department for Social and Economic Affairs, March 2011, http://www.un.org/en/development/desa/policy/capacity/output_studies/roa87_study_egt.pdf.

140. World Bank, "Egypt Country Data," http://www.worldbank.org/en/country/egypt.

141. World Bank, "Population Growth Chart," http://data.worldbank.org/indicator/SP.POP.GROW; Bel Trew, "Multi-billion Dollar Project Will Not Solve Egypt's Housing Crisis," *Al-Monitor*, March 25, 2014, http://www.al-monitor.com/pulse/originals/2014/03/egypt-housing-uae-arabtec-shortage.html#.

142. Associated Press, "Egypt in State of Emergency as Clashes Leave 278 Dead," August 13, 2013, http://www.cbc.ca/news/world/egypt-in-state-of-emergency-as-clashes-leave-278-dead-1.1303479.

143. Kareem Fahim and Mayy El Sheikh, "Memory of a Mass Killing Becomes Another Casualty of Egyptian Protests," *New York Times*, November 13, 2013, http://www.nytimes.com/2013/11/14/world/middleeast/memory-egypt-mass-killing.html.

144. Human Rights Watch, "All According to Plan: The Rab'a Massacre and Mass Killings of Protesters in Egypt," August 12, 2014, https://www.hrw.org/report/2014/08/12/all-according-plan/raba-massacre-and-mass-killings-protesters-egypt.

145. Amnesty International, "Egypt: Generation of Young Activists Imprisoned in Ruthless Bid to Crush Dissent," June 30, 2015, https://www.amnesty.org/en/latest/news/2015/06/egypt-generation-of-young-activists-imprisoned-in-ruthless-bid-to-crush-dissent/.

4 The New Intellectual in Egypt's Revolutions

Shereen Abouelnaga

PERHAPS WE SHOULD examine the prerevolution position of the intellectual and determine whether there were factors that led to the open encounter witnessed on the Egyptian scene between the cultural community and the Islamist authorities. This encounter evolved in a manner that made it appear like a conflict between the religious and the cultural, which in turn deepened the sharp divisions in the community. What is it that sparked this encounter between the cultural and the religious? Of course, these frictions have always lurked behind the scenes, but they were subtle. Indeed, everything that took place before the roar "The people want" resounded has contributed to the enfeeblement of the intellectuals and the impairment of their tools, stripping them of the ability to defend the culture of the country. It was a completely paradoxical issue, as the state that afforded thorough protection, on its own terms, of intellectuals and spared them any violent confrontation with radical Islamism has vitiated them and eliminated the possibility of their communicating with the masses, which could have afforded them protection at the moment of confrontation. The official cultural institution had a major role in weakening the intellectual. For decades, the cultural field has been subordinate to the political field, and perhaps it has not been independent at all since its inception at the hands of Muhammad Ali.

In her accurate analysis of such a relationship between the state and the intellectual, Samia Mehrez elaborated in her book *Egypt's Culture Wars* on the relationship between the cultural community and political authority, concluding that the "cultural" is the political.[1] No wonder, then, that the marvelous writer Naguib Mahfouz attributed a significant position to the intellectual in his narratives, introducing the opportunist intellectual in *Al-Lis wa al-Kilaab* (The thief and the dogs), the confused intellectual in *Qalb Al-Layl* (Heart of the night), the idealist intellectual in *As-Sukkariyya* (Sugar Street), the contemplative intellectual in *Al-Tareeq* (The road), and other models of intellectuals who either adapt to new developments or violently confront them. The intellectual's relationship with authority, be it conciliatory or counteractive, seems inevitable. Yet, because they resorted to a depoliticized epistemology, based on strict specialization and noninterference, as termed by Edward Said, all their intellectual labor was rendered ineffective. The main feature of weakness is the lack of "a dialectical response from a critical consciousness worthy of its name," and so, "instead of noninterference and specialization, there must be interference, crossing of borders and obstacles, a determined attempt to generalize exactly at those points where generalizations seems impossible to make."[2] That is why one cannot delve into any definition of the intellectual. In the Egyptian context, the intellectual is defined by his position and aspirations.

Prior to the eruption of the revolution, intellectuals always had the dream of "marching down the streets" to "lead" the masses and enlighten them. This is probably the most harmful illusion on which the intellectuals have wasted their time. In 1972, in a conversation between the two post-structuralist critics Michel Foucault and Gilles Deleuze, Foucault referred to what happened to intellectuals during the May 1968 events in France, saying, "The intellectual discovered that the masses no longer need him to gain knowledge: they know perfectly well, without illusion; they know far better than he, and they are certainly capable of expressing themselves." Therefore, "the intellectual's role is no longer to place himself 'somewhat ahead and to the side' in order to express the stifled truth of the collectivity; rather, it is to struggle against the forms of power that transform him into its object and instrument in the spheres of 'knowledge,' 'truth,' 'consciousness,' and 'discourse.'"[3]

It is possible to understand the reason behind the limited options for grappling with authority if we recall the reality that stiflingly besieged the intellectual/citizen. The manifestations of corruption were everywhere, and the cultural domain fared no better than the political domain. Numerous agonies have escalated and accumulated over the last decade, to the extent that no person could have ignored them. Corruption was augmented by the aid of the philosophy of the ex-minister of culture Farouk Hosni, who had announced in 1982 that he was to "bring in all intellectuals into the barn."[4] Apparently, he succeeded to a large extent, and those who adamantly remained outside "the barn" were marginalized and deprived of all privileges. This situation explains the unprecedented increase in the number of literary seminars immediately prior to the outbreak of the revolution, as such seminars became the only safe area, providing a rhetorical margin where the cultural and the political, and sometimes the religious, conjoined.

None of the definitions of the intellectual advanced by philosophers, critics, or politicians are applicable to the intellectuals who "ruled" the cultural scene in Egypt prior to the revolution. The state had managed to control them by imposing a strict division of labor, and by almost forcing them to abide by the rule that the state "can run the country, and we [intellectuals] will explicate Wordsworth."[5]

After the People Cried for Change

Have the events of February 11, 2011, constituted a shock or a fulfilled dream for intellectuals? Were they ready for what happened that day? To a great degree, the pressures and impediments restricting their discourse have vanished, and the scene is ready to receive new blood. Unfortunately, however, what the Hosni Mubarak state had done over the previous three decades left intellectuals no sufficient power or energy to confidently move into the scene, and this rendered their faltering in the face of the multifarious "violent" discourses and movements quite understandable. Thus, the intellectuals find themselves exposed to a severe attack by groups that understood their fragility, and in turn followed up with successive accusations, reaching a level of criticism and detraction. In the end, the tone of degradation prevailed. Subsequently, the intellectuals only found refuge in attempts to organize small protest gatherings, which were totally ineffective. Moreover, the intellectuals' dialectical discursive practices could not attract the attention of a populace that was fed up with a vague vocabulary and "arrogant" discourse. More attractive was the clear and simple right-wing discourse that was "defending" Islam, and the intellectual could not compete. Briefly, intellectuals were equally confused and shocked. They wanted to "purge" the cultural institutions (a term that at the end simply meant a change in leadership), they were threatened by radical Islamists, they were trying to carve their own space in the constituencies of decision making, and they were busy defending and presenting their views to the media. Unfortunately, it was only the final task that they could do successfully.

On the other side, the political scene was transforming rapidly, and the extreme fluidity never allowed intellectuals any time to reach a minimal degree of agreement on any of their urgent concerns. Whether to cooperate with cultural institutions, whether to agree on a single statement, whether to accept the transitional rule of the military, and whether to run for the elections as one bloc remained contested issues. Amid these hesitations and petty power conflicts, the Freedom and Justice Party (FJP), the political arm of the Muslim Brotherhood, declared its program in which culture won a full section. It is impossible not to notice that religious preferentiality generally controls the party program, especially in the most controversial areas, like tourism, culture, and family, even if the discourse in form reflects the contrary.

In the beginning of the section addressing culture and art, the program clearly reflects the party's vision as follows:

> Culture relates to religion in an undeniable manner, and Egyptian culture is formed in its totality on the basis of Islamic identity, without exclusion or neg-

ligence of cultures that contributed during a historical stage, and that "still does," to the formation of the community, with its distinctive features, like the ancient Egyptian and Christian cultures. Islamic civilization has also constituted a framework for the unity of the nation that allows plurality and preserves internal diversity and multiplicity of creeds. Hence, there is no room for cultural conflict; but rather acculturation, interaction and blending of cultures.

The Egyptian culture, with its foregoing features, also represents an invincible fortification against the means of destructive intellectual invasion and the wiles of cunning assimilation by western cultures that corrupt, and reform not, and that contribute to the dilution of Arab and Egyptian national affiliation. Our culture, with its originality and flexibility, can extract from incoming cultures that which complies with it and contributes to the renaissance of the nation. It can also develop the legacy of predecessors through re-reading and modernizing it.[6]

This excerpt proposes religious preferentiality as a culture-delimiting framework. And though it firmly denies the existence of a "cultural conflict" at the local level, it confirms manifest hostility toward the global, which embodies the attributes of the invader who aims at diluting belongingness. Whatever comes from outside Islamic religious preferentiality is thus discarded, being representative of "western cultures that corrupt, and reform not." In the words of Amin Maalouf, these are "deadly identities"[7] (if fanatics of all kinds manage so easily to pass themselves off as defenders of identity, it is because the "tribal" concept of identity, which is still prevalent all over the world, facilitates such a distortion). This rejects acculturation and in the meantime endorses it in its discourse; such a principle basically undermines the concept of art.

The problematic issue is clearly manifested when different cultural and ideological discourses clash with religious discourse; even before a genuine ideological clash occurs, it seems as if there is one discourse advocating Islam and another opposing it. Polarization gradually emerged between a liberal discourse calling for openness toward others cultures and a conservative right-wing religious discourse calling for a cultural enclosure with the purpose of preserving identity. Following the logic of this dichotomy, the liberal discourse is charged with betrayal of the nation's culture, while the religious discourse suggests that it seeks to preserve it. Such a problematic issue is not new, and these fixed classifications are not surprising, considering the populace's relation to intellectuals, in particular, as well as to culture in general, prior to the January 25 revolution.

Upon considering the details of the FJP's cultural preferentiality, what is striking is that it presupposes the unity and homogeneity of Egyptian culture, as the cultures preceding "Islamic civilization" are acknowledged by way of accumulation and cross-fertilization, while diversity in cultural practice as a current fact is an unpropounded supposition. This imagined homogeneous culture is not only deadly for the talent, diversity, and richness expected from any culture, but also a suppressive instrument for all, especially when the discourse broaches "the means of destructive intellectual invasion and the wiles of cunning assimilation by western cultures that corrupt, and reform not."

The problem with these criteria is that they are loose enough to allow branding whatever is dissimilar to such partisan politics as a destructive invasion. It is impossible, in a world that communicates from the Far East to the West through modern means, to determine the form of "invasion" or to indicate the "authentic" local. It is no longer possible to make such arbitrary separations, though it is possible to consciously integrate the local and the global in order to produce new artistic forms that preserve originality and engage with the global until it turns into resistant forms. This is manifested in most of the artistic forms that crystallized in Tahrir Square during the massive (eighteen-day) sit-in and after. It was not an ideological conflict between a secular camp and a religious one, as was imagined and depicted by some (including the media, which intensifies the polarization), but rather was, and has always been, a conflict between the local and the global.

Such conflict has roots in all fields, though it primarily presents itself in the cultural field. In his famous book *Modernity at Large: Cultural Dimensions of Globalization*, Arjun Appadurai illustrates how multimedia projects recycle images in a way that creates an important role for the imagination.[8] Here, imagination does not mean the adoption of myths or immersion in rituals detached from reality. Similarly, it is not the imagination that constitutes a mere reaction to the certainty of reality. Rather, it is the imagination that establishes new social projects and transforms the fixity of place into a momentum that drives large groups to improvise mechanisms of alliance and resistance. Therefore, when imagination acquires a collective nature, it becomes able to stimulate action. (How did the revolutions break out in the Arab region, for instance?) In other words, this imagination, which is derived from and based on images, builds up a joint community of visions, sentiments, actions, and objectives. Paradoxically enough, while non-Islamists (the term *liberal* is a misnomer) formed their own "imagined" community, Islamists did the same. Each camp adhered to a specific "imagined community."[9] But while non-Islamists exhibited their convictions discursively, Islamists managed to recruit and convince the populace materially.

In this conflict, the idea of freedom of opinion and expression occupies a considerable space, though we must recognize that the controversy over it was never in the interest of the freethinker and intellectual. It can be recalled that the crisis over Salman Rushdie's novel *The Satanic Verses* has become a symbol for, and an indicator of, the conflict between Tehran and the West.[10] Likewise, it cannot be forgotten that several crises were raised in the former parliament and its predecessor around movies, novels, and poems.[11] Most importantly, one should never attribute this to religious trends alone, since censorship of creative works, and sometimes confiscation of them, receives the support of the press and the populace on the grounds of art's connection to interest and morals. Moreover, if this raised controversies and arguments in the past, it has now turned into a partisan item, for in the section titled "Some aspects of the cultural life," the FJP's program stresses the following:

> 1) The party adopts non-separation between the ethical, moral aspect and the creative act in all its forms. Within this framework, the party emphasizes freedom of creativity and protection of the community's morals, ethics, proprieties and customs alike.
> 2) The party emphasizes the importance of the Egyptian citizen's self-censorship, and the development of a culture of self-immunization that is based on the values of nationalism virtue, right and goodness, and that is capable of distinguishing the wheat from the chaff, as a civilized alternative to the culture of banning and authoritarian censorship.

The affirmative-emendatory statement is repeated, as the freedom of creativity is established; yet the creative act is a mirror for "the ethical, moral aspect." As for authoritarian censorship, it would be replaced with self-censorship, which is harsher and more arduous that authoritarian censorship. Therefore, the objective is that the community embraces equality between the creative act and the moral act, and then reproduces these visions without any authoritarian institutional interference. Hence, the mechanisms of extending the domination of the religious discourse are manifested, being focused on exporting the idea that it is necessary for the creative work to have a worldly interest and moral grounds, in a community suffering economic crises. In short, all the Mubarak censorship returned, cloaked this time in a religious tone. This does not mean that nothing had changed; on the contrary, there was a radical change in the interplay of power relations and political actors, and in the position of intellectuals vis-à-vis the rule of the military—the last resort at the time.

While the conflict between intellectuals and the various Islamic factions lacked equity, the intellectuals, who had always been protected and patronized by the Mubarak regime, were not willing to accept the fact that the world they had always known was gone. True, the attack on intellectuals, their discourse and practices, their writings, and their trajectories was escalating, and, I would add, it was frightening since it involved attacks on the intellectuals' personal safety. However, that situation required not only new strategies and practices, but also an autonomous vision that would allow the initiation of a "new" world. The lack of equity, along with the absence of the will to sacrifice, to confront, to lose, and, most importantly, to support the revolutionary discourse and practices of the rising generation, led intellectuals to seek protection in the bosom of the state that they have always known, and whose restraints they have long dreamed of dismantling.

By the beginning of 2012, the grand imam of Al-Azhar, Ahmad al-Tayeb, invited most of the cultural and political actors (non-Islamists) to draft a public freedoms document. Following the approval of all participants, the document was issued, and it included four key items: freedom of faith, freedom of scientific research, freedom of opinion and expression, and freedom of artistic creativity. In the beginning, the document stressed that attainment of these items requires "ceaseless effort where enlightened religious discourse would interweave with rational cultural discourse."[12] Thus, initially, the obstacle was clearly in the linking of the religious discourse to its cultural counterpart in a relation marked by rivalry, since the religious ranks high and assumes the role of trusteeship. Likewise, it is impossible to link both while maintaining the peculiarities and premises of each. This is because the religious departs from fixed preferentialities, while creativity seeks to plunge into other worlds that are completely different. Miraculously, all those who participated in drafting the document somehow forgot that it was the Al-Azhar institution that has always issued fatwas against works of art.

The entire course of the transitional phase has demonstrated the difficulty for the cultural community to reach an agreement on such objectives, as intellectuals never faced the "real" responsibility of attaining them. The defining moment comes when the question long avoided is raised: Which shall prevail, the religious or the cultural? Accordingly, what the document proposes has already received much public interest, though it stumbled at articulating artistic and creative exception. The document calls for freedom, yet it does so only to a certain extent, and for free thinking, yet within certain boundaries. It also encourages creativity, provided that it does not conflict with the ethics of the community in general.

Shortly thereafter, it became clear that all written documents do not offer genuine guarantees of creativity. It seems that this was not the concern of intellectuals. Their problem revolved around who was producing the discourse and setting the rules. There is not much difference between the FJP's rhetoric and that of Al-Azhar. The core is similar: art is secondary to society and public opinion, and the definition of culture is tied to other discourses. When the Egyptian Creativity Front organized a march in January 2012, no new discourse was heard. The front submitted recommendations that they drafted regarding freedom of creativity to parliament. It is noticeable that the fourth term of the document took Al-Azhar's document into account as a common ground. Generally, the front received a quasi-consensus, which allowed it to make alliances that could counter persistent attacks on art and creativity.

Hence the "cultural" did not pursue full independence from religious institutions, as the Azharite legitimacy kept granting it a sense of security. Besides, the intellectuals did not want to face the hard-line religious groups without any "legitimate" cover, so they did not build up an independent preferentiality. The whole cultural situation was going back to square one. Yet, a new discourse was in the making. Then, at the threshold of the presidential elections, the Egyptian scene plunged into severe division between the rigid and conflicting binaries. In his discussion of German society in the 1970s in his book *The Neoconservatives*, Peter Steinfels notes that division—as a mechanism for dominance—was imposed by the right-wing discourse. "The struggle takes the form of exposing every manifestation of what could be considered an oppositionist mentality and tracing its 'logic,' so as to link it to various forms of extremism,"[13] he states.

A New Intellectual Is Born

While the intellectuals, call them traditional, old, or patriarchal, were attempting to reform what had previously existed, there emerged a new intellectual, whose political consciousness was formed in the town square and whose rhetoric sprang out of the core of the revolution. This young intellectual was totally indifferent to the institution and all the chances for symbolic or economic capital that were available to him or her. The "pulse of the street" was the guiding compass for the new intellectuals, who remained in constant engagement and communication with the political fluidity, getting inspiration from successive incidents. Hence, their imagination and expression kept parallel to such incidents. On the other hand, the traditional intellectuals kept trying to revive the spirit of revolution in well-worn institutions, believing that such institutions may eventually respond. Thus, they fixed their vision without moving a step forward.

Gradually, the new intellectuals managed to restore some art forms to the public—a public that had been completely alienated from arts due to the former regime's policies. The new intellectuals continue to advance and gain new spaces, in the real and the symbolic sense, while the "old" intellectuals return to their "old" lives, which are dependent on holding seminars, writing articles, and issuing calls for conferences that aim at uniting the cultural community. Meanwhile, the right-wing trend has continued its fierce attacks on freedom of art and creativity.

It should be noted that the generations that took to the street on January 25 and developed a political consciousness did not emerge from the womb of the cultural or political institution. Consequently, following the revolution, the official cultural institution earnestly tried to assimilate those youth through official statements affirming that it is the youth who will take the lead, or announcing the formation of a youth committee and the like; statements that affirm formal existence, but that fail to assimilate such a massive energy of youth—a youth who have employed a totally new language that is unintelligible to the institution. Hence, their forms of expression seemed wild and predominant, and by definition grounded in the rejection of institutionalization. As the emergence of these generations was surprising for all, experts and analysts started to affirm that all the youth who took to the streets were "unpoliticized," as if engagement in politics were a suspicion that must be warded off. In addition, it seems that the definition of politics adopted by analysts and experts was so narrow and classical that it failed to encompass the new nature of political work carried out by those youth. Protesting on January 25 and raising certain demands was a political action par excellence that everyone sought to black out, since acknowledgment of it meant the failure of the policy of nonrecognition adhered to by all politicians regarding the parallel world that had been forming in front of them, but which they dismissed as "virtual."

January 25 was the turning point in the definition of the intellectual. The new intellectual, who grew out of the spirit of January 25, appeared to be that youth who would write a poem, face the bullets, move along the streets denouncing the practices of authority, and then return to sing with a band. Therefore, with the outbreak of the revolution on January 25, it was confirmed that there were thousands who would express their opinions in various forms, provide analyses for what was going on, and offer alternative choices and new approaches. They all chose to take a stance instead of remaining silent. What is more, from the margins to which they were confined, they managed to disturb the center and even penetrate it. In fact, the rhymed chants, bearing strong objections to and a total rejection of current policies, replaced the subtle and detached political analyses that had abounded in the media under state control.

Besides, Twitter and Facebook comments allowed immediate commentary on any official speech, so much so that in some cases the authority had to comment in reply or harass the commentators. To a certain extent, modern means of communication turned into an alternative arena for fueling the conflict in the era of the Muslim Brotherhood. Moreover, there was an increase in independent gatherings that assumed different means of expression and that did not attempt to cooperate with official sites, as was done by the old intellectuals, who participated in events held by organizations such as the Independent Culture Coalition, which would hold an artistic ceremony on the first Saturday of each month. The new generation renounced the institution, which is a key point in cultural analysis of the status quo, and proceeded to smash the concept of symbolic figures, which largely confounded the institution. Thus, through a vision involving minimal agreement on the basics, at least politically and culturally, the patriarchal authority was transformed in most cases into a target for ridicule and cynicism. Yet, what is more important is that the institution lost credibility among a new generation, for whom its restrictions were no longer acceptable.

The rejection of the institution expresses the revolutionary choice that allowed the new intellectuals to fully declare their opposition to the military through all available means: marches, sit-ins, posters, blogs, chants, short films, and testimonies. Yet, the art of graffiti remained among the most important forms of expression, and even transformed into an area of conflict between the new intellectuals and authority. The graffiti drawings that covered the walls of Cairo were registering stances, expressing protest, and establishing a new discourse. Therefore, it was natural that the authority set out to scrub off the drawings, only for them to be redrawn by the revolutionaries the next day. Graffiti artists have become targets of an authoritarian regime.

The trajectory of the new intellectuals is reminiscent of that described in the article written by the American cultural critic Cornel West, who participated in the 1960s civil rights movement. In the article, titled "The New Cultural Politics of Difference," West addressed the policies adopted by the black cultural activists in presenting their culture and creativity to the community, which led him to elaborate on the challenges that faced them. He pinpointed three challenges: intellectual, existential, and political. Since the new intellectual shares marginalization with the black intellectual—of course in a different political context—the three challenges mentioned by West can be utilized in order to understand the present Egyptian context. Here, the intellectual challenge depends on how theorization is carried out and, in turn, on understanding these new avant-garde policies and how the circles surrounding the work are magnified.[14] As for the existential challenge, it lies in the way the new intellectuals manage to afford the resources for their persistence and to procure symbolic capital in the cultural field; that is, the essential and necessary skills in the field. Yet, West adds, discipline and perseverance are necessary for success, without an undue reliance on the mainstream (taste or the institution in this case) for approval or acceptance.[15] Regarding the third challenge, the political one, which the vanguard managed to handle proficiently, the objective was right before their eyes. This vanguard has made staunch alliances for the realization of democracy and freedom in their society. This needs more explanation since it was the challenge that underlay the whole endeavor.

The protesting actions of the new intellectuals suggest a different relation between art and politics. Recently, critics such as Gerald Raunig have used the term *transversality*[16] to describe new terrains of open cooperation between activist, artistic, social, and political practices. Such new alliances, even if temporary, set to de-territorialize the disciplines and fields they work across. Transversality is not a form or an institution that one joins, but rather it is continually constituted through events that require and trigger certain acts of alliance where art and the revolution connect. It is a relation that manifests itself in practices that spring from every place, with no center and no reproduction. They emerge in the cracks, the in-betweens, and in the most unexpected moments; yet, they are not linear at all. There is no hierarchy either for art or for the revolution; on the contrary, there are temporary overlaps that Raunig describes as "micropolitical attempts at the *transversal concatenation* of art machines and revolutionary machines" (italics added).[17] They are carried out by different factions of society, and they are immediate struggles in the sense that people criticize instances of power that are closest to them. Most important, they conquer, by accumulation, the totalization and individualization of the regime. Foucault explains that such struggles assert the right to be different, and they undermine everything that makes individuals truly individual.

On the other hand, they attack everything that separates the individual, break his links with others, split up community life, force the individual back on himself, and tie him to his own identity in a constraining way.[18] Having managed to redress the gap between the individual and the collective is one of the most notable successes of the new intellectuals. To lobby collectively while protecting individual identity has subverted the discourse of the regime that has always tried to cement the discursive, social, and cultural barriers so as to keep its power intact. The point of strength of these "new" protests is that they are transversal; they are works of art that are not works of art. They are "collective actions undertaken by non collective actors," as Asef Bayat has stated.[19]

Over time, since 2011 and up until now, the concept of "the intellectual" has changed, being no longer confined to the writer or thinker, but rather extending to include all the new expression and protest forms pursued by the new generation. It seemed as if the new intellectuals had managed to achieve an accumulation of experience and to develop their discourse, though they did not reject the idea of just retaliation for martyrs, which is directly linked to the concept of justice. From the outset, the new intellectuals rejected any form of domestication, either within a party or an institution (Félix Guattari has developed the concept of transversality in face of the "party" as the ultimate political organization), which made most blocs emerge in the form of a "movement" without any conventional organizational framework, as can be seen in the April 6 Movement, ultras groups, Bahiya ya Masr (Beautiful Egypt), Askar Kadhibun (Lying Generals), Ikhwan Kadhibun (Lying Brotherhood), and many others. This rendered the emergence of the Tamarrud Movement understandable in light of the poor performance of Mohammed Morsi's government,[20] regardless of the fate of such a campaign.

The use of the word *youth* in reference to the new revolutionary generation bore many patriarchal characteristics, as it implied vigor and lack of experience in the face of reason and wisdom. At a defining moment, the term even turned into a tactic in President Morsi's penultimate speech, when he declared that a youth assistant would be appointed for every minister in an attempt to placate the youth, who did not accept simulated solutions and were not lured by the president's positions at any stage since the outbreak of the revolution. The only option in their eyes was the original concept on which the revolution was established: bread, freedom, and social justice. However, the problematic issue for the new intellectuals, who adopted a radical discourse and a different vision, and who pursued unprecedented means of expression that combined the local and the global (including even the Black Bloc Movement), remained: others' incomprehension of the new intellectuals' attitude, whether that other be the old intellectual, the military authority, the Muslim Brotherhood, or even the recent regime headed by Abdul Fatah el-Sisi.

Of course, the old patriarchal intellectuals were somehow in solidarity with the new generation, and forcefully supported them in certain contexts, though they maintained political neutrality, watching and analyzing, until authorities directly assaulted them. And so they started protesting against the "Brotherhoodization" of culture. What is strange about the role of the intellectuals is that the process of state Brotherhoodization had actually begun earlier, but the threat did not seem pressing for them until such a process extended to the "cultural" sector.

Hence, it can be said that the new intellectuals have managed to build the foundation for a new world, which was not easy, since they paid a high price (detention, assault, defamation, death, and legal and military trial). Thanks to these new intellectuals, who imposed through their persistence a different political discourse, the populace's cultural discourse started to produce a different vocabulary in form and content. Despite such a largely manifest novelty, the institution remained tenaciously wedded to its old discourse, which gives full credit to the "youth" in press releases, but totally forgets them in real practices. Thus, the institution was (and still is) aware of the importance of new forms and means of expression, and the new intellectuals were (and still are) convinced of their being a sheer tool for the implementation of an old agenda. Therefore, the schism between the old and new still exists, and the task of resolving it, not to mention the cost of undertaking such a challenge, is huge.

Notes

1. Samia Mehrez, *Egypt's Culture Wars: Politics and Practice* (Cairo: American University in Cairo Press, 2010), 1–13.

2. Edward Said, "Opponents, Audiences, Constituencies and Community," in *The Anti-Aesthetic: Essays on Postmodern Culture*, ed. Hal Foster (New York: New Press, 1998), 181.

3. Quoted in Joseph Kay, "Intellectuals and Power: A Conversation between Michel Foucault and Gilles Deleuze," libcom.org, September 9, 2006, http://libcom.org/library /intellectuals-power-a-conversation-between-michel-foucault-and-gilles-deleuze.

4. Ali Ahmed Ali, "Ihtikam hatheera Farouk Hosni," Masress, May 30, 2013, http://www .masress.com/altaghieer/134463.

5. Said, "Opponents," 181.

6. "Birnameg Hizib Horiya Wa a'dala," Ikhwanwiki, http://www.ikhwanwiki.com/index .php?title=%D8%A8%D8%B1%D9%86%D8%A7%D9%85%D8%AC_%D8%AD%D8%B2%D8%A 8_%D8%A7%D9%84%D8%AD%D8%B1%D9%8A%D8%A9_%D9%88%D8%A7%D9%84%D8% B9%D8%AF%D8%A7%D9%84%D8%A9 (accessed August 2, 2016).

7. In 2004, a translation of Amin Maalouf's book *Deadly Identities* was issued (Beirut: Dar al-Farabi). It raised a fuss at the time because of its rejection of a "fixed" identity, a concept that was new to the Arab world, which has always sought a unitary, fixed identity.

8. Arjun Appadurai, *Modernity at Large: Cultural Dimensions of Globalization* (Minneapolis: University of Minnesota, 1996), 4.

9. Benedict Anderson, *Imagined Communities: Reflections on the Origin and Spread of Nationalism* (New York: Verso, 1983).

10. Sadik Jalal al-Azm, *The Mental Taboo: Salman Rushdie and the Truth within Literature* (London: Riad El-Rayess Books, 1992).

11. In the year 2000, a crisis erupted following the publication of Haidar Haidar's novel *Banquet for Seaweed*, and then similar crises arose around various novels, movies, poems, and magazines. Later, social outcry centered on actresses' public statements (for example, the crisis of Farouk Hosny's statement on the Hijab) and their wardrobes (for example, Yousra's famous dress).

12. Document available at http://www.islameiat.com/Pages/Subjects/Default.aspx?id=7605 &cat_id=108 (accessed August 8, 2016).

13. Peter Steinfels, *The Neoconservatives* (New York: Simon and Schuster, 1979), 65.

14. Cornel West, "The New Cultural Politics of Difference," in *The Cultural Studies Reader*, ed. Simon During (London: Routledge, 1993), 213.

15. Ibid., 214.

16. The term *transversality* was first developed by Félix Guattari in 1964 as a result of his experience at the La Borde clinic in France. His theory takes as its point of departure the forced relationship of the various segregations between the world of the insane and the rest of society and the need to avoid at any cost taking the object of institutional therapy "out of the real context of society. Guattari sought to introduce open collective practices that worked across the confines of the institution itself." See in particular Félix Guattari, "Transversality," in *Molecular Revolution: Psychiatry and Politics*, trans. Rosemary Sheed (Harmondsworth, UK: Penguin Books, 1984).

17. Gerald Raunig, *Art and Revolution. Transversal Activism in the Long Twentieth Century* (New York: Semiotext[e], 2007), 18.

18. Michel Foucault, "The Subject and Power," *Critical Inquiry* 8, no. 4 (Summer 1982): 781.

19. Asef Bayat, *Life as Politics: How Ordinary People Change the Middle East*, ISIM Series on Contemporary Muslim Societies (Amsterdam: Amsterdam University Press, 2010), 97.

20. All the information relating to this campaign can be found on its official site: http://www.tamarud.net.

5 The Muslim Brotherhood

Between Opposition and Power

Dalia Fahmy

THE MASS UPRISINGS that spread across the Arab region in 2011 and ultimately toppled long-entrenched authoritarian regimes were composed of ordinary citizens. The people who came together calling for change transcended ethnic, religious, ideological, and gender lines. It seemed that ideologically based social movements, long perceived to be the agents of social and political change, had failed to bring about such change. For a brief moment it seemed that these movements might lose their cachet as the symbolic agents of change, replaced by nonideologically committed coalitions of ordinary citizens.

In the case of Egypt, it was not the Muslim Brotherhood, the country's largest and most organized social and political movement, that brought about the revolution; on the contrary, they were late in officially joining the ideologically diverse revolutionary forces. However, following the removal of Hosni Mubarak, when the arena of contestation moved from the street and the square to negotiations with the Supreme Council of the Armed Forces (SCAF), and ultimately to the ballot box, Egypt's nonideological coalitions were replaced as the primary actors by the Muslim Brotherhood. This chapter traces the changes and adaptations made by the Muslim Brotherhood during three significant political moments: the authoritarian regime of Mubarak, military rule under the SCAF, and the democratically elected Islamist government of the Muslim Brotherhood under Mohammed Morsi. The chapter will also examine if and how structural changes altered the political commitments and ideological rhetoric of the Muslim Brotherhood.

The Brotherhood under Mubarak

During the more than thirty-year reign of President Mubarak, the Muslim Brotherhood went through periods of political openness and repression, which led to significant changes in its political behavior and strategies. Following the assassination of Anwar Sadat by militant extremists in 1981, the Mubarak regime followed a policy of appeasement toward the brotherhood. Mubarak released many brotherhood members imprisoned under Sadat, including the general guide, Omar al-Tilmisani, and began building a relationship aimed at utilizing the brotherhood as a counterweight to growing extremism in Egypt.

Although Mubarak allowed the brotherhood to remain socially and politically independent, the organization was still officially banned from direct political participation. After Mubarak came to power, the brotherhood began making attempts at becoming a recognized political party. It applied for recognition in 1984 and again in 1987 after minor electoral victories, only to be turned down. Nevertheless, during the 1980s, the state maintained a strategic relationship with the brotherhood: the brotherhood would be allowed to operate through grassroots activism and social welfare programs as long as it refrained from politically contesting the state and voicing harsh criticism of President Mubarak. For much of the decade the brotherhood cooperated with Mubarak's regime and focused primarily on "the improvement of society,"[1] but it did attempt to take advantage of new opportunities to express themselves politically.

Noting the brotherhood's general cooperation with the regime and avoidance of challenging state politics, the state began to allow it more exposure and a louder voice in the public sphere. This allowed the brotherhood not only to voice its positions on social issues, but also to compete publicly with its secular opposition. The regime hoped that this strategy would reveal the brotherhood to be a weak movement whose social vision would be rejected by the public.[2] This strategy of challenging the popularity of the brotherhood, which was barred from returning the challenge to the state, thereby exposing the brotherhood as a weak movement, continued until 1984. However, in 1984, when the brotherhood formed a political alliance with the secular Wafd Party and as a result made remarkable gains during the parliamentary elections, the regime decided it could no longer continue to ignore the brotherhood's activities.[3]

The results of the 1984 parliamentary elections surprised both the regime and the brotherhood. The brotherhood fielded twenty-two candidates, and eight of them won seats. According to the brotherhood's then general guide Tilmisani, "We would have been satisfied if only five of them won."[4] The brotherhood's surprise emergence on the political scene, through an alliance with a secular opposition group, forced the regime to reconsider its position toward it. The brotherhood's unexpected display of power "alerted the regime to the potential political force of the Brotherhood and prompted it to closely examine the organization's activities."[5]

Much to the regime's surprise, the brotherhood was changing strategies. It would no longer focus on social issues and on the improvement of society, but would begin turning attention to regime activity and attempting critiques of government policy. Yet, while brotherhood leaders endeavored to make such bold statements, the party accomplished very little else. Its efforts to introduce Sharia in parliamentary discussions were often ignored, and as a result its new parliamentary status did not offer it any new political power. The regime remained unthreatened by it.[6]

Since the small victory of 1984 did not result in any real political power, the brotherhood shifted strategies again, and by the 1987 parliamentary elections, it had allied with both the Liberal and the Liberal Socialist Parties. This alliance allowed for the three parties to collectively hold thirty-six seats, demonstrating the increasing popularity and influence of the brotherhood among the electorate. It expanded its reach, not only to gain representation in the People's Assembly, but also to strengthen and utilize its network of social services in neighborhoods and villages. Its initiatives aimed at filling gaps in government services created an enormous degree of popular support for it without directly challenging the government, and its growing societal influence would come to change the nature of its relationship with the regime. In April 1989, the then interior minister, Zaki Badr, forever changed the relationship between the brotherhood and the regime when he alleged that the brotherhood had links to radical Islamist groups. After this official denouncement in 1989, there emerged a more determined state effort to confront the organization in response to its noticeably more independent position and its increasingly confident opposition to the regime.

In the 1990s, the Muslim Brotherhood amplified its criticism of the government and its policies, redefining its nature as well as its relationship with the regime. What was once a movement focusing primarily on social services was now developing itself into a more formal party with political ambitions. In 1990, it took a clear position against the regime and joined the opposition party, al-Wafd, in its boycott of the upcoming parliamentary elections, which were seen as flawed because they were not representative or democratic. In a joint statement released by the boycotting parties in October 1990, they refused to "contribute to the creation of a false democratic façade."[7] This stance was seen by some as aiming to embarrass the regime.

Following the 1992 earthquake, during which President Mubarak was out of the country, the weakness of the state apparatus became apparent, and the brotherhood's social service structure and reach came to the fore. Because the state apparatus could not deal with social demands, brotherhood rescue teams struggled into the night to dig out survivors and provide alternative shelters, food, and potable water; the brotherhood, through its own organizational structure, emerged as heroes to the victims of the earthquake.

The ability to mobilize quickly allowed the brotherhood to publicize its political ambitions. The fact that it had resources in rural areas and a presence in urban areas led to the effective distribution and rapid mobilization of its efforts in a manner that proved it to be more effective than the state. Its success was noted by both CNN and BBC, furthering the perception that the brotherhood was growing both in power and in numbers. Alongside the brotherhood's relief efforts, the same political banners displaying its slogan of "Al-islām huwa al-ḥāl" (Islam is the solution), which were used in the run for the 1987 elections, were once again displayed in public as the brotherhood conducted relief efforts, again tying the political activities of the brotherhood to its social success. Despite its increasing social clout, the 1990s were marred with a period of great repression of the brotherhood, resulting in a period of electoral boycott by the organization as much of its leadership was in prison. Subsequent elections in the decade would not result in increased political activity.

However, in 2000 and subsequently in 2005, during a period of limited political liberalization, the brotherhood sought to reassert itself on the political and electoral scene. If electoral outcomes were at times almost certain, then why would opposition candidates and parties take parliamentary elections seriously? In Egypt, elections are opportunities for opposition parties to publicly present electoral platforms and vigorously campaign in the public sphere. This was especially the case during the 2005 election cycle. In Egyptian politics, elections—the very essence of procedural democracy—serve as a moment of strategic interaction between the opposition and the state. And thus, elections are seen as an opportune moment for the opposition movements to directly oppose the state.

The Muslim Brotherhood's electoral success in 2005 provides insight into the question of what happens when Islamists win. Just as its 2005 electoral platform focused on reform, right after its electoral gains the brotherhood issued a statement asserting that its top priority in parliament would be to press for general political reform in Egypt, or *iṣlāḥ*. The platform of *iṣlāḥ*, although seen as ambiguous, was a far cry from the previous platforms based primarily on instituting Sharia principles.

In the 2005 election, eighty-eight members of the Muslim Brotherhood were elected to parliament, representing twenty-one of Egypt's twenty-six governorates, whereas only seventeen brotherhood members were seated after the 2000 election. The eighty-eight members—or the Brotherhood Bloc, as they came to be known—took their role in parliament and the power of parliament more seriously than the ruling party had in the past, with interesting consequences. The entire Brotherhood Bloc moved into a hotel in Cairo in order to work and live together while the People's Assembly was in session, and most importantly, to attend parliamentary sessions regularly. Their visibility in parliament challenged and changed the dynamic of what was not a powerful legislative body, but what, according to Saad al-Katatni, then head of the Brotherhood Bloc, had "been for so long just a rubber stamp on the actions of the President. . . . The NDP [National Democratic Party, the state party] [had] such a stronghold, because of the joint-benefits the Party [had] with the President. We intend[ed] to change that."[8]

Before the 2005 election, fewer than thirty NDP members would be present by the end of a parliamentary session; during the first sessions, at least one hundred had to be present to outnumber the Muslim Brotherhood members. "Our presence in the parliament, and our persistence, dictates that a similar number of the National Party must be present, so the total number of members in parliament [present in session] went from 30 to 200—allowing for real work and real debate to occur."[9] Another consequence of the Muslim Brotherhood's attendance was not only the attendance of NDP parliamentarians, but also an improvement in their level of preparedness. By 2008, it could be said that "for the first time, everyone comes ready to work."[10]

In the span of five years—2005 to 2010—brotherhood parliamentarians sought to alter the image of parliamentarians in the eyes of their constituents by becoming effective politicians. The brotherhood parliamentarians' reform agenda aimed to expose the regime's fraud. "Seats were not the goal," said Mohamed El Biltagy, a brotherhood parliamentarian, but "active participation, getting people together for reform and change—that is the goal."[11] Their first move was to interact with their constituents on a regular basis. According to member Hazem Farouq Mansour, from the Shubra al-Kheima district, "We want the people to see a politician that interacts with his constituents on the street instead of avoiding them, a politician who reports to parliament in the morning and argues for the public's demands—setting the example for what it means to be a productive parliamentarian."[12]

The 2005 Committee on Education exhibited an example of the effect of attendance on parliamentary activity. The committee had fifty-three members, twelve of whom were from the Muslim Brotherhood. In the attendance roster of the Nineteenth Congress, the twelve members of the Muslim Brotherhood and the chair of the committee, Sharif Amer, were the only MPs who regularly attended. The brotherhood MPs directly affected the discussion and implementation of draft proposals. Katatni asserts that health, industry, and consumer protection committees all followed this pattern.[13] The strategy of the Muslim Brotherhood seemed quite simple—to be effectively distributed in committees so as to have an overall presence. It always had at least two MPs participate in every discussion, leading to a tangible effect in a few committees that do not garner great attendance. According to Katatni, this participatory strategy, which was maintained from 2006 to 2008, led to a "change in the work mechanism. Not only did our work become visible, but the [parliament] became visible as an active legislative body."[14]

This strategy did not go unnoticed by the Mubarak government, and the increased committee activity led to a change in media coverage of parliament. Before the increased presence of the Brotherhood Bloc in parliament, a state-owned television station used to broadcast council sessions live, "but that was banned in order to prevent the public opinion from observing the conduct of the Muslim Brotherhood bloc in the council."[15]

During the 2006 legislative session, the brotherhood gained seats in twenty of the twenty-three legislative committees, and it took majority control over the following legislative committees: education, executive, economic, health care, human rights, and industry. It did not pursue a majority of seats in committees with a social or cultural affairs focus. For example, in the Cultural Affairs Committee, it held only two seats, or 6 percent, whereas the National Democratic Party held twenty-three seats, or 75 percent. This strategic commitment to pursue seats on committees dealing with economic and governance issues rather than on social committees signifies a marked difference with the brotherhood's past strategy of focusing on social issues.

According to the minutes of the 2006 parliamentary assembly, brotherhood MPs submitted over 207 out of a total of 221 questions and interpellations on education alone, equaling 94 percent of the work on that committee,[16] even while the brotherhood had only 42 percent representation on the committee and the NDP enjoyed 53 percent representation. According to Katatni, because of the consistent presence and attendance of the brotherhood members, they were able to take part in discussing, drafting, and addressing all the decisions and laws pertaining to the Education Committee. Similar situations played out in the health, industry, and economic committees. For Katatni, the strategy was to ensure that the brotherhood members were "well distributed among the committees, and yes, we have a relatively large presence in some of the committees that we see as important, and a smaller one in others, but our presence is effective."[17]

Given the enormity of its mandate, days after election the brotherhood filled a four-story building in the Minyal district of Cairo with experts on parliamentary issues, dedicating entire floors to social, economic, and political legislation.[18] Symbolically, the building sits on a major road in a bustling neighborhood, signaling to both the regime and the masses the public nature of the brotherhood's work. The first floor of the building has a reception area to welcome guests and hold media interviews. A separate room for conferences (with a separate entrance) allows the brotherhood to hold roundtable discussions, invite guests from various think tanks and universities, and record statements made by brotherhood parliamentarians that are broadcast on the internet. The Brotherhood Bloc also launched its own website, nawabikhwan.org (no longer in existence), to provide information on their activity and voting behavior, stream video conferences, and offer taped broadcasts to various media outlets. The website further signaled to the masses that the once private, underground organization was now public, with a presence that could be monitored by anyone interested. The brotherhood ran on a platform of transparency and had now, in the name of transparency, become the most visibly organized political group in the country.

The secondary strategy of the brotherhood was to focus on three primary issues: corruption, social services, and political reform. This strategy was two-pronged, as the group established early on that it would commit itself to two levels of work: one, *riqābī*, to monitor parliament's previous work and review it for effectiveness, corruption, and maintenance of the national interest; and another, *tashrī'ī* (legislation), to submit new proposals and discussions on new issues.[19] The task of closely investigating the legislative work of past assemblies while simultaneously establishing a work agenda for its present legislative session was an enormous one. Uncovering the work of the past assemblies was seen as key to the group's primary goal as laid out by the electoral platform—political reform and ending the culture of corruption.[20]

The pragmatic approach to politics that the brotherhood took in the mid-2000s stood in stark contrast to the approach taken by the brotherhood members in parliament who came before them. Whereas previous members would voice opposition in the Cultural Affairs Committee on issues like Egypt joining the Miss World competition, or discuss the content of schoolbooks, now brotherhood parliamentarians were no longer perceived as hard-liners. Rather, they were more open to working with other groups to forge compromises, and even garnered support from secular members for their opposition to the extension of the country's emergency law, and their support of human rights reform. The brotherhood also pushed for the independence of the judiciary and lobbied for increasing press freedoms. These goals and attitudes, however, were not well received by the Mubarak regime.

In 2007, the regime responded with the mass arrest of brotherhood members. Eighteen brotherhood legislative staffers drafting education and health-care-reform bills were among the hundreds of members arrested. Mubarak followed this with a brutal crackdown not on the organization's hard-line leaders but rather on the movement's moderates. It seemed that they had emerged as the regime's largest threat. The brotherhood's history of social activity and now its strong political presence were beginning to highlight the gross incompetence of the Mubarak regime, setting the stage for what was to become the most crushing political defeat the brotherhood would suffer. In the rigged 2010 parliamentary elections, the brotherhood did not win a single seat in the People's Assembly. The overwhelming defeat of the brotherhood, or more precisely its moderate members, pushed its members out of Egypt's political institutions.

The ideological moderation and political activity of the brotherhood that, rather than centering on religious and social issues, focused on transparency and good governance, emerged as the new face of political Islam in Egypt, and also served to be the very undoing of the Mubarak regime. One month after the 2010 parliamentary elections, millions of Egyptians descended on Tahrir Square, among them moderate members of the brotherhood. Eighteen days later, on February 11, 2011, Mubarak was gone, ending his more than three-decade-long reign over Egypt. But the question remained: What would this mean for the brotherhood?

The Muslim Brotherhood during the Revolution

During the revolution, the brotherhood was not at the forefront of political activity and did not officially get involved in the initial protests. Instead, they seemed to take a strategic political position to provide support to the protesters, all the while not serving as leaders of the antigovernment movement. In fact, they deliberately allowed non-Islamists to be the leaders of the protests. The organization seemed to be eager to avoid upsetting either the protesters or the government, unsure where the revolution might lead. On February 6, the "Brotherhood [said] in a statement that it '[had] decided to participate in a dialogue round in order to understand how serious the officials are in dealing with the demands of the people.' "[21] Moreover, some senior members of the party took an official position that "backed off its demand that Mr. Mubarak step down immediately and make other concessions, for apparently little concrete in return."[22] This move, which seemed to be an attempt to avoid a direct challenge to Mubarak, produced a strong backlash within Egyptian society, as well as increasing tensions within the brotherhood itself and among the youth of the brotherhood who had formed alliances in the street.

It was not that the brotherhood supported the government, as they historically have been major challengers to the Mubarak regime, but rather that it seemed to be aware of the political costs that would be associated with serving as the leading (and openly direct) opposition to the Mubarak regime during this time. In fact, "the Brothers, ever cautious and aware that they bear the brunt of regime repression when they join protests, were slow to participate in the demonstrations that broke out on Jan. 25 and have struggled to craft a united front ever since."[23] And during the funeral of Mustafa Sawi, the first person killed in the 2011 Egyptian protests, the brotherhood was not visible in an official capacity. The organization itself "insists it is little more than a bit player in the outpouring of resistance to the regime of President Hosni Mubarak."[24] For former brotherhood general guide Mohammed Mahdi Akef, "this is on purpose. . . . We want to be part of the fabric of society."[25] Therefore notions of the brotherhood's religious or ideological politics were obscured during the uprisings.

Indeed, where, exactly, it would emerge after the revolution had yet to be seen, for it had strategically and ideologically taken a backseat during the uprising, refusing to confront the regime head on.

The Muslim Brotherhood under the SCAF

On February 11, 2011, with recently appointed vice president Omar Suleiman's announcement that President Mubarak had resigned and that authority would now be transferred to the SCAF, it seemed that a new era had begun in Egypt. And though during the revolution the military refused to turn on the revolutionary forces, and chants of "The people and the army are one" filled the streets, the main coalition of January 25 revolutionaries submitted thirty-five demands to the military leadership that, in addition to calling for reform of the economic security and social sectors, demanded the quick transfer of power from the military SCAF to civilian leaders.

The military leadership responded by stating that they would meet the demands of the revolutionary forces; however, they did so in very limited ways. The military council dissolved the parliament that had been fraudulently elected under Mubarak just a few months earlier. They also arrested three former cabinet ministers for corruption, and called on the state prosecutor to begin investigating the network of crony capitalists that had flourished under Mubarak. However, because the SCAF was not willing to reform the security apparatus that had historically been integral to the regime's ability to control the political scene, was not willing to actually convict the Mubarak-era crony capitalists, and was not willing to reform the media that continued to shape public perception without true independence, the SCAF's commitment to reform seemed merely symbolic, and it quickly began to lose favor with the revolutionary forces.

While the transitional period highlights the deep entrenchment of the SCAF in the political process and ultimately in the Egyptian state, this period also marked a great shift in the brotherhood's political strategy. In the wake of the revolution, it found itself caught between the dual commitments it had struggled with over the past decade: whether to remain engaged in politics or return to its roots of *da'wa* (religious outreach) through a movement relegated to the social sphere that aimed to foster pious Muslims through preaching, social services, and integrity by example. This bifurcation in vision culminated with the ideological divide that had been emerging in the brotherhood during the 2005–2010 parliamentary sessions.

The divisions within the brotherhood were further exacerbated in postrevolutionary Egypt by the organization's youth, whose participation in the protest movement was not only essential to the success of the revolution, but also gave them a sense of legitimacy in the eyes of the brotherhood leadership that they previously did not enjoy. Thus, the brotherhood found itself trying to hold on to its activist youth, who during the revolution began to see their leadership as increasingly out of touch, while trying to forge a new path ahead by shaping Egypt's political future. This moment of tension also coincided with the release from prison of more hard-line members of the brotherhood such as Khayrat al-Shatir, whose release was due to youth activity, but whose vision for the future of the brotherhood in Egypt stood in stark contrast to theirs.

On the political front, the revolution led to the establishment of several political parties that emerged as ideological competitors of the brotherhood. On February 19, 2011, the first party to gain recognition by the courts in postrevolution Egypt was the previously illegal Center Party (al-Wasat Party). Founded by Abul Ela Madi and other former members of the brotherhood, along with Coptic leaders and women, the Center Party's political vision for Egypt is seen as inspired by conservatism but not articulated through Islamism. Members of the Center Party were integral in the 2004 popular uprising that led to the establishment of the Egyptian Movement for Change, or Kefaya.

On February 23, 2011, the Muslim Brotherhood's Guidance Bureau announced that it would be establishing a political party separate from the movement called the Freedom and Justice Party (FJP), led by Katatni, former head of the Muslim Brotherhood's parliamentary bloc from 2005 to 2010. And though the new party would still be banned due to its articulation of religion as its source of guidance (an indication of the resilience of the political status quo, which still saw the party as illegal in Egypt), on March 29, 2011, the party invited youth, Copts, and women to join its membership. However, the strategy did not work, and much of the revolutionary youth remained alienated from the new party.

On March 26, 2011, high-ranking Muslim Brotherhood Guidance Bureau member Abdel Moneim Abul Fotouh announced to a gathering of Muslim Brotherhood youth that he would be forming a more liberal Islamic party that still reflected the core ideals of the Muslim Brotherhood (piety and social justice), but that would move ideologically beyond the Muslim Brotherhood and embrace "liberal Islamism." Another high-ranking Muslim Brotherhood member widely respected by the brotherhood youth, Ibrahim al-Zafaarani, announced the establishment of the Nahda Party (the Revival Party), which aimed to become a party that was rooted in Islam with political pluralism and democracy as its aim.

As younger Islamists began to distance themselves from the Islamist political identity of the Muslim Brotherhood and move toward a pluralistic framework in which the past signified a bygone era of the strategic evolution of Islamism, the brotherhood found itself in a predicament. It was no longer perceived as the primary voice advocating for political Islam in Egypt; in an era of pluralism, there was now competition. And the new Egyptian political landscape had opened up not only the political arena, but also the marketplace of ideas in which different Islamisms were now emerging. Islamism, as a reaction to alienation from the state, was being replaced by pluralistic approaches to justice and development on one hand and, for the first time in Egypt's modern history, the surfacing of more hard-line Salafi political perspectives on the other. Salafists, who rejected the notions of democracy and political processes, were coming to the forefront and competing in politics, trying to gain for themselves a larger stake in Egypt's political future. And increasingly marginalized on both ends of the spectrum were the revolutionary youth, who were resistant to engaging with the brotherhood.

With the military in power, Egyptians seemed divided over the timing of the elections. The secularists and revolutionary coalitions wanted to postpone elections, giving them time to organize and campaign, while the Muslim Brotherhood, under the newly formed FJP, wanted elections held as soon as possible. While the stated intent of the brotherhood's push for early elections might have been to move the SCAF out of power, it was perceived by many Egyptians as a collusion between the brotherhood and the SCAF in which the brotherhood, the largest organized political group in the country, would surely win a majority of the seats in parliament. The secularists also wanted to hold off on the parliamentary elections until a constitution was written, fearing that an Islamist-dominated parliament would lead to an Islamist-dominated constitutional assembly responsible for drafting Egypt's postrevolutionary constitution. The SCAF chose to hold the constitutional drafting period between the parliamentary and presidential elections.

Egyptian parliamentary elections are unique in that they are supervised by the judiciary, and, due to the vastness of the country and the limited number of judges, the SCAF moved to hold elections over a period of four months. Several smaller parties joined the FJP to form the Democratic Alliance. After two rounds of elections, it became clear that the Democratic Alliance would be in the majority, consistently winning over 50 percent of the seats. In this regard, the brotherhood made several symbolic mistakes by emerging as the largest, most organized, and most publicly visible group during the parliamentary campaigning period, to be followed only by the Salafi Nour Party. Historically, the brotherhood had maintained modest electoral objectives, contesting not more than a third of parliamentary seats. According to former secretary general of the brotherhood and the current interim general guide, Mahmoud Izzat, "We are not after power, rather we want to have influence in parliament, to reflect the will of the people that elect us to those positions."[26] One-third of parliamentary seats would also allow the brotherhood to meet the minimum threshold necessary to veto any constitutional changes.

But it became apparent that the brotherhood was more interested in achieving political presence than it seemed to let on. And after the declaration of the FJP as a separate political party, a heavy campaign to promote the FJP began. Prior to the parliamentary elections, polls were placing the brotherhood support at 20–30 percent.[27] However, after a few short weeks of heavy campaigning, through an extensive reliance on the brotherhood's vast networks, the country was plastered with images of candidates campaigning under the FJP banner, with a logo, it should be noted, that more closely resembled the 2008 Barack Obama campaign logo than the Muslim Brotherhood logo. More importantly, there were very few religious symbols in any of the FJP campaign posters. However, the public was getting mixed messages about who was in charge of the FJP. Although it had established itself as an entity separate from the Muslim Brotherhood, and it occupied its own building in Cairo's Muqqatam district, the statements issued relating to the parliamentary elections were released from the Office of the Muslim Brotherhood Guidance Bureau, in the Minyal district. It was clear to the public that the FJP could easily be equated to the Muslim Brotherhood, and that the Guidance Bureau was running the party as a political wing of its organization.

Furthermore, the historically successful strategy of not contesting more than 30–40 percent of seats, which had worked to ensure the brotherhood a place at the table with some modicum of power without being perceived by the public as a usurper, was repeatedly undermined in the run-up to the parliamentary elections. Despite announcements coming out of the Guidance Bureau stating that the brotherhood was not after domination but rather participation, the perception was not such among the public. The general guide of the Muslim Brotherhood, Muhammad Badie, announced on its website and in speeches during April 2011 that the brotherhood "was from the people, with the people and for the people"[28] and wanted to effect change in parliament, not dominate it. Yet on April 30, the brotherhood announced that it would not contest more that 45–50 percent of seats.[29] Coupled with the entry of the Salafi Nour Party into the competition, this announcement was perceived as threatening to undermine the loosely allied liberal coalitions. By mid-October, the brotherhood had announced that since not enough candidates were running on certain lists, it was going to increase the proportion of seats it was contesting to 60 percent,[30] and a few days later, it announced that it would field candidates in every race, contesting 100 percent of seats in parliament.[31] In the end, the FJP won 47.2 percent of the seats, and 24.7 percent went to the Salafi Nour Party, resulting in Islamist control of 72 percent of parliament.[32]

The Islamists' success in the parliamentary elections was met with a direct response from the SCAF, who appointed a new advisory council headed by Kamal al-Ganzouri, prime minister from 1996 to 1999 under Mubarak, and populated it with liberals, secularists, and heads of political parties who had not fared well in the elections. After initially joining, the FJP withdrew from the assembly, seeing it as an appointed body that was created as a counterbalance to parliament, the body actually elected by the people. Thus, the brotherhood and the FJP continued to find themselves caught between the public's outcry at the demise of their former policy of limited participation and a transitional authority seeking to undermine any perceived political gains by Islamists.

Through this exclusion, the SCAF was successful in creating a level of alienation of the brotherhood from the revolutionary forces and other political groups. It was also able to utilize the vast resources at its disposal, including private and public media outlets and Mubarak-era businessmen and crony capitalists capable of contributing vast sums of money, to offset brotherhood popularity and further alienate the revolutionary forces, often turning them on each other. The public very quickly not only grew weary of the brotherhood, but also began longing for the old regime.

The brotherhood responded in late March 2012 by announcing that it would field a presidential candidate, after it had continually officially stated throughout the year since the start of the revolution that it was not after the leadership. According to brotherhood leader Badie, the new Egypt "is under a serious threat" because its current military-led government "has failed to represent the will of the people."[33] The brotherhood sought to run Shatir, a longtime financial backer and member of the Guidance Bureau who initially denied any intentions of entering the presidential race.[34] He then resigned from the brotherhood to run for president. On April 14, the Supreme Presidential Electoral Commission announced Shatir's disqualification as a presidential candidate, as he faced charges of belonging to an illegal organization—the Muslim Brotherhood. The brotherhood responded by fielding a former parliamentarian, Morsi, as its presidential candidate.

Morsi had been the primary negotiator between the brotherhood and the state security apparatus, the very means through which the Mubarak regime monitored and infiltrated the brotherhood. Morsi had negotiated with state security to ensure the brotherhood's participation in various political matters, such as parliamentary elections. In this regard, he seemed to be a candidate with the ability to both legislate, as he once did in parliament, and make inroads with the SCAF.

Morsi had less than two months to run, as the first round of elections was to take place at the end of May. The brotherhood argued that they were not after power, but to the public it clearly seemed that they were. The brotherhood controlled both the upper and lower houses, and was now after the presidency. The SCAF responded by threatening to dissolve parliament in order to check the power of a rising brotherhood. Revolutionary groups that were growing increasingly insecure in the face of the brotherhood's control over two branches of government echoed this sentiment. The High Constitutional Court responded by dissolving parliament two days before the presidential election.

While the SCAF intended to undermine the brotherhood through several strategic steps, what became increasingly apparent was that the transition from military rule was not a part of the military's strategic program. Consequently, on June 14, the military occupied the parliamentary building and claimed all legislative powers for itself. The Ministry of Justice then reinstituted the emergency laws that had been lifted after Mubarak's fall. And during the final round of presidential elections on June 17, the SCAF issued a constitutional declaration transferring much of the presidential power to itself and stripped the president of his role as commander in chief of the armed forces—placing it in the hands of Field Marshal Mohamed Tantawi. It then began to dissolve the one-hundred-member constitutional writing committee recently appointed by parliament, granting itself veto power over any presidential decree. Finally, Tantawi appointed one of his assistants, another military general, as chief of staff of the president. Basically, the new president had a diminished role in the face of the rising power of the military. Morsi had won, but it was not clear what he had won.

The transition period from Mubarak to Morsi was marred by a political power struggle between the brotherhood and the SCAF. It was also marred by the brotherhood's perceived abandonment of its commitment to principles of moderation and its political strategy of limited participation, as well as the formation of new alliances that seemed to undermine its previous commitments. Perhaps the most damage was done to the image of the brotherhood in the eyes of the public, wherein the SCAF was able to draw a picture of an ambitious and incompetent group that was not to be trusted. In this regard, the SCAF shaped public perception in a way that stacked the deck against the brotherhood.

Morsi and the "Brotherhoodization" of the State

On Friday, June 29, 2012, newly elected president Morsi entered Tahrir Square. His entry was met with eruptions of "Allahu Akbar" (God is great). The chants continued, interspersed with nationalist rallying cries, but a heavy religious undertone that was absent in the square during the revolution became palpable. President Morsi addressed the crowd, and in a show of confidence he opened his jacket to prove he was not wearing a bulletproof vest, stating that he had nothing to fear as the legitimate representative of Egypt's uprising and also of the Egyptian state. He promised to be a "president for all Egyptians," declaring that "the revolution must continue until all its objectives are met."[35] Morsi also made reference to the diminished presidential powers that the military under the SCAF had just decreed, stating, "I promise you that I will not give up on any of the powers given to the president." While it was clear from the outset that the Morsi administration was entering a hostile political landscape, it was not clear if the brotherhood was ready for governance. What the subsequent year would come to show was that Morsi and his administration were quite often not in control.[36] The political landscape had shifted in the sixteen months since the revolution, and the SCAF had ensured its position of power and ability to both undermine Morsi's authority and sway public sentiment to its side. It seemed that it was easy to capitalize on the public perception that the brotherhood was out to "Brotherhoodize" the state—that is, to enter into an institution they historically were excluded from, and seize control of it.

The standoff between Morsi and the SCAF began immediately. Two weeks after taking office, in a move to demonstrate his commitment to governance that reflected the will of the people, Morsi sought to assert his power and to reinstitute the previously dissolved parliament. However, the Supreme Constitutional Court (SCC) overturned his decree and handed over legislative authority to the SCAF. This caused Morsi to commit one of his first political mistakes: he vowed to respect the SCC's judicial ruling, a move he would reverse in the coming months. Publicly, Morsi began to appear weak.

Within a few months in office, Morsi began to discuss the massive Egyptian political bureaucracy, and publicly stated that it was replete with corruption, especially since the Mubarak-era loyalists (or remnants, *fulool*, as they became known) still controlled much of the political scene. The *fulool* composed much of the state security apparatus, the business elite, and the Egyptian media empires. They stood to lose much of their control of the state and the economy if Morsi continued to challenge them, and thus they embarked on an extensive media campaign to project Morsi and his administration as incompetent.[37]

The prosecutor general, a Mubarak appointee assigned to oversee the trials of those being prosecuted for the violence against civilians during the revolution, was acquitting many of the perpetrators. Morsi responded by dismissing him. However, after much outcry from other senior judges, who accused Morsi of executive overreach, the prosecutor general was reinstated. This move again caused Morsi to appear as an indecisive and weak leader.

However, the major battleground between Morsi and his opponents, who now came to include the secularist and the revolutionary forces, emerged during the constitutional drafting process. With the gap between Islamist forces, which now included members of al-Wasat Party, the Nour Party, and the Brotherhood, in clear view, secularists accused the Islamists of trying to "Islamize" and ultimately "Brotherhoodize" the state. The 2012 constitutional draft was almost identical to the Mubarak-era constitution. However, the main point of the 2012 constitution was Article 2, which stated that the principles of Sharia would continue to be the main sources of legislation, as had been the case since 1971, during the presidency of Sadat. Salafi members of the committee pushed for a more literalist interpretation of Sharia, while secularist wanted nothing of the sort. Secularists also pushed for greater discussion of constitutional clauses that remained unclear regarding the role of the state institutions in the judiciary, the independence of the judiciary, and military control.

The deadline for the completion of the drafting process was set for December 12, and with several debates not yet concluded, members of the constitutional drafting assembly began to resign. Those that resigned included former presidential candidate Amr Musa; leader of the liberal al-Ghad Party, Ayman Nour; leader of the liberal Wafd Party, Al-Sayid Badawi; members of the revolutionary forces (including members of the April 6 Movement); and representatives of the Coptic Church. It seemed that the only members left in the process were the Islamists. If the December 12 deadline was not met, the SCC would issue a new assembly, and on December 2 the current assembly was due to be reviewed. This situation positioned Islamists against many of the other political voices, and threatened to undo the assembly. While the secular forces may have hoped that the SCC would push for a new assembly, what they did not foresee was Morsi's response—an act of power that may have been the tipping point that ultimately led to his fall.

In an attempt to thwart the SCC's dissolution of the assembly on November 22, Morsi issued a constitutional decree in which he limited the tenure of the prosecutor general from a lifetime appointment to a four-year term. He followed this by appointing a new prosecutor who, unlike his predecessor, was critical of the Mubarak regime. Morsi canceled all not-guilty verdicts that took place under the former prosecutor general, and appointed a fact-finding committee to investigate the crimes that had occurred during the revolution. However, in his greatest show of power, Morsi extended the December 12 deadline for the drafting process by two months, and to prevent the SCC from overturning this, he banned any judicial review of the president until a new constitution was passed and a new parliament was elected. But the decree would go even further: there would be no judicial review of parliament by the SCC. While this could have been seen as increasing the legislative power of parliament, it was also seen as an attempt by Morsi to issue himself more power and then protect a parliament that was sure to be overwhelmingly composed of brotherhood members. While he may have been trying to protect an increasingly faltering political process, it seemed that Morsi was indeed Brotherhoodizing the state. And while he explained to the Supreme Judicial Council that this decree was temporary and would only apply to sovereign decisions and not administrative ones, it was too late. Morsi had given the SCAF, the secularists, the *fulool*, and, most importantly, the revolutionaries, a reason to return to Tahrir, which lead to his removal from power by the military on July 3, 2013.

While the Muslim Brotherhood accepted the principle of democracy, it is not clear that it had anticipated electoral success, especially in a political climate that had for so long seen it as insular and untrustworthy. Though the ideological reform, political commitments, and organization of the brotherhood built under authoritarianism pushed it to the forefront of postrevolutionary Egypt, it seemed that its hard-line rhetoric in the face of increasing repression was making a comeback. The brotherhood, whose long-term political strategy was to participate in politics in order to influence but not usurp them, quickly became perceived as abandoning this strategy.

Although the brotherhood had been able to continue its commitment to Egypt's increasing democratization, it remains unclear if it was ready for governing. Its political strategy of not contesting more than 30 percent of seats in parliamentary elections had proven to be an effective tool under Mubarak. However, in postrevolutionary Egypt, the system had changed, and the brotherhood no longer stood as a challenger to an authoritarian regime. Rather, it emerged as a challenger to a deeply entrenched military apparatus. With their vast control of the economy, the military had more power and much more political leverage than Mubarak did.[38] Yet, more importantly, because the military was perceived as a facilitator and ally during the initial revolution, it also enjoyed a degree of public support the Mubarak did not. In this regard, the deck was stacked against the brotherhood and any group that stood to challenge the new political order.

The success of the brotherhood in the decade prior to the revolution may have helped lay the groundwork for an uprising that would ultimately topple Mubarak, but the deep state remained. And the political strategies that were successful during the limited political contestation could not be used to challenge the new political order, let alone lead to a strategy of governance. Ultimately, the conditions that led to the rise the brotherhood also led to its fall.

Notes

1. Gilles Kepel, "Islamists versus the State in Egypt and Algeria," *Daedalus* 124, no. 3 (Summer 1995): 115.
2. Ahmed Abdalla, "Egypt's Islamists and the State: From Complicity to Confrontation," *Middle East Report*, no. 183 (July-August 1993).
3. Dia Rashwan, "'A Trial at the Polls,'" *Al-Ahram Weekly* 21, no. 27 (September 1995).
4. Quoted in "Muslim Brotherhood Leader on Elections, Policy," *Al-Majallah* 9, no. 15 (June 1984): 9–10.
5. Rashwan, "'A Trial at the Polls,'" 2.
6. Barry Rubin, *Islamic Fundamentalism in Egyptian Politics* (New York: St. Martin's, 1996), 23.
7. "Egypt Election Concerns," *Middle East Watch*, November 15, 1990, 8.
8. Author's interview with Saad al-Katatni, Cairo, August 4 and 6, 2008 [audio recording].
9. Ibid.
10. Author's interview with Hazem Farouq Mansour, August 3, 2008 [audio recording].
11. This remained the strategy in the 2010 election cycles as well. Kristen Chick, "Egypt Election Routs Popular Muslim Brotherhood from Parliament," *Christian Science Monitor*, December 1, 2010, http://ca.news.yahoo.com/egypt-election-routs-popular-muslim-brotherhood-parliament.html.
12. Author's interview with Hazem Farouq Mansour, August 3, 2008 [audio recording].

13. "In 70–80% of committees the MB [Muslim Brotherhood] is in control through their attendance." Author's interview with Saad al-Katatni, Cairo, August 4 and 6, 2008 [audio recording].

14. Ibid.

15. Ibid.

16. *Akhbar al-Majlis* [Official documents of the parliament] (Cairo: Majlis Al-Sha'b, 2007).

17. Author's interview with Saad al-Katatni, Cairo, August 4 and 6, 2008 [audio recording].

18. However, in 2007 eighteen brotherhood legislative staffers drafting education and health-care-reform bills were among the hundreds of members arrested. Charles Levinson, "'Brothers' in Egypt Present Two Faces," *Wall Street Journal*, February 15, 2011, http://online .wsj.com/article/SB10001424052748704629004576135882819143872.html?mod=WSJ_hp _LEFTTopStories.

19. Muslim Brotherhood Parliamentary Bloc, *Adwaa ala adaa nuwwab al-ikhwan* (Spotlighting MB parliamentary members' performance) (Cairo: Alakhbar English, 2010).

20. Muslim Brotherhood, "Birnamij Al-Intikibat 2005" [The 2005 parliamentary election platform], Muslim Brotherhood's Official English Website, http://ikhwanweb.com/.

21. "Timeline: Egypt's Revolution," *Al Jazeera*, February 14, 2011.

22. Dan Murphy, "Egypt's Protests: Muslim Brotherhood's Concessions Prompt Anger," *Christian Science Monitor*, February 7, 2011, http://www.csmonitor.com/World/Middle-East /2011/0207/Egypt-protests-Muslim-Brotherhood-s-concessions-prompt-anger.

23. Ibid.

24. Will Englund, "Muslim Brotherhood Says It Is Only a Minor Player in Egyptian Protests," *Washington Post*, January 31, 2011, http://www.washingtonpost.com/wp-dyn/content /article/2011/01/30/AR2011013003308.html.

25. Ibid.

26. Author's interview with Mahmoud Izzat, July 11, 2008.

27. Dalia Mogahed, "Winning Back the Revolution," *Foreign Policy*, November 18, 2011, http://www.foreignpolicy.com/articles/2011/11/28/winning_back_the_revolution?page=full.

28. "MB Chairman: We Seek to Participate, Not Dominate Elections," Ikhwanweb.com, April 20, 2011, http://www.ikhwanweb.com/article.php?id=28432.

29. "Jamā'atu-l-ikhwān tunāfis 'ala 50 percent min maqā'id al-barlamān wā 'an taqdīm al-hizb murashahh li-ri'āsati-l-jumhurīyya amrun mahhalu-niqāsh," http://elmokhalestv.com /index/details/id/3124.

30. "Al-ikhwān tunāfis 'ala akthar min 60 percent min maqā'id al-barlaman," http://www .nmisr.com/vb/showthread.php?t=360601.

31. "Qawā'im al-ikhwān tunāfis 'ala jamī' al-maqā'id al-barlamānīyyah," http://www .alqabas.com.kw/node/23510.

32. The brotherhood controlled 15.8 percent of parliamentary seats in 2000, and 22 percent in 2005.

33. Mohamed Fadel Fahmy, "Egypt's Muslim Brotherhood to Field Presidential Candidate," CNN.com, April 1, 2012, http://www.cnn.com/2012/04/01/world/meast/egypt-brotherhood -president/.

34. Interview on Al Jazeera TV's program *Without Limits* (Bilā ḥudūd), with host Ahmed Mansour, February 8, 2012. Video of this interview can be found on YouTube: http://www .youtube.com/watch?v=MhvouWONOiY.

35. Link TV, "Mosaic News - 06/29/12: Egypt's Morsi Takes Presidential Oath in Cairo's Ionic Tahrir Square," YouTube, July 2, 2012, http://www.youtube.com/watch?v=vvEmj5s3jHU.

36. According to Wael Haddara, senior adviser to President Morsi, "We were in office, we were never in power." Author's interview, May 2, 2014, Toronto, Canada.

37. See chapter 7 of this volume.

38. With estimates of the military control of the economy ranging from 5 to 40 percent, it is difficulty to get a clear picture of what Robert Springborg calls "Military, Inc." *Egypt Independent*, October 26, 2011. And with reporting on the economic assets and footprint of the military nearly impossible, it is unclear how deep the military influence over the economy really runs. See Shana Marshall and Joshua Stacher, "Egypt's Generals and Transnational Capital," *Middle East Report* 262 (Spring 2012) and Shana Marshall, "Egypt's Other Revolution: Modernizing the Military-Industrial Complex," *Jadaliyya*, February 10, 2012.

6 Copts' Role in Modern Egypt

Mai Mogib Mosad

ONE OF THE distinctive subthemes of the Egyptian uprising on January 25, 2011, has been the proliferation of Coptic political participation in the country. Christian movements and political participation had largely, though not entirely, been guided by the church during the Mubarak era. During the January 25 "revolution," Christian Egyptians joined their Muslim counterparts as "one hand" to challenge state authorities in pursuit of "freedom, bread, social justice and human dignity." After successfully deposing the former president, many of these Christian Egyptians continued on with their revolutionary ambitions.

> For years Copts presented their demands to the state primarily through the person of Pope Shenouda. When pressed to demonstrate for their demands, either by events or by clergy, they did so mostly within the confines of church walls. The revolution changed this equation, however, and the unity expressed in overthrowing Mubarak gave Copts a new sense of participation in rebuilding Egypt. Some Christian participation remained along the lines of revolutionary values, enveloped fully in the youth movements that populated Tahrir Square. Others began sensing a threat to their full participation from the emergence and ascendency of Islamists groups, and rallied behind a liberal and civil cause. Still others took the opportunities afforded to them by the revolution to organize and demonstrate for particular Coptic issues.[1]

Regardless of these differences, newly arisen variables influenced the position of Copts in contemporary Egypt: the rise of political Islamist tendencies, the frequent sectarian clashes and incidents, the church's retreat from political affairs, the politics of the new pope and Egypt's newly elected president Mohammed Morsi, and, finally, the Copts' participation in the June 30 demonstrations and its impact on both the political and social circumstances of Coptic society and the Copts' relationship with the newly elected president.

This chapter seeks to analyze the triangular relationship between the regime, the church, and the Copts. This triangular relationship helps in understanding the position of Copts before and after the so-called revolution and in uncovering the key factors that influenced these three actors after January 25. Among the factors to consider are how this triangular relationship was framed by the media, the impact of the relationship on the Coptic community as a whole, and the governing regime's approach to the Copts as a single, homogeneous bloc represented by the pope. This chapter discusses the prerevolutionary history of the regime-church-Copts relationship, traces its development after the fall of Mubarak, and examines the current factors and events that influence such an interrelated and complicated rapport.

Copts: A Consolidated "Minority" Perception

Christianity in Egypt[2] dates from the time of Saint Mark the Evangelist. From that time, the whole of Egypt was Christian until Islamic rule began in the seventh century. Egyptian Christians were called Copts (*Qibt* or *Aqbat*), from the Greek *Aigyptos*. The transformation from Christianity to Islam and the Arabic language occurred steadily throughout the centuries. Now, to be a Copt is to be a native Egyptian Christian, in contrast to Egyptian Muslims and to non-Egyptian Christians.

The perception of what constitutes a "minority" is constructed through some important insights about networks of association and lines of division among different groups in society. Minorities tend to assert special needs and advocate for legal acknowledgment of their rights and special status in society. Minority claims may be acknowledged or violated as the existence of a minority becomes socially and institutionally embedded. To be considered a minority, a group must be an integral element in broader society while remaining sufficiently outside its sociopolitical core. To be a minority is to lack access to the kinds of power and status conferred on those who abide by the dominant norms in that society. The significance of minority status thus differs from society to society. It is dependent on which social characteristics come to be treated as critically distinctive, and on whether there are disadvantages accompanying this distinction.

In practical terms, the categories of "minority" and "majority" are meaningless. The more pertinent category is power—namely, how the majority and the state use their power vis-à-vis the minority population. The more pertinent question is whether a government represents the entire population or just one particular segment of society.[3] A minority is a group that cannot be dominant in a society and in that society's polity. A group can be deemed a minority when its values and worldviews are either excluded from or insufficiently reflected in the public sphere and in the constitution of societal norms. This kind of exclusion signifies marginalization and exclusion. Marginalization is a perception, among individuals or a group, of a lack of belonging to the predominant social structure and an inability to effect change within society.[4] Because religion embodies a clear delineation of culture, a religious group may rely on religion to consolidate its minority status.

Accordingly, social identities are, to a certain extent, constructed and maintained through shifting social boundaries. The demarcation of these boundaries is negotiable. In a sense, the Christian identity of Copts does not, then, signify the exclusion of Copts from Egyptian society or its sense of "Egyptian-ness" but rather stresses their distinct identity from that of the majority.[5] Indeed, the issue of minority rights in Egypt is by definition a political one, with the minority and its corollary, the majority, often implicit in political discourse. That is, in Egypt, the category of the minority tends to be represented in religious terms. Thus, the Christians are a "minority community" since religion is treated as the definitive component of culture.

Yet, in Egypt, the Copts are not defined a religious group, per se. The Egyptian state groups its subjects into the categories of a legally privileged majority and a legally protected minority; a distinction that identifies the former with the Egyptian nation and the latter as simply residing within that nation, though not fully a part of it. The most striking change in Egyptian political culture during the past fifty years has been the apparent increase in its commitment to Islam, due in large part to the success of Islamist groups in providing services (that is, relief from substandard living conditions) where governments have been slow to respond. The signs of growing Islamic identity are everywhere—in dress, in behavior, and in the country's publications—and seem to have had an impact on the degree of piety among ordinary Egyptians.

Common Assumptions and Some Clarifications

Before delving further into the discussion presented in this chapter, key terms and concepts need to be defined in order to dispel some common assumptions and misinterpretations.[6] First, it should be noted that Coptism is not a religion. The term *Copts* (*al-aqbat*) has, historically, denoted all Egyptians. Coptism, or the state of being Coptic (*al-qubtyah*), does not to belong to a specific religious sect, but rather refers to Egyptians in general. In this chapter, however, the designation "Copts" refers to all Christians in Egypt. The term *Coptism* is used as a symbolic indication of Christianity.

Second, any focus on Egyptian Orthodox Copts to the exclusion of Protestant or Catholic Copts is predicated on the false assumption that the attitudes of the Catholic or Protestant Church are distinct on political or social levels from those of the Orthodox Church. It is true that the three churches certainly differ on doctrinal matters, and that unlike the Anglican Church, the Catholic and Orthodox Churches did not declare any clear support for the January 25 demonstration. But the variation in doctrine and degree of willingness to publicize the respective churches' political views has not significantly influenced the groups' political positions. As such, the foregoing analysis will simply focus on the Orthodox Church, which represents the vast majority of Copts.

Third, the Copts are not an insular, homogeneous group of people. Different social groups within the Coptic community vary in terms of both social standing and political engagement—they represent different social classes and espouse different political ideologies. Copts are found among peasant farmers and urban professionals alike. The only uniting characteristics among Copts are their nationality—they are all Egyptians—and their broad religious affiliation—they are all Christians. They have different interests, sociopolitical ideas, and biases and, accordingly, do not take a unified position toward public issues.

Fourth, it is important to distinguish between Copts as a religious group represented by the church and Copts as a social group enmeshed within the Egyptian national fabric. Since Egyptian Copts differ in their political, social, and sectarian affiliations, they cannot be treated as one cohesive group. However, a long history of internal religious tensions eventually leading to greater cohesion between the community and its official religious institutions has forced religious leaders to play multiple roles in defending the interests of the Copts as well as representing them in the public sphere.

Fifth, the terms *Coptic group*, *Coptic issue*, and *Coptic question* give an impression that Copts have a socioreligious system parallel to that of the Egyptian Muslim majority, who, it should be noted, are also heterogeneous in their politics and social beliefs. Also, these concepts suggest that Copts form a group that is currently in the process of transforming into a political lobby of religious affiliations.[7] Use of these terms in this chapter is not intended to affirm either impression. Instead, this chapter is intended to both underline the heterogeneity of the group and more accurately describe its common features.

Regime-Church-Copts: A State-Society Approach

The state-society approach is the ideal way to analyze the regime-church-Copts relationship introduced above. Theoretical treatments of state-society relations discern five main steps or stages that transform these relations. First, the theory posits a state that manifests Thomas Hobbes's emphasis on the importance of the national state as a tool to control society and protect it from the "war of all against all." Second, it posits a secular state that aims to abolish differences and spread societal homogeneity. Third, it posits a state that recognizes diversity and thus encourages the revival or survival of different cultures and identities. Fourth, it posits the retreating state, which witnesses the rise of primordial and sectarian powers. Fifth, it calls on the concept of "mutual empowerment," as described by Joel Migdal,[8] in which the state is a part of society and any governing regime—democratic or autocratic—cannot be isolated from its society.

Accordingly, the more the state is in retreat, the more it experiences the forces of separation and disintegration. It is at this intersection of retreat and separation that religion often surfaces as a social fact,[9] bringing people together in organizations that have political influence, but also becoming a source of political and social conflict at the same time. Hence, in order to analyze the regime-church-Copts relation, key variables must be considered.[10] First, the structure of the community within the state is significant: If Copts are regarded as the largest Christian sect, their religious leader could potentially be regarded as a rival to the state. A powerful church leadership makes it difficult for the state to challenge it, which forces the state to adopt a policy of rapprochement backed up by repression if necessary. Alternatively, if different sects of the same religion exist, it is less likely that the state will perceive the religion as a threat.

Second, the structure of the Christian community as a whole in relation to the rest of society is also important. In states like Egypt that exhibit a clear majority-minority divide, Christians are inclined to perceive themselves as more vulnerable to changes that take place within the majority community. However, the existence of other minority groups can offer the minority community some space to articulate its concerns. Third, church-state relations are affected by both regime policies toward the presence of the Christian community and perceptions held by Christians regarding the impact of these policies on their security.

Fourth, there is the security problem. The church is faced with the dilemma of whether to defend the communal rights of its followers or exercise self-censorship, given that the regime is the ultimate provider of its security. Correspondingly, if this guarantee of protection is not fulfilled, it is more likely that church leaders will be outspoken on particular issues.

Finally, the existence of competitors within the community can influence the activities of the church, often resulting in a desire for a close relationship with the state in order to secure patronage, or a distance between the state and the community.

Religion in State and Society

Egyptians often describe their society as a religious one, and indeed religion plays a prominent role in public life in Egypt. However, there are grounds here for tension as well as consensus.[11]

Socially, there are periods when tension between religion and politics becomes more acute, and periods when it subsides. One might define moments of low tension, or relative equilibrium, as moments when neither the religious nor the political side seeks major modification of the relationship. At other moments, one side or the other seeks revision.[12] Indeed, the relationship between religious and political institutions in Egypt remains unstable for two key reasons: First, there is constant social and economic change in the form of urbanization, social mobility, and improved communication. These changes have increased pluralism and produced conflict within the religious sphere. Some elements of the religious sphere have sought to make religion a more prominent, or even a dominant, part of the state. Second, in return, the Egyptian state has responded by seeking to further suppress religious institutions.

In addition, by restricting political participation and representation through-out society, Egypt's authoritarian leadership has diverted internal tensions toward other spheres of life: cultural, social, economic, and legal. In particular, by denying its citizens access to political space and either refusing or failing to uphold its end of the social contact—providing for social needs such as poverty reduction, infrastructure development, and employment (to name a few) in ex-change for its continued authoritarian rule—the Egyptian government has rein-forced the authority of the Islamic establishment, which has evolved in response to changing political opportunities, gaining influence and power along the way.[13] Moreover, while the religious and political spheres have not yet fully agreed upon an ideological foundation for the Egyptian state, there does seem to be some nar-rowing of ideological differences. The Islamist movement has succeeded in creat-ing a more religious society and in goading the state to greater religious sensibility. In defending itself against the "Islamic rise," the Egyptian state has itself become significantly more religious in orientation. Thus, Islamist ideology has penetrated the Egyptian state, and the state has produced a reshaping of Islamist ideology.[14]

How then does this heavy dose of Islam affect those Egyptians who are not Muslims? Egyptian Copts pride themselves on being one of the oldest Chris-tian communities in the world, and many often note that the words *Copt* and *Egypt* have the same etymology. But while Egyptian Christians often com-plain of marginalization, few have called for the complete separation of religion and state.

Copts under Mubarak

According to the parameters of state-society dynamics, the Egyptian state under Hosni Mubarak may be characterized as weak at the political level but fierce at the security level. Society suffered divisions that impaired the ability of its citi-zens to confront the state, a tension that boiled over during the mass revolts of January 25, 2011, which were directed not only against the state, but also against the social structure itself, against the marginalization and exclusion endured for so long and by so many.

The government's handling of violence against Copts[15] during Mubarak's reign also shows its failure to protect its citizens. Several attacks on Copts and their churches reinforced the view that so-called religious violence was a major threat to the prospect of Egyptian democracy. The Mubarak regime had always maintained that it was the only force capable of ensuring "religious peace" because it suppressed religious extremism (the claim that Mubarak successfully bottled up Islamists is sometimes repeated in postrevolutionary Egypt). In actuality, how-ever, and in a policy of "divide and rule" designed by Egypt's security forces to divert attention from its corrupt political and economic management, the Mubarak regime attempted both to satisfy and keep the Islamists in check by operating under a formula in which the state continued to rule from the top, while the radical Islamists determined and supervised social norms from below (that is, from within Egyptian society). In a regime whose priority was its own survival, Copts have therefore become symbolic victims.

Mubarak's ability to maintain such complicated relations with Egypt's religious factions is linked to two issues: the desires of the "Islamic street" movement and corruption.[16] The Islamic street movement is growing stronger and demanding greater Islamization, and the regime has met these demands in order to increase its own legitimacy, power, and domination. The Muslim Brotherhood, which influences and leads the movement in Egypt, has a rather complex relationship with the regime. Aware of the possibility, which has manifested itself periodically, of repression as well as their own relative weakness, the Islamists avoided challenging the regime in any significant way. At the same time, the regime tried to buy off the Islamists and preoccupy them by giving them a large measure of power over the establishment of Egypt's social and cultural norms and by tolerating, if not encouraging, the oppression of Copts. Second, corruption had become one of the pillars of the regime, with a powerful oligarchy firmly in place, and was in large part responsible for its inability to confront Egypt's escalating societal, demographic, and development problems in a satisfactory manner.

Concern that other actors would be less tolerant of the Copts' religious community was therefore not misplaced, and this, with perhaps also an eye also toward protecting the privileged position of the church, led the Coptic Orthodox pope, Shenouda III, to support the Mubarak regime. Indeed, Shenouda III was granted significant autonomy over the Coptic community on the condition that this power base was not to be used to challenge the state. However, the willingness and ability of the state to guarantee protection of the Coptic community were increasingly challenged in the latter years of Mubarak's presidency. Recurring issues have included the lack of political representation and participation and sporadic outbursts of violence that are often related to societal inequalities.[17]

Concerning the place of Copts between the state and society, the contention that political problems were created by the previous regime and used to guarantee church support against the potential ascendancy of Islamists was supported. This created a societal crisis between Muslims and Christians and transformed the church into the sole representative of Copts at the political level, which deepened religious polarization.

The relationship between Copts and the regime was one in which the state treated and regarded Copts as a closed and homogeneous bloc that was represented by the Coptic Church both politically and spiritually. Factors such as the charismatic character of Pope Shenouda III and worries over the Islamic alternative further confused the relationship despite the refusal of numerous Coptic secular activists and movements to be manipulated. Also, the patriarchal system of governance inherent in the traditional churches endorses church involvement in political and societal matters, especially through the church figurehead, the patriarch himself.

Accordingly, Christians were forcefully confronted with the importance of defining the relationship between communal loyalty and national identity, not only in the realm of ideas but also in their daily lives. In light of the challenge to the authoritarian model, which erupted in 2011, the church hierarchy's support for the regime reflects this assumption that the authoritarian status quo was preferable to democratic uncertainties. However, the unexpected and powerful emergence of popular movements on January 25 invited Copts to privilege civic solidarity over primordial ties.

The Coptic Church and the January 25 Revolution

One of the powerful images that came to define the Egyptian protests of 2011 was that of Christians and Muslims praying together in Tahrir Square in Cairo. That image helped shape the understanding of what was being portrayed as a liberal and secular uprising, one that stood in dramatic contrast to the region's traditional dichotomy of politics as a choice between the authoritarian regimes and the Islamists. The overriding aim of leaders in the Coptic Church of protecting their communities led to a modern variation of the historical millet system that provides them public status in exchange for their acquiescence to regime policies. This security guarantee, combined with wariness toward other potential political actors and the desire to protect their privileged position from communal challengers, has resulted in the church's preference for the authoritarian status quo rather than the promotion of democracy.

Having experienced the brunt of Islamic radicalism and government acquiescence, the church had little doubt that the Mubarak regime, while not perfect, provided a stable environment for Copts to maintain their faith. Indeed, the patriarch publicly supported Mubarak until his resignation in February 2011. Fearing that the uprisings would be Islamist led and serve to undermine the rights of Copts, leaders of the three major Coptic sects in Egypt denounced the participation of their followers in the January 25 protests. Bishop Morcos, the spokesman of the Coptic Orthodox Church, said, "We don't know the goal of these demonstrations, its details, or who stands behind them." Similar attitudes were expressed by Andrea Zaki, head of the Evangelical Church deputy, and Bishop Antonious Aziz, the representative of the Coptic Catholic Church.[18]

Since the Copts are not a homogeneous group—as mentioned—many objected to such a relationship between the church and the regime. Many had concerns about the increasingly political role of the church and its impact on citizenship. They felt that they engaged with the state according to the guidance of the church and not as independent citizens.

With respect to the Egyptian revolution, the stance of Copts has been varied, with some participating in protests, others defending the authoritarian regime, and most remaining on the sidelines. In the month leading up to the events of January 25, the symbol of the crescent and the cross resurfaced in light of the tragic church bombing in Alexandria on December 31, 2010, which left about thirty dead and several hundred injured. Essentially, the period between this tragic incident and the onset of the protests saw the emergence of a widespread national debate concerning the rights of the Copts, the role of religion in the public sphere, and the need to tackle the issue of so-called extremism. The symbol of the crescent and the cross was seen on banners in the streets; it covered the pages of newspapers and was broadcast on national television. Copts' actions during this time proved that the church leadership's control over them became very tenuous. Copts' participation in the protests challenged the notion that Pope Shenouda III was the sole legitimate representative of the Coptic citizenry's political demands, and showed that the demonstrations took place independently of the church's will.

In Tahrir Square, the protesters primarily sought to delegitimize the Mubarak regime's alleged guardianship of national unity in Egypt in order to show that the population did not need the protection of the state to remain united. It was a tactical form of resistance aimed at delegitimizing the state and encouraging Egypt's religious groups to join the protest movement. The banner proclaiming "Muslim, Christian, One Hand" was raised during the eighteen days of the uprising. By insisting that both Coptic identity and Muslim identity should contribute equally toward the construction of the Egyptian national identity, many Copts thus emphasized their adherence to the national cause.[19]

On the morning of Tuesday, February 15, 2011, after Mubarak's resignation, Pope Shenouda III issued the following statement: "The Coptic Church salutes the honorable youth of Egypt, the youth of January 25, who led Egypt in a strong, white revolution and sacrificed for this cause precious blood, the blood of the nation's martyrs, who have been glorified by the Egyptian leadership and armed forces as well as the entire population. We offer our condolences to their parents and members of their families. The Coptic Church also salutes the brave Egyptian army and the Supreme Council of the Armed Forces in its efforts for securing Egypt internally and externally."[20]

There is little doubt that any hierarchal institution, of which the church is an example, by its nature does not believe in revolutions. A hierarchal institution considers obedience one of its main principles (which is to say, it is difficult to blame the church for opposing the revolution).[21] However, the January 25 protests illustrated the failure of the divide-and-rule strategy adopted by the Mubarak regime. Coptic churches were not threatened at any time throughout the eighteen days of the uprisings despite the absence of state security forces to protect them.

Participation by Copts in the uprisings was testament to their sense of belonging and their ability to defy political isolation.

The Rise of Islamic Tendencies and Sectarian Attacks

It is a common notion in Egyptian modern history that, after its reemergence on the political scene back in the 1970s, the Muslim Brotherhood has been the main opposition force in Egypt. Given the events in the country in January 2011 we must ask: Has the Muslim Brotherhood represented a real alternative to Mubarak's regime? To what extent was the Muslim Brotherhood able to shape or at least influence the Egyptian political and social agenda?

The brotherhood was the main opposition force in Egypt, but it has generally employed a moderate approach toward the political establishment. Acting as an opposition force, it was an integral part of the regime, but this is not to say that it ever had the power to induce any systematic change throughout Egyptian society. Based on the powerful argument of I. William Zartman, some scholars have argued that opposition supports authoritarian rule and its resilience.[22] On one hand, this "accommodating" strategy has allowed the Islamist organization to survive and even flourish in certain periods but, on the other, it has exposed it to accusations of lacking political initiative and unduly compromising with the regime.

The Muslim Brotherhood is, however, well known for its social activities, which are considered to be the key to the Islamists' success in popular mobilization, in contrast to the Mubarak regime's declining legitimacy. With increasing poverty and social inequalities as one of the most challenging issues facing Egyptian politics, the brotherhood may, at least in theory, be better placed than other political actors to capitalize on social discontent.[23]

It was clear that the Muslim Brotherhood was deliberately presenting a face of restraint because its leaders were aware that many Egyptians feared that it might take advantage of the post-Mubarak open era to dominate the political landscape and impose conservative Islamic practices. Moreover, the Salafists, who had been apolitical for decades, appeared on the political scene, demanding an immediate debate on religion, guided by their belief that the new constitution and the political system should be based on precepts of the Holy Qur'an. Salafists showed little concern for compromise or diplomatic sound bites.[24]

In the weeks after Mubarak's departure, as the brotherhood and the Salafists obtained legal recognition,[25] their political ambitions—including constitutional amendments and talk of "collusion" and a "bargain" between the brotherhood and the military—had increased brotherhood and Salafist involvement in electoral politics. The brotherhood even reversed its decision to withhold a candidate from the 2012 presidential race. Indeed, the ability of the Islamists to perform well in elections owes something to a reputation for serving the needs of the public.[26]

The myths associated with the Egyptian revolution are numerous, but none is perhaps more damaging than the quite modern debasement of the concept of free society in which it is defined—essentially and simply—as the holding of elections. Following the events of January 25, the ballot box was perceived as a magical solution from which free speech, free enterprise, and religious freedom would necessarily follow. Egypt's elections (parliamentary in 2011 and presidential in 2012) witnessed the rise of Islamic tendencies, with the consequence that issues were no longer debated in terms of choices between alternative solutions with advantages and disadvantages, costs and benefits. The only question became whether something was halal or haram, permissible or forbidden in Islam, as if religion had somehow come to preside over life itself.[27]

The increase in "Islamic attacks," the widespread re-Islamization of Egyptian society, and the development of state policy with strong "Islamic" overtones aroused an increasing sense of danger among the Copts, who responded by trying to suppress internal differences for the sake of defending their identity. Non-Islamist opposition forces also took every opportunity to reaffirm their support for their Coptic copatriots and vigorously denied the existence of tension between Copts and Muslims.

However, church fears came true to an extent: the Muslim Brotherhood, which for decades had built a network of social and religious programs for the public, quickly became the nation's most potent political force. Moreover, Islamists reversed the logic of the nation-state discourse by arguing that Islam is the solution for all problems. Hence, the equality Christians yearned for was defined as incompatible with "Islamic" values.[28] The Salafists and the brotherhood have not emphasized the Islamic duty to protect Christians as "people of the book." Instead, in the years since the start of the revolution, Egypt has witnessed church burnings, attacks, and the murder of over two hundred Copts in their homes and churches by Islamic fundamentalists.[29] The state, especially the governments led by Morsi and the Supreme Council of the Armed Forces (SCAF), did not punish the perpetrators.

The diminishing role of the state in dealing with sectarian crises continued under the rule of the SCAF. Sectarian crises were treated informally through the mediation of clergy and figures from the political elite, while the actual causes of the tensions between Muslims and Christians were not addressed directly. Thus, the path to democracy in Egypt suffered setbacks at all levels, politically, socially, and culturally; the same changes that the Copts had demanded under Mubarak continued to be necessary.

The slogan "Raise your head high, you are Egyptian" was changed by many to "Raise your head high, you are a Muslim," and during Coptic protests against the rise of political Islam under Morsi, the slogan "Raise your head up high, you are a Copt" also became popular. Indeed, the demise of the spirit of the January 25 revolution and the discourse of national unity was deeply felt. Ten months on, the image of Muslim and Christian leaders sharing the podium in Cairo's Tahrir Square had faded from popular memory.[30]

Sectarian attacks increased in Egypt after Mubarak's ouster. The number of incidents rose by a third in 2011 compared to 2010, and was double the number of incidents in 2009 and 2008.[31] The victims were targeted because of their religious affiliation. These new attacks involved radical Islamists who sought to force their vision of Egyptian society on the public at large and on Copts in particular. Increasingly, Copts living in poorer neighborhoods found themselves forced to abide by certain Islamic practices or face possible punishment. The government, meanwhile, showed a continued lack of interest in protecting Christians. The solution of the SCAF to the burning of a church in Atfih in March 2011, for example, was to invite Salafi preacher Mohamed Hassan to the area to try to calm down the local Muslims.[32]

The greatest sectarian confrontation, known as the "Maspero Massacre," took place in October 2011;[33] it resulted in the death of twenty-seven civilians and represented a critical moment in the history of Egyptian politics. It also reflected the gap between the Coptic civil movements and the church leadership over the church's crisis management. Just before the death of Pope Shenouda III, the church leadership suffered a serious blow after the Maspero Massacre. When the church was celebrating Christmas Eve, and the pope was greeting the army generals, members of the youth movements shouted "Down, down the military rule." It became very clear that Copts were no longer retreating behind the church walls, and they were propelled into the streets. The animosity between the Coptic people and the army worked, ironically, in the favor of the Islamists at the time.[34]

Presidential elections took place in May 2012. The Muslim Brotherhood candidate, Morsi, won the presidency, which emboldened Islamist groups on the streets to enforce public compliance with their moral codes. They acted openly, under Morsi, on their religious beliefs in ways that would have been more covert during Mubarak's era.[35] The main targets were Coptic churches and buildings of the church. Besides these targets, the believers themselves were also in danger. The discourse of aggressive Muslim elements (whose slogan is "Egypt is a Muslim country") reinforces, and is in turn reinforced by, the discourse of a separate Coptic identity—each seeing in the other proof of religious provocation. Muslim suspicions of Coptic intentions are met by Coptic slogans of self-assertion ("We are the original owners of the land").[36] Accordingly, this has led to suspicions among elements in the Muslim "majority" (expressed in organized demonstrations) that there are plans to divide up Egypt, and among the Coptic "minority" that the Islamists want to exclude them and act against their existence in Egyptian society.

Faced with these hardships, it is no surprise that the Copts began questioning whether there is a future for them in the new Egypt. In particular, younger members of the Coptic community refuse to accept their inferior status in society, and thus many participated in the June 30 revolution and, once again, demanded the removal of the president.

The Changing Spiritual Leadership of the Coptic Church and the Ouster of an Elected President

The strategy of the Coptic Church's leadership in the post-Mubarak regime was not to engage in politics. Because of the gap between the institution and its followers that emerged as a result of the institution's support of Mubarak's son as the successor to the presidency, and the changing reaction of the church toward the January revolution, the church was "on hold," and it reversed its political stance, especially in the face of the high level of political vulnerability and insecurity.[37]

Moreover, Pope Shenouda III died, and Bishop Tawadros became the church's 118th pope four months after President Morsi was elected.[38] Pope Tawadros II inherited a church that had suffered greatly under the Islamists. Yet, the new spiritual leader had also come into power during an era that was witnessing a reconfiguration of power within the Coptic community due to the revival of Coptic citizens' political activism. Copts, who had been adrift since Shenouda's death, were concerned about the demands by ultraconservative Islamists to filter the country's new constitution through Sharia, or Islamic law. The new constitution, issued in December 2012, gave little room for religious equality, and many young, politically active Christians no longer want to rely on the church to advance their rights.

One of the most famous sectarian confrontations took place on April 7, 2013, when fighting erupted after a mass funeral for five Copts who had been killed during violent clashes in a north Egyptian town in Greater Cairo on Friday, April 5, during which a Muslim man was also shot and killed. The attacks in Al-Khusus continued and spread to Saint Mark's Cathedral in central Cairo, placing hundreds of Christians under siege inside the Coptic cathedral after the funeral. This anti-Christian violence brought chilling validation to the concerns Copts harbored.

President Morsi said he gave orders for the cathedral and citizens to be guarded, and announced, "I consider any attack on the Cathedral as an attack on me, personally."[39] The attack set a most dangerous precedent in the history of the relations between the state, the church, and the community. It reinforced the idea of the inferiority of Copts, and thus challenged not only their rights but also their existence. As the grassroots anti-Morsi Tamarrud (Rebellion) Movement gained steam, Copts were among the millions calling for Morsi's early removal from office and new elections.

Due to the failure of the new president and his government to achieve any real political or economic change, millions of Egyptians—Copts included—demonstrated against the regime on June 30, 2013, and demanded early presidential elections. The symbol of the cross and the crescent reappeared in the streets. At the July 3 news conference, attended by both the pope of the Orthodox Church and the head of Cairo's Al-Azhar Mosque, the minister of defense, Abdul Fatah el-Sisi, announced the military would back the will of the people. Unfortunately, the appearance of the pope at the conference also reinforced grand conspiracies that Christians were working to derail the Islamist project.

Participants at the conference reinforced calls to remove Morsi from office and supported continued demands to hold early presidential elections to replace him. During this time, the pope also affirmed his support for the political interventions already put forth by Al-Sisi. An amended version of the 2012 constitution (previously adopted by the Muslim Brotherhood) was drafted. Following this, in an article printed in the state-owned *Al-Ahram* newspaper, Pope Tawadros II encouraged Al-Sisi to run for the presidency and insisted that Egyptians should approve the new draft constitution during a referendum scheduled for January 2014.[40]

However, sustained political and economic change would prove more difficult to ensure than proponents perhaps first assumed. In particular, the Coptic community, the military, and the old regime were quickly singled out by outraged Muslim Brotherhood supporters as the primary parties responsible for ousting Morsi.[41] Angry mobs took to the streets of Dalga, near Minya, which resulted in injuries and the burning of Christian homes and shops. Hundreds stormed a local church, accusing Copts of treason. A few weeks later, attacks became especially rampant in Upper Egypt, where Copts constitute a disproportionately large part of the population.[42]

In reaction to General Sisi's call to the Egyptian people to come out into the streets on July 26 and support the interim government's goal to fight terrorism, the pope tweeted to his flock that "the national responsibility of the Coptic Church of Egypt demands us all to support the measures that protect our country and achieve our freedom without violence or recklessness. Long live Egypt, safe and secure."[43]

The events of August 14,[44] when the state security forces dispersed Muslim Brotherhood sit-ins, invited more retaliation against Christians. More than seventy Orthodox, Catholic, and Protestant churches were attacked, many of them looted and then completely demolished. Mobs also destroyed several Christian convents, monasteries, orphanages, schools, homes, and shops.[45]

New Regime, Old Problems

In late January 2014, Sisi received an endorsement from the SCAF, Egypt's highest military body, for a potential presidential run. Though the church did not directly address the possibility of Sisi's candidacy, Pope Tawadros II gave his approval, sending Sisi a telegram congratulating him on receiving the military's political support.[46]

Following the election of Sisi, the church tried to regain its role as the champion of the Coptic community. Yet, such efforts to act on the behalf of the Copts carry significant risks: not all Copts have embraced the church's intent to fulfill its role in this capacity, particularly youth who wish to define and defend their interests as politically engaged Egyptian citizens.[47] The church should focus instead on being an institution of civil society that defends universal ideals such as human rights and social justice, and on supporting developmental projects for both Muslims and Christians.[48]

In January 2015, President Al-Sisi surprised many Egyptians by making an unannounced visit to Cairo's Abbasiya Cathedral, becoming the first Egyptian president to attend Christmas Mass. It was a televised event in which Al-Sisi urged Egyptians everywhere to remain united as "one hand" as the world, he noted, was watching Egypt.[49] However, the newly restored relationship between the pope and the president was made readily apparent during Al-Sisi's visit to Saint Mark's Coptic Orthodox Cathedral, in which he reinforced his call for Egyptian unity. "What kind of Egyptian are you?" he asked those gathered in the crowd before him. "It is not right to call each other anything but 'the Egyptians.' We must only be Egyptians," he concluded.[50]

The tone and nature of Al-Sisi's speech reflects the state's attempts to reestablish and reaffirm an Egyptian nationalism that was suppressed under Mubarak's regime and the Muslim Brotherhood.[51] Yet, although many Copts continue to support Al-Sisi and believe him to be their saviour from repressive Islamic rule, attacks against Copts nonetheless persisted even after Al-Sisi's rise to power as president. As it stands, it seems that only time will tell whether or not he will truly support their struggle for full rights and equality as citizens.[52]

In an interview during his campaign for president, Al-Sisi revealed some interesting views he had about the future of Copts in Egypt. In the interview, he was questioned about key issues impacting the Copts,[53] including discrimination in government institutions (i.e., the military and the judiciary) and the "Hamayouni Decree"[54]—a rather contentious law enacted under the Ottoman empire that has been challenged by those seeking a more unified law for the preservation and upkeep of places of worship. Al-Sisi avoided any concrete response that would have illuminated his position on these issues, choosing instead to vaguely praise the Copts for fulfilling "a patriotic role after June 30." When pressed for a clearer answer, Al-Sisi merely stated that: "We will try to offer a comfortable climate for everyone in Egypt."[55]

In another interview in which he was questioned about the place of religion in the state, Al-Sisi responded by addressing his own position towards this issue, rather than that of the state itself. According to Al-Sisi: "The president of the state is responsible for everything in the state, including religion, which is Islam according to the first article of the constitution. I'm responsible for the values, principles, ethics, and religion."[56]

Indeed, if historical experience has shown anything regarding the relationship between religion and the state in Egypt, it is that strategies employed by its leaders to confront Islamists will very likely end poorly for the country's Coptic minority. President Al-Sadat, in particular, tried to dispel Islamic critique through the introduction of Article 2 in the constitution, which states that the main source of legislation in Egypt is Islamic Sharia. Near the end of his tenure, Al-Sadat went so far as to order the banishment of Pope Shenouda III to a monastery and jailing a number of clergy. Yet, despite these efforts, Copts continued to face discrimination throughout Al-Sadat's reign and beyond that through Mubarak's regime and—as this chapter has argued—must *still* fight for their rights as full citizens under Al-Sisi.[57]

In all revolutionary situations there is uncertainty, and suspicion flourishes and promotes the idea that forceful actions related to terminologies and their political context are necessary. Accordingly, definitions and their reflections acquire new urgencies. The term *Copt* refers to different groups with different trends and orientations, and the term *Islamist* actually covers heterogeneous class origins that are rarely distinguished: not only are all "Islamists" not potential terrorists, they are not all businessmen or neoliberals, and their views on politics are not the same.

A historic perspective, shared by many watchers of the Egyptian political landscape, has led many to think that free elections are the main requisite for democracy, ignoring the important roles of political culture and institutions, which take time to develop on the complex path to democracy. G. O'Donnell suggests that one can distinguish between "political democratic freedoms," which are provided by regular elections, and "basic liberal freedoms," which encompass much more than voting on election day.[58] Democracy requires a culture, a state of mind, and an organizational structure that at the moment simply do not exist in Egypt.

This does not mean that only a dictatorship can guarantee the rights of minorities, but the culture of the "tyranny of the majority," highlighted by Alexis de

Tocqueville,[59] has become enrooted in both the practices of Egyptians and the political system over the last four years, creating a kind of tyranny in which being in a "minority," with all its levels, starts to seem unacceptable, and even presents a threat to the majority. As a result, the theory of electoral democracy is based on some hidden, convenient fictions:[60] it reinforces state power, disempowers the grassroots, and does not work very well to present serious challenges to prevailing power systems in Egypt, which is why Egyptians may not be ready for democracy.[61] Electoral methods may be one of the most exciting political developments in Egypt recently, but in entering electoral politics the country may have limited the potential for bringing about radical change.[62] In fact, it ensured continuing reliance on the old system of politics as practiced under the Muslim Brotherhood in dealing with the rights of "minorities."

It is difficult to draw a line between state and religion in Egypt, but observing that difficulty does little to define the many ways that the state expresses, supports, pursues, contains, and defines religion, or the ways that religion informs, limits, guides, and infiltrates state authority. In postrevolutionary Egypt, the complexity of the relationship is growing, but even more notable is the fact that religion is providing a conduit for a decline in the distinction between state and society.

The church is no longer the political representative of Copts, and it did not speak out on their behalf against the state throughout the first year after the revolution, especially in the face of the new norms presented by the rise of political Islamist trends and the drafting of a new constitution, in addition to community pressures for more flexible rules on certain social issues, such as second marriages. But it is clear that the churches have learned to adapt to changing situations, and the overriding objective of the Coptic Church will continue to be to secure the survival and prosperity of its community according to security imperatives.

But the church's support for the military's 2013 intervention has given it a privileged position in the new regime, prompting it to try to revive the old pact it had with the Mubarak regime. And changes carried out by the state have helped the church regain its position as the only representative of the Coptic community. As the new political authority has tightened its control over the public sphere, youth movements, including the Maspero Youth Union, have lost their ability to mobilize. Coptic politicians have also lost their influence, as the new regime seems to see few roles for parties. However, the church's former strategy brought with it many problems, and, in the current environment of political and societal polarization,[63] a return to that approach could have harmful consequences for the Coptic community.

First, this approach, based on backdoor channels between the church and the political authority, often failed to resolve Coptic grievances in the past. It also denied Copts their rights as Egyptian citizens, because the church and the regime have often tried to reach compromises outside the framework of the law. These compromises have often been intended to contain religious tensions, but not to address their causes. The church should withdraw from this type of negotiation and ask for the law to be applied to all problems involving Christians. If the government fully enforced the principles of citizenship and the rule of law, Copts would have a chance to claim their religious and political rights as Egyptian citizens, instead of waiting for the church to negotiate with the political regime on their behalf.

Second, by encouraging church members to depend on Coptic leaders to channel their political and social demands, the Copts' isolation is deepened and they are discouraged from joining political parties or movements. This hinders their interaction with other political forces and their integration into civil and political society, leaving them engaged only in activities organized by the church. The church should refrain from representing the Copts politically and instead allow lay Coptic actors to defend their interests in the political sphere. Even with the new restrictions on political and civil society in Egypt, Coptic actors should join other political parties and movements in their struggle for a democratic regime.

Third, the church's past strategy reinforces the perception that Copts are one homogeneous group. The church has worked to unify the Coptic community's voice within the political sphere in order to maximize the Copts' influence in political debates. This leads to a situation in which church decisions can put the lives and property of any individual Copt at risk, even if he or she did not actually participate in making a political choice. There is no need for the Copts to speak with one voice. In fact, it would be productive for them to take part in different groups and movements according to their own political preferences.[64]

In Egypt, the relationship between political and religious authorities looks neither like what it was before the revolution nor like what it should be in a modern secular state. The religious authorities now have returned to control a more influential social machinery.

Still, there is little evidence to suggest that Christians' future would be protected under a military-led regime. The Maspero Massacre against Christians in October 2011 was an atrocity committed under the SCAF's watch. The same can be said of the families' murder that occurred at Alexandria's Two Saints Church on January 1, 2011, under the rule of Mubarak.

The future of Copts is related to the future of political actors who might make democratic life a daily reality. This would necessitate viable and energetic political institutions and organizations dedicated to the values of democracy. Beyond representing the legitimate aspirations of the various groups and sectors in society, these institutions would have to channel the expressions of these aspirations in an orderly political competition.

There are widespread fears that in the near future, the Muslim Brotherhood—now outlawed and excluded from electoral politics—will resort to violence on a greater scale, along with other militant groups operating in Sinai and in Egypt's largest cities. At the same time, the Arab world is ridden with turmoil caused by an ongoing civil war in Syria and the rise of isis (the Islamic State) in Syria, Iraq, and Libya.[65] Under these circumstances, many Egyptians see a strong security state under Sisi's command as the only thing that can protect them from the chaos, terror, and sectarian extremism engulfing other countries in the region. As a non-Muslim minority, Egyptian Copts are particularly fearful of these threats. As long as they are believed to be real, these threats provide a powerful impetus for Copts to keep supporting Sisi despite any nondemocratic practices.

Egypt remains in a state of flux, but a return to law and order will give the people a chance to gain some normalcy in their lives. At the least, the election of Sisi shows that Egyptians are momentarily weary of fighting and violence, and that bodes a little better—just a little—for the religious minorities in the country. If the current cohort of leaders—officers and civilians—wishes to protect and include all Egyptians, it will need to enact the legal and security reforms that Sadat, Mubarak, Mohamed Tantawi, and Morsi failed to undertake. Such efforts could help rebuild a national sense of "Egyptian-ness" that has waned under secular and Islamist rulers alike.

Notes

1. Jayson Casper, "Mapping the Coptic Movements: Coptic Activism in a Revolutionary Setting," http://www.arabwestreport.info/en/mapping-coptic-movements-coptic-activism -revolutionary-setting.

2. There are thirteen Christian sects actively engaged in religious activities in Egypt: Orthodox Copt, Catholic Copt, Protestant Copt, Roman Catholic, Roman Orthodox, Armenian Catholic, Armenian Orthodox, Syrian Catholic, Syrian Orthodox, Latin Catholic, Maronite Catholic, Chaldean Catholic, and Anglican Protestant. This large multiplicity of sects springs not only from creedal differences in regard to the nature of the Christ, but also from the proliferation of numerous nationalities and ancient peoples who belong to these sects.

3. T. H. Eriksen, "Ethnicity, Race and Nation," in *The Ethnicity Reader: Nationalism, Multiculturalism and Migration*, ed. M. Guibernau and J. Rex (Cambridge: Polity, 1997).

4. Fabrizio Butera, *Coping with Minority Status: Responses to Exclusion and Inclusion* (Cambridge: Cambridge University Press, 2009), 59. See also Evelyn Kallen, *Social Inequality and Social Injustice: A Human Rights Perspective* (Basingstoke, UK: Palgrave Macmillan, 2003), 32. Over the years, in teaching courses on majority-minority relations, I have found that the widespread lay use as well as the political use of the terms *majority* and *minority* refers to social inequalities. Students tend to become confused when these concepts are applied to unequal power relations, because they think of inequality in terms of the relative size of a social group as a percentage of a country's total population. In the present work, I would like to make absolutely clear to the reader that my analysis of unequal relations between groups focuses on

unequal power relations and not on inequalities in numbers (population size). The term *dominant* refers to any population whose members have the power to impose their will and their laws on society at large and who are able to exercise the greatest degree of political, economic, and social power in society, thus controlling the destinies of invalidated subordinate populations. The term *subordinate* refers to members who are invalidated and categorically discriminated against by dominant authorities; are subject to violations of their fundamental human rights to freedom, equality, and dignity; and become collectively disadvantaged and come to occupy a marginalized social status in society.

5. Frederick Barth, *Ethnic Groups and Boundaries: The Social Organization of Culture Difference in Ethnicity* (Bergen, Norway: University of Bergen, 1969), 7–9.

6. Mai Mogib, "Copts in Egypt and Their Demands between Inclusion and Exclusion," *Journal of Contemporary Arab Affairs* 5, no. 4 (October–December 2012): 535–555.

7. E. J. Chitham, *The Coptic Community in Egypt: Spatial and Social Change* (Durham, UK: University of Durham, 1986), 42.

8. Joel S. Migdal, ed., *State Power and Social Forces: Domination and Transformation in the Third World* (Cambridge: Cambridge University Press, 1994), 1–4.

9. Jonathan Fox, ed., *Religion, Politics, Society and the State* (Oxford: Oxford University Press, 2002), 1–9.

10. Fiona McCallum, "Religious Institutions and Authoritarian States: Church-State Relations in the Middle East," *Third World Quarterly* 33, no. 1 (2012): 109–124.

11. Pippa Norris and Ronald Inglehart, *Sacred and Secular: Religion and Politics Worldwide* (Cambridge: Cambridge University Press, 2004).

12. Robert Hefner, *Civil Islam: Muslims and Democratization in Indonesia* (Princeton, NJ: Princeton University Press, 2000), 17. Hefner makes this point about Indonesia, but it applies to many other Muslim states.

13. See Jakob Skovgaard-Petersen, *Defining Islam for the Egyptian State: Muftis and Fatwas of the Dar al-Iftaa* (Leiden, Netherlands: Brill, 1997).

14. See Norris and Inglehart, *Sacred and Secular.*

15. According to statistical analysis, Egypt witnessed fifty-three sectarian events per year till January 2011; this violence represents only the tip of the iceberg regarding policies of discrimination and exclusion, which feed into the cycle of violence. Ami Ayalon, "Egypt's Coptic Pandora's Box," in *Minorities and the State in the Arab World*, ed. Ofra Bingio (Boulder, CO: Lynne Rienner, 1999).

16. Adel Guindy, "Symbolic Victims in a Socially Regressing Egypt: The Declining Situation of the Copts," *Middle East Review of International Affairs* 14, no. 1 (March 2010): 80–90.

17. Fiona McCallum, "Muslim-Christian Relations in Egypt: Challenges for the Twenty-First Century," in *Christian Responses to Islam: Muslim-Christian Relations in the Modern World*, ed. A. O'Mahony and E. Loosley (Manchester: Manchester University Press, 2008), 66–104.

18. Quoted in Emad Khalil, "The Three Churches Denounce the 25 January Protests and Call upon the Copts Not to Participate," *Al-Masry Al-Youm*, January 24, 2011.

19. Dina El Khawaga, "The Political Dynamics of the Copts: Giving the Community an Active Role," in *Christian Communities in the Arab Middle East: The Challenge of the Future*, ed. Andrea Pacini (Oxford: Clarendon, 2004), 172–190. The revolution seemed to bring out the best in interfaith relations, with incidents such as Christians forming a human shield to protect prostrated Muslims in prayer from attacks by armed Mubarak loyalists, and Muslim youth guarding churches against looters after the security forces abandoned their posts.

20. A statement of the Coptic Church, February 15th, 2011, http://st-takla.org/News/Holy-Synod-Statements/2011-02-15—January-25-2011-Revolution_.html.

21. Magdi Guirguis, "The Copts and the Egyptian Revolution: Various Attitudes and Dreams," *Social research* 79, no. 2 (Summer 2012): 511–530.

22. I. William Zartman, "Opposition as Support of the State," in *Beyond Coercion: The Durability of the Arab State*, ed. Adeed Dawisha and I. William Zartman (London: Croom Helm, 1988), 61–87. In several statements the Muslim Brotherhood's Murshid al-Amm (general guide), Mohammed Mahdi Akef, welcomed the regime's reform proposals and even announced support for another presidential term for Mubarak. Moreover, Akef dismissed any plans on the part of his movement to found a political party in the foreseeable future. Jack Shenker and Brian Whitaker, "The Muslim Brotherhood Uncovered," *Guardian*, February 8, 2011.

23. Daniela Pioppi, "Is There an Islamist Alternative in Egypt?," Instiuto Affari Internazionali, *IAI Working Papers* 11, February 3, 2011.

24. Jeffrey Flieshman, "Egypt's Copts Fear for Rights; Emerging Political Islam Has Christians Feeling More Isolated," *Los Angeles Times*, December 12, 2011.

25. Here, a clarification should be made concerning the difference between the Muslim Brotherhood and the Salafists regarding their perceptions about the Copts. Salafists clearly declare that Copts are nonbelievers, but the brotherhood's statements give the sense that it is more moderate and committed to the preservation of Coptic rights. However, its commitment was apparently abandoned when it formed a majority in parliament and when President Morsi came to power. On the contrary, although the president vowed to be "although the president vowed . . . events proved that this was not the case," the Coptic Cathedral fell under siege in April 2013 after a mass funeral for five Copts that were killed during violent clashes in north Egypt in Al-Khusus. Coptic movements were met by the Morsi government with extreme repression, which subsequently spawned radicalized offshoots. See Mariz Tadros, *Copts at the Crossroads: The Challenge of Building Inclusive Democracy in Egypt* (Cairo: American University in Cairo Press, 2013), 249.

26. Nathan Brown, "Contention in Religion and State in Post-revolutionary Egypt," *Social Research* 79, no. 2 (Summer 2012): 531–550.

27. Bassma Kodmani, "The Dangers of Political Exclusion: Egypt's Islamist Problem," *Carnegie Papers, Middle East Series*, no. 63 (October 2005): 1–28.

28. Samuel Tadros, "The Coptic Winter," *National Review*, November 14, 2011, 25–26.

29. Dina El Khawaga, "The Political Dynamics of the Copts: Giving the Community an Active Role," Christian Communities in the Arab Middle East: The Challenge of the Future, ed. Andrea Pacini (Oxford: Clarendon, 2004), 172–190.

30. Mariz Tadros, "Sectarianism and its discontents in Post-Mubarak Regime," *Middle East Report*, Summer 2011.

31. Emad Gad, "The Amiriya Incident Is Sectarian, You Philosophers of Denial" [in Arabic], *Al-Tahrir*, February 21, 2012.

32. Tadros, "The Coptic Winter," 25–26. There was a kind of distrust, among Copts, of the Muslim Brotherhood. This is partly due to the lack of effort on the part of the Morsi presidency to establish trust between the brotherhood and the Coptic community (except for broad statements that Islamic Sharia guarantees non-Muslims their freedom). Some Copts suspected that the Muslim Brotherhood was trying to show that Christians betrayed the revolution.

33. Disputes emerged in Aswan concerning a church in Al-Mirinab on September 30, with the province's governor announcing that the Copts were to blame, noting that the land belongs to the state and not to the church. Copts responded with protests in Maspero, Cairo, rejecting the governor's statement, followed by a confrontation between the army and the protesters.

34. All the organized political forces in the country—all presidential candidates and parties, including the Muslim Brotherhood's Freedom and Justice Party—condemned the massacre.

35. Pew Research Center, "The World Muslims: Religion, Politics, and Society," April 30, 2013, http://www.pewforum.org/uploadedFiles/Topics/Religious_Affiliation/Muslim/worlds -muslims-religion-politics-society-full-report.pdf.

36. Talal Asad, "Fear and the Ruptured State: Reflections on Egypt after Mubarak," *Social Research* 79, no. 2 (Summer 2012): 271–298.

37. Tadros, *Copts at the Crossroads*, xi–xiv.

38. Soon after his election as pope on November 18, 2012, when it became clear to Tawadros and all the Copts that their concerns were not even at the bottom of the president's agenda, he began to share his criticism openly in the press. Tawadros's critical stance seemed like a natural reaction to his people's apparent political marginalization, and it was easy to forget that it required a great deal of courage for a Coptic pope to stand up to the ruler. The Copts felt sidelined, ignored, and neglected under a government that did not even pretend to defend their religious rights. The reality is that during most of Egypt's history, Copts have had little choice but to accept whoever was in charge. This has been the case since Arabs replaced the Romans in 641 CE. Apart from guarding the faith, part of a Coptic pope's job has historically been to serve as the point of contact between his community and the Muslim authority. At the same time, he has also been expected to stay above politics in his dealings with the governing regime.

39. "Egypt's President Morsi: Attack on Cathedral is attack on me," Ahram online, Sunday, 7 April, 2013. http://english.ahram.org.eg/NewsContent/1/64/68720/Egypt/Politics-/Egypts -President-Morsi-Attack-on-cathedral-is-atta.aspx

40. Georges Fahmi, "The Coptic Church and Politics in Egypt," Carnegie Middle East Center, December 18, 2014, http://carnegieendowment.org/2014/12/18/coptic-church-and-politics -in-egypt-pub-57563.

41. Febe Armanious, "Egypt's Copts between Morsi and the Military," *Cairo Review of Global Affairs*, September 2, 2013, http://www.aucegypt.edu/gapp/cairoreview/pages/articleDetails.aspx ?aid=417.

42. Michael Adel, "Copts under Attack," August 24, 2013, *Al-Ahram Weekly*, http://weekly .ahram.org.eg/News/3481/17/Copts-under-attack.aspx.

43. Quoted in Jason Brownlee, "Violence against Copts in Egypt," November 14, 2013, http:// carnegieendowment.org/2013/11/14/violence-against-copts-in-egypt/gtsf.

44. In the middle of August, arsonists damaged or destroyed more than forty churches in Upper Egypt, in Beni Suef and Fayyoum. The proximate catalyst for the wave of church burnings was the military's August 14 killing of more than eight hundred civilians who were protesting the president's removal. The end of an Islamist government brought an immediate sense of relief to Coptic communities. It remains to be seen, however, whether the transition will deliver lasting rights and security or whether it will instead reproduce the old pattern of state officials exploiting sectarian tensions rather than addressing them.

45. Ayat Al-Tawy, "Churches Torched across Egypt in Anti-Coptic Violence," Ahram Online, August 15, 2013, http://english.ahram.org.eg/NewsContent/1/64/79124/Egypt/Politics- /Churches-torched-across-Egypt-in-antiCoptic-violen.aspx.

46. Asma Ajroudi, "Four Years on from Egypt's Uprising, Are Copts Better Off?," *Al Arabiya*, January 24, 2015, http://english.alarabiya.net/en/perspective/analysis/2015/01/24/Four -years-on-from-Egypt-s-uprising-are-Copts-better-off-.html.

47. Julianna Kaye Smith, "Coptic Papacy and Power in a Changing Post Mubarak Regime" (MA thesis, Ohio State University, 2013), 70–74, https://etd.ohiolink.edu/!etd.send_file?accession =osu1366214073&disposition=inline.

48. Peter Jesseser Smith, "Egypt Christians Greet revolution against Muslim Brotherhood," *National Catholic Register*, July 6, 2013, http://www.ncregister.com/daily-news/egypt-christians -greet-revolution-against-muslim-brotherhood/.

49. "Egypt's Sisi Becomes First President to Attend Christmas Mass" YouTube video, Al-Sisi's speech on Christmas Mass, posted by "From The World," January 6, 2015, https://www.youtube.com/watch?v=18XwiyevZF8.

50. "Egypt's Sisi Becomes First Egyptian President to Attend Christmas Mass," *Egyptian Streets*, January 6, 2015, http://egyptianstreets.com/2015/01/06/egypts-sisi-becomes-first-president-to-attend-christmas-mass/.

51. Ajroudi, "Four Years on from Egypt's Uprising."

52. Ashraf El-Sherif, "Egypt's Post Mubarak Predicament," Carnegie Endowment for International Peace, January 29, 2014, http://carnegieendowment.org/2014/01/29/egypt-s-post-mubarak-predicament-pub-54328.

53. Interview with Al-Sisi, posted by "Dream TV Egypt," May 19, 2014, https://www.youtube.com/watch?v=ko1QuZxjWWg&feature=youtu.be.

54. The "Hamayouni Decree" is a law enacted under Ottoman rule that regulates church construction and maintenance and is notorious for the obstacles it put in place.

55. Mina Fayek, "Copts in El-Sisi's Egypt," openDemocracy, May 29, 2014, https://www.opendemocracy.net/arab-awakening/mina-fayek/copts-in-el-sisis-egypt.

56. Interview with candidate Al-Sisi, posted by "M Sarhan," May 5, 2014, https://www.youtube.com/watch?v=DXqIQu4dDIY.

57. Ali Gokpinar, "Sectarianism and the Copts in Revolutionary Egypt," openDemocracy, June 30, 2013, https://www.opendemocracy.net/ali-gokpinar/sectarianism-and-copts-in-revolutionary-egypt.

58. G. O'Donnell, "Illusions about Consolidation," *Journal of Democracy* 7, no. 2 (1996): 45.

59. See John Stone and Stephen Mennell, eds., *Alexis de Tocqueville on Democracy, Revolution and Society* (Chicago: University of Chicago Press, 1980).

60. Thomas S. Martin, "Unhinging All Government: The Defects of Political Representation," *Our Generation* 20, no. 1 (Fall 1988): 1–21.

61. George H. Smith, "The Ethics of Voting," *Voluntaryist* 1, no. 1 (October 1982): 1, 3–5.

62. John Burnheim, "Democracy, Nation States and the World System," in *New Forms of Democracy*, ed. David Held and Christopher Pollitt (London: Sage, 1986), 218–239.

63. Jared Malsin, "Copts in a Revolutionary Age: Egypt's Last Secularists," *Revealer*, March 7, 2014, http://therevealer.org/archives/19090.

64. Fahmi, "Coptic Church and Politics in Egypt."

65. A massacre perpetrated by ISIS took place in Libya against twenty-one Egyptian Copts working there in February 2015. The ISIS-affiliated Tripoli Soldiers released photos showing the execution, according to ISIS's English magazine *Dabek*. ISIS said the mass execution came in response to the alleged abduction of Muslim converts in Egypt.

7 Egyptian Media Capturing the Revolution

Mohamad Hamas Elmasry
and Mohammed El-Nawawy

PREVIOUS RESEARCH INTO the Egyptian media has approached the subject from a number of angles. Studies have looked at the evolution of the national press system,[1] news production under former president Hosni Mubarak,[2] freedom of the press,[3] journalistic professionalism,[4] the political blogosphere,[5] journalists' perceptions and attitudes,[6] the politicization of television talk shows,[7] the structure of satellite broadcasting,[8] the role of Egyptian media in the 2011 uprising against Mubarak,[9] and the role of social media,[10] among other salient issues.

To date, however, scholarship has not focused on critically comparing Egypt's news media across three important periods in the nation's recent political history—the late Mubarak era, the military-led transition period, and Mohammed Morsi's presidency—nor has this scholarship offered practical suggestions on restructuring the press system to be more conducive to a democratic state. Such a comparison is important given the political turbulence Egypt has faced since the January 2011 uprising against Mubarak. Both the military-led transition period and the yearlong Morsi presidency were tumultuous, and news media were seen as playing a crucial, and arguably deleterious, role in Egypt's attempted transition to democracy.[11] Additionally, current Egyptian president Abdul Fatah el-Sisi has been accused by analysts and human rights organizations of heavy-handed repression of journalists,[12] some exceptional cases of critical media coverage notwithstanding.[13]

This chapter will comparatively examine the role and performance of the Egyptian press during the late Mubarak period, the military-led Supreme Council of the Armed Forces (SCAF) period, and the Morsi period in Egypt, and attempt to explain what Egyptian news media may have been able to do differently in order to play a more productive role in Egypt's democratic transition. Issues of journalistic professionalism, news ideology, media education and training, concentration of ownership, government influence on the content of the press, and the structure of the media will be examined in turn and with reference to each of the three periods in question. The chapter, which will conclude with suggestions on how the Egyptian press system might be restructured to better serve an Egyptian democratic project, may serve as a useful guide if and when Egypt takes a meaningful democratic turn.

The Press under Hosni Mubarak

Mubarak took over as president of Egypt in 1981, immediately after the assassination of his predecessor, Anwar Sadat, and ruled the country until a large protest movement forced him from power in 2011. Mubarak had inherited a fairly repressive and restrictive press structure from his predecessors, Sadat (1970–1981) and Gamal Abdel Nasser (1956–1970).[14] Some occasional criticisms of the government notwithstanding, state-run media dominated the news system and remained loyal to Mubarak and the government line.[15] The independent press, meanwhile, while significantly freer than the state-run press, also faced restrictions.

The Mubarak regime exerted its powerful control over state-run media outlets through policies that allowed the government to directly appoint editors.[16] The regime also used a broadly repressive legal umbrella—which included the Press Law, the Emergency Law, the 1971 constitution, and the penal code—to effectively control press output. For example, the Press Law stipulated prison sentences for journalists who published "false news," and granted the president the right to censor news content that threatened "public safety and national security."[17] The Emergency Law gave the government the right to censor "newspapers, publications, drawings and all means of expression" in matters related to its own definition of "national security."[18] Moreover, the penal code outlined strict punishments—including heavy fines and/or prison sentences—for insulting the president or public officials and for blasphemy.[19] The 1971 constitution, meanwhile, gave the president sole discretion for declaring states of emergency and allowed for the continual renewal of states of emergency—indeed, successive Mubarak decrees put Egypt in a state of emergency for virtually the entirety of his thirty-year presidency. Finally, the Emergency Law gave the president complete power to censor "all means of expression," and to shut down printing houses.[20] Other articles in the 1971 constitution further restricted press content by tasking the press with preserving "the genuine character of the Egyptian family" (Article 9) and "safeguarding and protecting morals" (Article 12).

The Mubarak-era legal umbrella did include a fair amount of freedom-granting provisions to the news media, contained mostly in the Press Law and the 1971 constitution, which included, for example, Constitutional Article 47 and its guarantee of "freedom of the press."[21] The Mubarak regime was nonetheless able to use its more expansive and powerful array of repressive provisions to effectively cancel out many of the freedoms alluded to in these documents. Journalists who attempted to transgress government-imposed limits were often repressed harshly. Many were sentenced to jail and physically assaulted during Mubarak's rule.[22]

Yet, in spite of its repressive legal framework, there was arguably more press freedom during the Mubarak era than during the Sadat or Nasser periods. Much of the increased freedom can be attributed to a 2004 government concession granting private Egyptian citizens the right to own news-publishing licenses,[23] which served to open up the Egyptian press system at least to some extent.[24] Privately owned news outlets were more likely to challenge the Mubarak government's narrative. Kenneth Cooper's study, for example, found that *Al-Masry Al-Youm*, a privately owned newspaper, devoted more coverage to human rights abuses and corruption (among other topics unfriendly and unflattering to the Mubarak government), than did state-run outlets.[25]

Still, although the independent press was allowed more latitude than state-run outlets, predetermined red lines prevented these news outlets from going far out of bounds and thereby more substantively fostering a potential democratic turn in Egypt. Another limiting factor to the democratic transition was that wealthy businessmen, relatively friendly to the Mubarak government, owned many of the new private news outlets. These included the moguls Salah Diab, Naguib Sawiris, Mohamed Amin, and Al-Sayid Badawi, all of whom appeared to maintain editorial biases against crossing any red lines.

Egypt's Mubarak-era press also suffered from a general lack of professionalism, including a relatively low quality of journalism education and only minimal training programs. Many journalists working during this period in Egypt did not have degrees in journalism or journalism-related disciplines. Other research suggests that Mubarak-era journalism was plagued by a lack of commitment to the principles of fairness, balance, and objectivity,[26] and was rife with nepotism, which prevented merit-based hiring practices.[27]

It was not until near the end of the Mubarak presidency that social media and blogging influenced Egyptian news and politics in meaningful ways, most markedly during the 2011 uprising that eventually ousted Mubarak. Indeed, internet penetration increased rapidly during the 2000s, and the Mubarak regime struggled to keep pace with the burgeoning online political activism. In retrospect, it seems almost inevitable that young activists would use blogs and Facebook to organize protests and help spark the 2011 uprising.[28]

The Press under the Supreme Council of the Armed Forces

Following nationwide anti-Mubarak protests held from January 25, 2011, to February 11, 2011, Egypt's SCAF ousted Mubarak and assumed executive power in Egypt. The military leadership oversaw Egypt's post-uprising transition period for approximately a year and a half, until June 30, 2012, the day Morsi was inaugurated as Egypt's fifth president.

It is during this period that a transition toward democracy would have been aided by major changes to both Egypt's draconian press law and the nation's penal code, including articles restricting free expression and freedom of the press. Making such changes would have been within the SCAF's power because, in the aftermath of the uprising and following the dissolution of Mubarak's parliament, the military leaders also assumed legislative power.[29] In addition to an overhauling of the nation's legal framework, Lina Atallah suggested that Egypt's state media also needed to be "purged" in the aftermath of the January 2011 uprising.[30]

Initially, the SCAF promised to put an end to the Emergency Law and to make other changes to promote a free press.[31] However, it eventually opted for the status quo, keeping the Emergency Law and other restrictive laws on the books. The lack of media law reform during this time may have been the product of a genuine desire on the part of military authorities to manipulate the press and stifle dissent. It may also be the case that military authorities did not have sufficient time to reform a deeply flawed press industry during what was to be a relatively short transition to civilian rule. Ultimately, however, there seems to have been little appetite for legal reform.

After a very brief honeymoon period immediately following the ouster of Mubarak, tensions rose between the SCAF and January 25 revolutionaries, who became critical of the military's road map for Egypt's future. By summer and fall 2011, press criticism of the military authority had become commonplace.[32] The SCAF responded to attacks on their policies by summoning journalists to appear before military courts, reactivating the Emergency Law, and using intimidation tactics to stifle dissent. Moreover, the SCAF used existing media laws to prosecute journalists and send bloggers and protesters to military trials.[33] On two separate occasions during SCAF rule, for example, Egyptian police raided the offices of Al Jazeera Mubashir Misr, an Al Jazeera affiliate dedicated to news about Egypt, and physically assaulted staff members on at least one occasion.[34]

The Committee to Protect Journalists (CPJ) also noted that the military authorities temporarily shut down the live broadcasts of two news networks, detained workers, and prevented the printing of multiple newspaper editions. CPJ's report also highlighted the sentencing of blogger Maikel Nabil Sanad to three years in jail for "insulting the military."[35] In February 2012, exactly one year after the fall of the Mubarak regime, Human Rights Watch proclaimed that the "climate for free expression in Egypt has worsened since Hosni Mubarak was ousted."[36]

One reason for increasing hard-line tactics and repression during SCAF rule may have been the increasingly aggressive nature of reporting about government activities in the aftermath of the January 2011 uprising. As 2011 wore on, press attacks on the military authorities increased in both frequency and intensity, possibly as a result of the revolutionary moment's breaking of the "fear barrier."[37] Writing five months after the January 2011 uprising, Joseph Mayton argued that

Egypt's newsroom mentality had changed, and that journalists were being "more forceful and brave" in their reporting of human rights abuses. As 2011 progressed, Mayton wrote, there was "growing criticism of the military in almost all Arabic dailies."[38]

The SCAF did, however, fulfill its promise of holding parliamentary elections in late 2011 and early 2012, and Egyptians voted their first post-uprising parliament into office in January 2012. Islamists, led by the Muslim Brotherhood, dominated the polls, taking about 70 percent of parliamentary seats overall.[39]

The newly elected Islamist-dominated parliament also chose not to repeal repressive press laws, although the new legislative body did put an end to the Emergency Law in May 2012.[40] Like the military, the Muslim Brotherhood–dominated parliament was accused of betraying revolutionary and democratic principles,[41] with the brotherhood specifically accused of making a power-sharing pact with the SCAF and serving an antidemocratic, military agenda.[42] The parliament was disbanded only four months into its term,[43] and it seems that it lacked sufficient time for more comprehensive legal reforms.

The Press under Morsi

Morsi took over as Egypt's first post-uprising president, and also its first-ever democratically elected president, on June 30, 2012. In an informal inauguration speech held at Tahrir Square on June 29, 2012, he said that power resided with the people and promised to govern Egypt democratically.[44] In another reassuring proclamation shortly before his election, Morsi said, "No one will touch media freedoms. There will be no pens broken, no opinions prevented, no channels or newspapers shut down in my era."[45] Less than two months into his term, Morsi pleased many journalists and activists when he outlawed the "pretrial detention of people accused of press crimes."[46]

In the eyes of some analysts, however, Morsi's brief term was characterized more by repression of the press than by freedom of the press. Morsi did not eliminate restrictive Mubarak-era media laws and, in fact, like the SCAF, he used them at times to restrict some forms of speech. Some analysts argued that Morsi's treatment of the press demonstrated that he was simply another in a long line of Egyptian dictators.[47]

During the first several months of his term, private lawyers supportive of Morsi filed numerous lawsuits against journalists and other media figures for "insulting the president."[48] In fact, there were more "insulting the president" lawsuits brought during Morsi's brief stay as president than during the entire thirty-year Mubarak era. Also during the Morsi period, state newspaper editors antagonistic to the Muslim Brotherhood were sacked and replaced with figures more sympathetic to the group,[49] and some newspaper issues were confiscated.[50] These facets of Morsi's governance prompted media scholar Rasha Abdulla to argue that Egypt experienced an "unprecedented lack of freedom of expression" under Morsi.[51]

Other analysts have suggested, however, that while many of Morsi's media-related moves may have been misguided and reflect some of his more reactionary tendencies, freedoms during his brief term were relatively high, as evidenced by the fierce demonization campaign launched against Morsi and the Muslim Brotherhood in the private media. From this perspective, Morsi's moves to silence critics were reactions to an irresponsible, and sometimes seditious, press. Analyst Eric Margolis argued that Morsi was "too soft" on the media and the rest of Egypt's "deep government," which Margolis claimed was actively "sabotaging the democratic government."[52] In the aftermath of open calls for an overthrow of Morsi, political scientist Shadi Hamid asked whether Egyptians should have the right to "call . . . for the army to depose an elected president."[53] Hamid noted that in the United States, such calls are not considered protected forms of speech and are prosecutable by law. Research by Abdallah Shleifer suggests that some Egyptian journalists conceived of themselves as political activists (prejudices therein included),[54] while in-depth interviews carried out by Mohamad Hamas Elmasry and Mohammed El-Nawawy suggest that journalists during the Morsi period intentionally biased reports against Morsi and the Muslim Brotherhood.[55]

Egypt's 2012 constitution was passed in December 2012, about six months into Morsi's term. The document was a point of contention among Egyptians, in part because many liberal political forces felt that Islamists unfairly dominated the constitution-building process. Many Egyptians also argued that Morsi used his controversial November 2012 presidential decree, which granted him temporary powers to exceed his legal authority, to impose a divisive constitution on the nation.[56] Critics of the 2012 constitution, which was written by a democratically assembled but Islamist-dominated body, argued that it unnecessarily restricted press freedoms, and that it could be used by the government to manipulate public opinion.

Although the 2012 constitution's demarcation of the freedom of the press represented a move forward from the 1971 constitution, it arguably did not go far enough to ensure that freedoms enshrined within it would be adequately protected. Article 45 declared that "freedom of thought and opinion are guaranteed" and that "every person has the right to express his opinion in speaking, writing, image, or otherwise." Article 48 guaranteed the "freedom of journalism, the press, the publishing industry, broadcasting, and other media." Article 49 provided all Egyptians the right to own newspapers without government permission, which represented a significant shift from the Mubarak-era issuing of newspaper licenses. Moreover, notably absent in the new constitution was a prominently entrenched emergency protocol, which Mubarak had used to eliminate freedoms granted in the 1971 constitution. Hence, whereas Mubarak had sole discretion over declaring states of emergency and could renew states of emergency more or less indefinitely, the 2012 constitution forced the president to obtain majority approval from both houses of parliament in order to declare a state of emergency. States of emergency were also limited to a maximum of six months.[57] After that, the constitution allowed the president to request no more than one additional six-month emergency period, but this could only take effect with public approval in a national referendum. These restrictions on the president's powers therefore made it more difficult for any president to use the Emergency Law to stifle dissent.

The 2012 constitution also contained some significant restrictions on press content and speech. Article 44 declared that it was "forbidden to insult any messengers or prophets," while Article 48 allowed for censorship with "a court ruling" and during "times of war or public mobilization." Article 48 also declared that freedom of the press would be placed within the "framework of the essential elements of state and society," which, according to the constitution's opening section, included "Islam" and "Islamic law." Thus, although the articles in this new constitution took some restrictive power away from the president and other elected officials, the courts still had the power to use these articles to narrow press freedoms, including restricting speech deemed to contradict Islamic principles.[58]

Article 215 of the 2012 constitution, which outlined the duties of the National Media Council, was also controversial, as this newly created body was given power over preserving "the pluralism of the media, preventing their concentration or monopolization," and protecting "the interests of the public." The council was also empowered with the discretion to "ensure that the different media abide by norms of professionalism and decency . . . and observe the values and constructive traditions of society." Once again, it seemed that the government was only willing to go so far in granting real freedoms to the press.[59]

In one sense, then, the Morsi period represented a partial democratic opening, particularly given that the state-run press was not as likely to toe the government line as they were during the Mubarak period. In another sense, however, the Morsi period highlighted both the need for more competent and progressive governance and a lack of journalistic professionalism that still needs to be addressed if Egypt's political system is to truly advance as a free and independent one.

Restructuring Egypt's Press: Building a Culture of Professionalism

Egypt's most critical journalism-related problems are those associated with the general lack of professionalism described above and the press restrictions related to Egypt's repressive political culture. Many of Egypt's problems stem from a journalism culture that does not seem to honor basic standards of professionalism. As noted above, journalism education and training are of a poor quality in the country, and some journalists conceive of themselves as political activists and thus do not adhere sufficiently to basic norms of balance, fairness, and objectivity. To address this problem, Egypt should invest in and focus more on modern journalism education, encourage news outlets to provide regular training workshops for their journalists, and, perhaps most importantly, institute independent monitoring of press performance.

In terms of education, Egypt must devote energy to forming both preuniversity- and university-level educational standards for journalism and media-related studies. At the primary level, schools should aim to enhance media literacy by requiring students to read and comparatively analyze news reports from diverse news outlets. Media literacy at this level should also be situated within a larger restructuring of Egyptian primary school education. Indeed, key pedagogical theories and ideas can facilitate the necessary changes and improvements. Connected learning, which "seeks to leverage the potential of digital media to expand access to learning that is socially embedded, interest-driven, and oriented toward educational, economic, or political opportunity,"[60] represents one such approach. Programs such as partnerships for twenty-first-century skills[61] and constellations of connections[62] could, for example, be employed to help encourage youth to become critical consumers of media.

At the university level, Egypt should integrate up-to-date journalism curricula and top-of-the-line news labs in journalism programs at colleges and universities. Journalism programs should also require their students to complete at least one intensive internship at a professional news outlet. Student newspapers should also be developed as on-campus venues for hands-on journalism experience. Finally, instructors with significant professional experience should be hired to teach professional skills courses in journalism programs. Fairness, balance, and detachment should be emphasized as key aspects of journalistic professionalism.

For their part, news outlets in Egypt should make more of a concerted effort to offer professional training programs and workshops, which are currently lacking. Funds should be allotted for the purpose of inviting veteran reporters from established news outlets inside or outside Egypt to conduct such programs at local Egyptian news outlets.

Perhaps most importantly, an independent media regulatory body consisting of journalism scholars and professional journalists should be established to ensure that basic journalistic principles and standards of ethics are understood and adhered to. The next section will discuss this independent body in some detail.

An Independent Egyptian News Media Regulatory Body

An independent media regulatory body must oversee, monitor, and regulate the performance of both the state and the private print and broadcast news media. Giandomenico Majone notes that independent media regulatory bodies are "specialized agencies, operating at arm's length from central government . . . as a way of enhancing the credibility of the regulatory strategies/policies emanating from this independent body."[63] Along the same lines, Mark Thatcher argues that a media regulatory institution is "a body with its own powers and responsibilities given under public law, which is organizationally separated from ministries and is neither directly elected nor managed by elected officials."[64]

Dumisani Moyo and Hlongwane Siphiwe also argue that independent media regulatory bodies should serve the "common good," defined by Media scholar Denis McQuail as "the complex of supposed informational, cultural and social benefits to the wider society which go beyond the immediate, particular and individual interests of those who participate in public communication, whether as senders or receivers."[65] The Freedom of Expression Institute has also set several criteria that would guarantee the independence of a media regulatory body. These criteria stipulate that the regulatory body "be located outside government, but not necessarily outside the state; have sufficient resources to enable it [to] discharge its mandate; have control over those matters directly connected with the functions it has to perform under its founding statute; and have the tenure of its members governed by appropriate appointment removal provisions which ensure that members are appropriately qualified, do not serve at the pressure of the Executive and can be removed only on objective ground relating to job performance."

Similarly, the Council of Europe highlighted the importance of having "specially appointed independent regulatory authorities for the broadcasting sector, with expert knowledge in the area. . . . [And] they should be defined so as to protect them against any interference, in particular by political forces or economic interests."[66]

In accordance with these provisions, Egypt's independent regulatory body must develop guidelines for journalistic professionalism and codes of ethics, and provide independent and equal training programs for both state-owned and privately owned news outlets. The body should also be given the power to grant press licenses, monitor news content, investigate and settle complaints, reprimand journalists and news outlets for violations, and suspend licenses of gross violators. Such a body would have played a useful role in Egypt's attempted transition to democracy in the aftermath of the 2011 uprising. In a heavily politicized and polarized environment, an independent news media regulatory body could have helped to ensure greater levels of accuracy and topic and source balance, and promote a less explicitly partisan and propagandist news coverage in the press.

A good example of an independent media regulatory body is the Consejo Federal de Communicacion Audiovisual of the Federal Council for Audiovisual Communication, established in Argentina, which has an "advisory body comprised of representatives from local government, private and non-profit media, unions, university broadcasters and indigenous groups, amongst others."[67] Another example is the Independent Communications Authority of South Africa

(ICASA), which "issues licenses to telecommunications and broadcasting service providers, enforces compliance with rules and regulations, protects consumers from unfair business practices and poor quality services, hears and decides on disputes and complaints brought against licensees and controls and manages the effective use of radio frequency spectrum." In theory, ICASA is an independent organ. However, "the Independent Communications Authority Act stipulates that, as an organ of state, it is accountable to the Minister of Communications through submitting its annual report."[68]

In Hungary, the National Radio and Television Commission monitors the functioning of privately owned radio and television networks and issues licenses to terrestrial, privately owned satellite channels. In addition, "it has around seven members, at least five of [whom] are elected by a simple majority of all members of parliament. The remaining two are nominated by parliamentary groupings (one member per 'grouping')."[69]

We argue that, like many regulatory news media organizations, Egypt's independent media regulatory body should also encourage the creation of a new code of journalistic ethics, although the body should not be given direct say over the code's content. In particular, media professionals and journalists would have to agree upon the code of ethics. In addition, the code would be "entirely up to the profession, and neither the government nor any regulatory body should have a say in this."[70]

Given Egypt's problems of economic inequality, and the likelihood that private press outlets will come to be owned by a narrow elite class of owners, we also believe that steps should be taken to reduce the negative effects of media concentration of ownership. Specifically, we suggest that news owners be stripped of all editorial control. This is important given the extent to which wealthy media owners have influenced news content in Egypt in the past. In this new system, then, working journalists at news outlets would elect editorial boards. News owners would not have influence over the composition of editorial boards or be allowed to influence their day-to-day work. The independent media regulatory body would be charged with the task of ensuring compliance.

Moreover, the independent media regulatory body would also play a role in restructuring Egypt's problematic press laws. The regulatory body would consult with an elected Egyptian parliament to revise press laws and constitutional articles in order to reflect the new democratic identity of the state. This legal restructuring would need to take place relatively early on in any transition. After all, "regulating the media can work only if the legal framework is in place. Apart from the general political will to liberalize the [media] sector, constitutional amendments or laws providing for the creation of a regulatory body are needed."[71] An example of a functional law that has revitalized the media scene in one country is the Audiovisual Communications Law (also known as *lev de medios*) in Argentina, which has played a critical role in "broadening the range of voices in [Argentina's] democratic debate."[72] Finally, Egypt's Syndicate of Journalists should be allowed to continue to function in any new media system. However, the organ should only look after and protect the rights of journalists and oversee the issuing of press memberships.

Managing Government Influence over the Press

Throughout Egypt's modern history, Egyptian governments have exercised varying degrees of control over the press, sometimes severely restricting the domain of free expression. In order to pave the way for a full transition to democracy, Egypt's press should be granted a significant degree of independence from the government.

The first step in this direction would be to abolish the Ministry of Information. Successive governments have used the information minister position as a tool to serve the narrow interests of the governing elite and to exercise control over media content. Eliminating this ministry is important and critical to the opening up of Egypt's press system.

Along these lines, and more generally, the sway of state-owned news outlets should be significantly reduced and independent press outlets should both be encouraged and allowed to flourish. Given the power that the Egyptian government (or any government) wields, it should not be granted the right to operate a disproportionate number of outlets or dominate the news environment. To this end, we suggest that the Egyptian government be allowed to operate a maximum of two newspapers and two broadcast channels. Limiting government-owned outlets to a total of four would allow the government to provide its perspective within the bounds of professionalism dictated by the independent media regulatory body discussed in the previous section and, at the same time, strictly limit the government's ability to dominate news output. Under this arrangement, the number of privately owned outlets would far exceed the number of government-owned outlets.

One potential obstacle to reducing the number of government-owned news outlets in Egypt is the enormous size of the current state-news apparatus. In order to facilitate the necessary changes, most of Egypt's state-owned news outlets would thus need to be privatized, and the total number of staff working at the Egyptian Radio and Television Union (ERTU) would need to be drastically reduced from its current total of forty-three thousand. ERTU staff could be reduced through a system that aims to vet out inefficient members and apply an incentive program where salaries and promotions are tied to performance. Taken together, these measures to professionalize Egyptian journalism and reduce the government's influence over press output could ensure a more democratic press and help facilitate Egypt's complete transition to democracy.

Notes

1. James Napoli and Hussein Amin, "Press Freedom in Egypt," in *Press Freedom and Communication in Africa*, ed. Festus Eribo and William Jong-Ebot (Trenton, NJ: Africa World Press, 1997), 185–211; Hamza Mohammed and Barrie Gunter, "News Consumption and News Agendas in Egypt," in *News Media in the Arab World: A Study of 10 Arab and Muslim Countries*, ed. Barrie Gunter and Roger Dickinson (New York: Bloomsbury, 2013), 83–104.

2. Mohamad Hamas Elmasry, "Producing News in Mubarak's Egypt: An Analysis of Egyptian Newspaper Production during the Late Hosni Mubarak Era," *Journal of Arab and Muslim Media Research* 4, nos. 2–3 (2011): 121–144.

3. Napoli and Amin, "Press Freedom in Egypt," 185–211; Kenneth J. Cooper, "Politics and Priorities: Inside the Egyptian Press," *Arab Media and Society* 6 (Fall 2008), http://www.arabmediasociety.com/?article=689; Noha Mellor, *The Making of Arab News* (Oxford: Rowman and Littlefield, 2005); Lawrence Pintak, "Satellite TV News and Arab Democracy," *Journalism Practice* 2, no. 1 (2008); William A. Rugh, *Arab Mass Media: Newspapers, Radio, and Television in Arab Politics* (Westport, CT: Greenwood, 2004).

4. Mohamad Hamas Elmasry and Mohammed El-Nawawy, "One Country, Two Eras: How Three Egyptian Newspapers Framed Two Presidents," *Global Media Journal: Mediterranean Edition* 9, no. 1 (2014): 27–39.

5. Mohammed El-Nawawy and Khamis Sahar, *Egyptian Revolution 2.0: Political Blogging, Civic Engagement, and Citizen Journalism* (New York: Palgrave Macmillan, 2013).

6. Jyotika Ramaprasad and Hamdy Naila Nabil, "Functions of Egyptian Journalists Perceived Importance and Actual Performance," *International Communication Gazette* 68, no. 2 (2006): 167–185; Hussein Amin, "Freedom as a Value in Arab Media: Perceptions and Attitudes among Journalists," *Political Communication* 19, no. 2 (2002): 125–135.

7. Naomi Sakr, "Social Media, Television Talk Shows, and Political Change in Egypt," *Television and New Media* 14, no. 4 (2013): 322–337.

8. Naomi Sakr, "Contested Blueprints for Egypt's Satellite Channels: Regrouping the Options by Redefining the Debate," *International Communication Gazette* 63, nos. 2–3 (2001): 149.

9. Sahar Khamis, "The Transformative Egyptian Media Landscape: Changes, Challenges and Comparative Perspectives," *International Journal of Communication* 5 (2011): 1159–1177; Naila Hamdy and Gomaa H. Ehab, "Framing the Egyptian Uprising in Arabic Language Newspapers and Social Media," *Journal of Communication* 62, no. 2 (2012): 195–211.

10. Rasha Abdulla, "The Revolution Will Be Tweeted: The Story of Digital Activism in Egypt," *Cairo Review* 3 (2011): 41–49.

11. Esam Al-Amin, "The Grand Scam: Spinning Egypt's Military Coup," *Counterpunch*, July 19, 2013, http://www.counterpunch.org/2013/07/19/the-grand-scam-spinning-egypts-military-coup/.

12. Nour Youssef, "How Egyptian Media Has Become a Mouthpiece for the Military State," *Economist*, June 25, 2015, http://www.theguardian.com/world/2015/jun/25/egyptian-media-journalism-sisi-mubarak.

13. Michael Georgy, "Media Push Back against Egyptian President Al-Sisi with Unprecedented Criticism," *Huffington Post*, May 13, 2015, http://www.huffingtonpost.com/2015/05/13/media-egyptian-president-sisi-criticism_n_7276318.html.

14. Munir K. Nasser, *Egyptian Mass Media under Nasser and Sadat: Two Models of Press Management and Control*, Journalism Monographs 124 (Columbia, SC: Association for Education in Journalism and Mass Communication, 1990).

15. Elmasry, "Producing News in Mubarak's Egypt," 121–144.

16. Karin Deutsch Karlekar, *Freedom of the Press 2005: A Global Survey of Media Independence* (New York: Freedom House, 2005).

17. Supreme Press Council of Egypt, *Law Number 96 of Year 1996 on the Organization of Journalism* [*Al-Hay'a al-'Amma li-sho'oon al-mataba' al-ameeriya*], 1998.

18. International Research and Exchange Board, "Media Sustainability Index 2005—The Middle East and North Africa," IREX, 2005, https://www.irex.org/sites/default/files/MSI05_MENA_EG.pdf.

19. Egyptian Council of Lords and Council of Representatives, "The Penal Law, Number 58 of 1937 (Modified by Law 147 of 2006): According to Its Latest Revisions," Dar al-Haqqaaniya, Cairo, 2008.

20. The Constitution of the Arab Republic of Egypt, 1971 (as Amended to 2007), http://www.constitutionnet.org/files/Egypt%20Constitution.pdf.

21. Ibid.

22. Amnesty International, "No Freedom—Journalists Stopped from Doing Their Jobs," May 3, 2009, http://www.amnesty.org/en/news-and-updates/feature-stories/no-freedom-journalists-stopped-doing-their-jobs-20090502; Supreme Press Council of Egypt, personal interview with a manager of Dawaayaat, Cairo, November 23, 2008.

23. Cooper, "Politics and Priorities."

24. Marsot Afaf Lutfi al-Sayyid, *A History of Egypt: From the Arab Conquest to the Present* (Cambridge: Cambridge University Press, 2007).

25. Cooper, "Politics and Priorities."

26. Chatham House, "Egypt in Transition: The Media's Role in Politics," Middle East and North Africa Programme, Workshop Summary, June 2011, London.

27. Elmasry and Nawawy, "One Country, Two Eras," 27–39.

28. Sakr, "Social Media, Television Talk Shows, and Political Change in Egypt," 322–337; Jose Antonio Vargas, "Spring Awakening: How an Egyptian Revolution Began on Facebook," *New York Times*, February 17, 2012, http://www.nytimes.com/2012/02/19/books/review/how-an-egyptian-revolution-began-on-facebook.html?pagewanted=all&_r=0.

29. "Egyptian Military Dissolves Parliament," BBC, February 13, 2011, http://www.bbc.co.uk/news/world-middle-east-12443678.

30. Lina Atallah cited in Sarah A. Tapol, "The Assault on Egypt's Free Press," *New York Times*, February 15, 2012, http://latitude.blogs.nytimes.com/2012/02/15/the-assault-on-egypts-free-press/?_php=true&_type=blogs&_php=true&_type=blogs&_r=1&module=ArrowsNav&contentCollection=Opinion&action=keypress&region=FixedLeft&pgtype=Blogs.

31. Mohammed, and Gunter, "News Consumption and News Agendas in Egypt," 83–104.

32. Joseph Mayton, "Military Unable to Silence Egypt's Media," Doha Center for Media Freedom, August 1, 2011, http://www.dc4mf.org/en/content/military-unable-silence-egypt%E2%80%99s-media.

33. Human Rights Watch, "Egypt: A Year of Attacks on Free Expression," February 11, 2012, http://www.hrw.org/news/2012/02/11/egypt-year-attacks-free-expression.

34. Committee to Protect Journalists, "Egyptian Police Raid Al-Jazeera Offices Again," Committee to Protect Journalists, September 29, 2011, http://cpj.org/2011/09/egyptian-police-raid-al-jazeera-offices-again.php.

35. Committee to Protect Journalists, "Egyptian journalists accused of 'insulting armed forces,'" Committee to Protect Journalists, March 9, 2012, https://cpj.org/2012/03/egyptian-journalists-accused-of-insulting-armed-fo.php.

36. Human Rights Watch, "Egypt: A Year of Attacks on Free Expression," February 11, 2012, https://www.hrw.org/news/2012/02/11/egypt-year-attacks-free-expression.

37. Mohamed Elshahed, "Breaking the Fear Barrier of Mubarak's Regime," Social Science Research Council, 2011, http://www.ssrc.org/pages/breaking-the-fear-barrier-of-mubarak-s -regime/.

38. Mayton, "Military Unable to Silence Egypt's Media."

39. David D. Kirkpatrick, "Islamists Win 70% of Seats in the Egyptian Parliament," *New York Times*, January 21, 2012, http://www.nytimes.com/2012/01/22/world/middleeast/muslim -brotherhood-wins-47-of-egypt-assembly-seats.html?_r=0.

40. "More 'Insulting President' Lawsuits under Morsi than Mubarak," Ahram Online, January 20, 2013, http://english.ahram.org.eg/News/62872.aspx.

41. Sara Khorshid, "Mohamed Morsi Has Turned His Back on Egypt's Revolution," *Guardian*, June 27, 2013, http://www.theguardian.com/commentisfree/2013/jun/27/mohamed-morsi -turned-back-egypt.

42. Wael Eskandar, "Brothers and Officers: A History of Pacts," *Jadaliyya*, January 25, 2013, http://www.jadaliyya.com/pages/index/9765/brothers-and-officers_a-history-of-pacts.

43. David Hearst and Hussein Abdel-Rahman, "Egypt's Supreme Court Dissolves Parliament and Outrages Islamists," *Guardian*, June 14, 2012, http://www.theguardian.com/world /2012/jun/14/egypt-parliament-dissolved-supreme-court.

44. CNN Wire Staff, "Egypt's President-Elect Promises to Put Power in Hands of the People," CNN, June 29, 2012, http://www.cnn.com/2012/06/29/world/africa/egypt-morsi/.

45. Quoted in Seifeldin Fawzy, "Morsi's Democracy Devoid of Press and Media Freedoms," *Jadaliyya*, December 19, 2012, http://www.jadaliyya.com/pages/index/9129/morsis-democracy -devoid-of-press-and-media-freedom.

46. Kareem Fahim and Mayy El Sheikh, "Egyptian President's Move Ends Detention of Critic," *New York Times*, August 23, 2012, http://www.nytimes.com/2012/08/24/world /middleeast/morsi-move-ends-detention-of-a-critic.html.

47. Rasha Abdulla, "Is Egypt Living in a Time of Unprecedented Freedom?," Ahram Online, March 26, 2013, http://english.ahram.org.eg/NewsContent/4/0/67754/Opinion/Is-Egypt -living-in-a-time-of-unprecedented-freedom.aspx; Fawzy, "Morsi's Democracy."

48. "More 'Insulting President' Lawsuits."

49. Erin Cunningham, "Mohamed Morsi vs. Egypt's Press," *Global Post*, August 23, 2012, http://www.globalpost.com/dispatch/news/regions/middle-east/egypt/120823/morsi-press -media-freedom-muslim-brotherhood.

50. Sara Elkamel, "Objectivity in the Shadows of Political Turmoil: A Comparative Content Analysis of News Framing in Post-revolution Egypt's Press" (MA thesis, American University in Cairo, Egypt, 2013).

51. Rasha Abdulla, "Is Egypt Living in a Time of Unprecedented Freedom?," Ahram Online, March 26, 2013, http://english.ahram.org.eg/NewsContent/4/0/67754/Opinion/Is-Egypt -living-in-a-time-of-unprecedented-freedom.aspx.

52. Eric Margolis, "So Much for Middle East Democracy," *World News Daily*, July 9, 2013, http://www.informationclearinghouse.info/article35491.htm.

53. Shadi Hamid, "Egypt's Uncomfortable Challenge: Balancing Security and Civil Liberties," *Atlantic*, August 20, 2012, http://www.theatlantic.com/international/archive/2012/08 /egypts-uncomfortable-challenge-balancing-security-and-civil-liberties/261260/.

54. Abdallah Schleifer, "Egypt's Media Quagmire Worsens," *Al-Arabiya*, April 3, 2013, http://english.alarabiya.net/en/views/2013/04/03/Are-Egypt-s-journalists-all-activists-.html.

55. Elmasry and Nawawy, "One Country, Two Eras," 27–39.

56. Richard Spencer, "Mohammed Morsi Grants Himself Sweeping powers in Wake of Gaza," *Telegraph*, November 22, 2012, http://www.telegraph.co.uk/news/worldnews

/africaandindianocean/egypt/9697347/Mohammed-Morsi-grants-himself-sweeping-new
-powers-in-wake-of-Gaza.html.

57. Nivien Saleh, "The 2012 Constitution of Egypt, Translated by Nivien Saleh, with Index,"
2012, http://niviensaleh.info/constitution-egypt-2012-translation/#part-1.

58. Ibid.

59. Ibid.

60. Mizuko Ito et al., "Connected Learning: An Agenda for Research and Design Summary
Report," Digital Media and Learning Research Hub, 2013, http://dmlhub.net/sites/default/files
/ConnectedLearning_summary.pdf.

61. Bernie Trilling and Fadel Charles, *21st Century Skills: Learning for Life in Our Times* (San
Francisco: Jossey-Bass, 2009).

62. Hannah R. Gerber et al., "From Mario to FIFA: What Qualitative Case Study Research
Suggests about Games-Based Learning in a US Classroom," *Educational Media International*
51, no. 1 (2014): 16–34.

63. Giandomenico Majone, "From the Positive to the Regulatory State: Causes and Consequences of Changes in the Mode of Governance," *Journal of Public Policy* 17, no. 2 (1997):
1391–1367.

64. Mark Thatcher, "Regulation after Delegation: Independent Regulatory Agencies in Europe," *Journal of European Public Policy* 9, no. 6 (2002): 954–972.

65. Dumisani Moyo and Hlongwane Siphiwe, "Regulatory Independence and the Public Interest: The Case of South Africa's ICASA," *Journal of African Media Studies* 1, no. 2 (2009):
279–294.

66. Achim Vogt, "Regulation and Self-regulation: The Role of Media Commissions and Professional Bodies in the Muslim World," *Political Communication* 19, no. 2 (2002): 211–223.

67. Robbie Macrory, "Dilemmas of Democratisation: Media Regulation and Reform in Argentina," *Bulletin of Latin American Research* 32, no. 2 (2013): 178–193.

68. Moyo and Siphiwe, "Regulatory independence and the public interest," 279–294.

69. Alison Harcourt, "The Regulation of Media Markets in Selected EU Accession States in
Central and Eastern Europe," *European Law Journal* 9, no. 3 (2003): 316–340.

70. Achim Vogt, "Regulation and Self-Regulation: The Role of Media Commissions and
Professional Bodies in the Muslim World," *Political Communication* 19, no. 2 (2002): 216.

71. Ibid., 212.

72. Robbie Macrory, "Dilemmas of Democratization: Media Regulation and Reform in
Argentina," *Bulletin of Latin American Research* 32, no. 2 (2012): 184.

8 The Egyptian Military and the Presidency

Continuity and Change

Dina Rashed

THE ESTABLISHMENT OF the first republic in Egypt in 1952 brought the country's military to the center of political life. Except for very brief periods, military men have monopolized the presidential seat for over six decades. However, the relationship between the presidency and the military has been anything but static. Gamal Abdel Nasser consolidated missions of external and internal security under the command of the military while his junta occupied the highest political positions in the state. Anwar Sadat sought to restructure the political system he inherited by civilizing the cabinet and redrawing the institutional boundaries between the state's institutions of force. Hosni Mubarak followed in Sadat's footsteps, intensifying efforts to disengage the military from domestic control, and depended extensively on the forces of the Ministry of Interior to enforce his authoritarian rule. In 2011, the Egyptian uprising brought the first republic to an end and created conditions for the revival of a direct military engagement with politics. Tumultuous and short lived, Egypt's second republic ended with a second mass uprising and the ouster of the first democratically elected civilian president. Mohammed Morsi followed a policy of official appeasement toward components of the security complex but could not forge real relations of trust and cooperation with either the military or the police. Abdul Fatah el-Sisi's policies aim to secure more political powers for the military and public support for the military's engagement in the state's economy.

Through examining the dynamic relationship between the military and presidents in Egypt, this chapter aims to identify moments of cooperation and contention and discuss their impact on Egypt's transition to democracy. Through discussions of the historical narrative, I intend to underscore two important aspects relevant to political transitions. First, I highlight an under-theorized form of military disengagement from politics: retreat from domestic control and involvement in economic activity. This partial disengagement differs markedly from trajectories of delegation of power and democratization that are often discussed in civil-military relations literature. Second, I show how in the post-regime breakdown of power, trust-building measures remain an integral part of the transition to democracy.

The chapter first discusses notable scholarship on military intervention in politics. It then engages with the historical narrative of the Egyptian republics, showing the dynamics of power between presidents and militaries. In the final section, I discuss how trust, and the lack of it, affected the country's transition from the Mubarak regime.

Militaries in Politics: Intervention and Disengagement

Militaries, like other strong institutions, strive to defend their interests and minimize infringements on their areas of influence. Studies of civil-military relations show that the organizational interests of militaries remain the most crucial factor in defining their intervention in politics. As disciplined armed organizations, militaries value the cohesion of, and autonomous control over appointments within, the officer corps. Generals care about the flow of sufficient funds and budgetary allocations to their institution as much as their monopoly over decisive force in society.[1] Most militaries prefer to remain outside politics as long as these interests are safeguarded. However, historical experiences show that interventions emerge out of civilian pressures to politicize the officer corps as much as they are produced by officers' grievances.[2] Factors such as the instability of the political system and civilian failure to resolve conflicts that shape the political culture of a country may produce hospitable conditions for generals' direct engagement with politics.[3]

Studies on officers' political behavior reflect little consensus with regard to how professionalism influences the decision to retreat from politics. Samuel Huntington has distinguished between professional and praetorian militaries based on their subordination to civilian rule, noting that professional militaries submit to civilian rule, while praetorian ones overtake political power.[4] Yet Morris Janowitz posits that professional officers must develop political-social insights to deal with political-military issues and the ambiguous nature of the security environment.[5] Examining the expanding political roles of the highly professionalized militaries in Latin America during the 1960s, Alfred Stepan finds that militaries concerned with threats of domestic revolution train their officers to acquire expertise in social, economic, and political issues, in addition to security matters.[6] These experiences reflect the centrality of the principal-agent dilemma in society-military relations.[7]

While most studies within the transition literature adopt the view that military subordination to civilians is a main feature of democratic transformation,[8] new research shows that coups could open the door to democratic governance.[9]

However, military disengagement from politics should not be conflated with subordination to civilians or with democratic transition. Researchers highlight two distinct trajectories of disengagement. The first is militaries' delegation of some authority to civilians without full retreat from politics. According to this framework, the military rules indirectly—or rules but does not govern.[10] The second trajectory associates military withdrawal with authoritarian breakdown. Research has shown that splits within the military prompt officers to return to the barracks and ultimately transition to democratic rule.[11] Junta members may consciously extricate themselves from politics or relinquish power under popular pressure in transitions to democratic rule.[12] In other cases militaries may extricate themselves temporarily from politics if the short-term costs of repression are high, and if future opportunities for their intervention are not foreclosed.[13]

Changes in domestic security arrangements under Sadat and Mubarak, as discussed in this chapter, demonstrate how the military retrenched from one sphere of power, particularly domestic control, and channeled more institutional energy into the economic sphere while maintaining external defense missions. Forsaking authority over domestic control is not a form of delegation, especially when decisions and policies about how, when, and whom to repress are made by another state apparatus and independently from the military. Both Sadat and Mubarak extricated the military from repressing dissent and relied more on the apparatus of the Ministry of Interior.[14] This partial disengagement from politics requires delicate balancing of the multiple roles of the different armed forces and the spheres through which they operate. The mass uprisings of January 2011 broke down this balance and brought the military back into the heart of domestic control.

The Military in the First Republic: Appeasement and Changing Interests

To understand the dynamics of Egypt's civil-military relations, it is important to briefly map out the country's security system. Egypt's current defense and security sector is made of three main institutions: the Ministry of Defense,[15] the Ministry of Interior, and the General Intelligence Service. The first two institutions each have controlled a separate surveillance apparatus: Military Intelligence and the State Security Investigation Service, respectively.[16]

Nasser (r. 1956–1970) endowed the presidential seat with extensive powers, including the right to appoint and dismiss vice presidents, prime ministers, ministers, and commanders of the armed forces at will. At the same time, he entrusted junta members with running the police force, surveillance apparatus, and paramilitary forces.[17] In 1954, the General Intelligence Service was established to monitor espionage activities, but eventually got enmeshed in the intra-junta rivalry and became part of the repressive machine of the regime.

The politicization of the junta came with a hefty cost for the officer corps and the presidency. Favoritism and a low level of professionalization characterized intra-corps relations. Ultimately, this posed a threat to the president's authority.[18] Nasser's rival was his closest associate and commander of the Egyptian Armed Forces, Field Marshal Abdel Hakim 'Amer. With a deep following within the officer corps, 'Amer worked to isolate Nasser and control access to information, especially about the military.[19]

President Sadat (r. 1970–1981) parted from his predecessor's policies and restructured missions and actors of the security sector. Recognizing the negative impact of officers' politicization, Sadat worked to sustain higher levels of professionalization through institutional independence. As early as 1971, Sadat selected his ministers of interior from within the police force, thereby ending two decades of military hegemony over the Ministry of Interior's leadership. He also shifted control of the antiriot units, the Central Security Forces, away from the Ministry of Defense and delegated it to the Ministry of Interior. Most importantly, he reassigned the responsibility of monitoring political activity to the State Security Investigation Service,[20] restricted the work of Military Intelligence to the monitoring of military officers, and reinstated the original mission of the General Intelligence Service. To further disengage the officers from politics, Sadat issued a decree in 1976 preventing all in-service officers from participating in public elections through vote or nomination.[21] Sadat's efforts to civilianize power included major changes to the makeup of the executive branch. Changes in the number of civilian cabinet members registered Sadat's effort to demilitarize governance. Of the total ministers who served under Nasser, 20.6 percent were officers and 14 percent officer technocrats, compared to 4 percent officers and 9 percent officer technocrats under Sadat.[22]

Mubarak (r. 1981–2011) followed Sadat's path. In his capacity as the supreme commander of the Egyptian Armed Forces, Mubarak screened the highest-ranking generals and appointed the least politicized to the most sensitive positions in the military while maintaining seniority.[23] He not only preserved but augmented the military's economic resources, thereby eliminating sources of institutional grievance. Throughout the 1980–2011 period, the military built a network of economic enterprises that guaranteed an undisrupted source of revenue.[24] These economic perks were only made possible through the generous military aid received from the United States, which allowed the Ministry of Defense to direct part of its budget to consumer goods without cutting allocation for training and equipment.[25]

This attention to the military's organizational interests paralleled an increased reliance on the police to control sociopolitical dissent, which explains why the Ministry of Interior witnessed extensive enhancement of its institutional capacity under Mubarak.[26] Yet, the meteoric political rise of Mubarak's son Gamal in the early 2000s[27] disrupted the delicate balance between state institutions and produced grievances on different levels. On one level, it put more pressure on the Ministry of Interior to suppress public dissent triggered by Mubarak's nepotism, thereby increasing public disaffection with the regime. On another, it created resentment within the officer corps toward what seemed an unjustified presidential succession for an unqualified candidate. Some unofficial military objections were aired as early as 2000,[28] and increased as influence of the younger Mubarak expanded into political appointments and economic policies.[29] The officers' apprehension was due to the limited political credentials of Gamal Mubarak and his lack of commitment to the state apparatus, of which the military is a central component.[30] However, the disapproval remained muted as the military's leadership preferred to refrain from direct intervention. It was only after the mass uprising that the military intervened to oust the unpopular president. In February 2011, political authority was wrested from Mubarak and into the hands of the highest collective body of the military, the Supreme Council of the Armed Forces (SCAF).

The Short-Lived Second Republic: Morsi's Troubled Relationship with the State

As a president, Morsi's relationship with the military differed from that of his predecessors. Not only was he the first democratically elected civilian, but, more importantly, he was a leading member of the officially banned Muslim Brotherhood. The history of Egypt's security arrangements vis-à-vis the Muslim Brotherhood complicated his relationship to the state's institutions of power. First under Nasser's military regime and then under Mubarak's police apparatus, the Muslim Brotherhood spent decades trying to adjust to, and at times infiltrate, the iron fist of the state.

However, the Muslim Brotherhood succeeded in forging a level of understanding with the SCAF during the early phase of the transitional period. Following Mubarak's ouster, the SCAF assigned a committee of legal experts to amend articles of the 1971 constitution as a basis for its transitional rule. The handpicked committee included Muslim Brotherhood leaders,[31] and in return the Muslim Brotherhood remained supportive of the military's policies,[32] despite the latter's governance-related missteps.[33] Both the military and the Muslim Brotherhood supported the status quo rather than radical change, often ignoring revolutionaries' demands.[34] This understanding may have been facilitated by the common traits that both enjoy and value: strict discipline as well as hierarchy and obedience among their members. The political dynamics under Mubarak may have also facilitated the emergence of a level of cooperation between the two. The military's disengagement from Mubarak's repressive practices[35] and Field Marshal Mohamed Tantawi's disinterest in direct political governance may have alleviated fears regarding the military's political ambitions.[36]

The early rapprochement gradually faltered after the parliamentary election gave Islamists over 70 percent of the People's Assembly, contrary to most predictions.[37] Two crises registered the deteriorating relationship between the popular movement and state institutions, in particular the military and the judiciary. The first crisis revolved around the right of the parliamentary majority to change the cabinet.[38] The second crisis revolved around the parliamentary election law, which allowed members of political parties to run for independent seats. Relations plunged as the Supreme Constitutional Court ruled unconstitutional one-third of parliament seats and recommended disbanding the assembly. Only days prior to the second round of the presidential election, the SCAF, still in its capacity as the official governing body of the country, dissolved the parliament and announced an addendum to its earlier constitutional declaration, reclaiming legislative authorities and minimizing the power of the incoming president over a broad range of issues including military affairs.[39] The measure indicated the deep crisis between the military and the incoming president, and ushered in a spiral of mistrust between those who controlled the state and those rooted within society.

Morsi won the presidency by a slim margin of votes. Aided by a powerless consultative body, the Shura Council, and having a shaky relationship with the state apparatus, his biggest support, outside his movement, came from the prodemocracy and revolutionary forces. Two months into his term, he formed a new government, annulled the SCAF's addendum, and exercised some control over military appointments. He introduced a limited but important reshuffle of top military and intelligence posts in the aftermath of the killing of seventeen Egyptian soldiers in Sinai in August 2012. Mubarak's longtime minister of defense, chief of staff, and General Intelligence Service head were all dismissed.

The removal of the old generals worked to the benefit of the military as it injected new blood into the upper echelons of its leadership. The new minister of defense, twenty years Tantawi's junior, wasted no time in reinvigorating the strong but stale institution. General Sisi adopted a strategy to meet the internal and external challenges facing the military. The strategy was based on three principles: to shield the institution from the surrounding political turmoil and prevent its fragmentation, to rebuild bridges with social and political forces and regain public trust in the military, and to prevent the infiltration of Muslim Brotherhood ideology into the officer corps. By focusing on the improvement of military preparedness, initiating joint military exercises with neighboring Arab states, and opening up military talks with great powers besides the United States, the new minister of defense seemed more responsive to the most important technical goals desired by the officer corps. Sisi also paid attention to the internal cohesion of the rank and file, increasing the financial and material benefits for active and retired personnel and their families. Freed from the burdens and volatilities of governance, the military also invested more energy in revamping its public image and mending connections with social and political forces, especially those who became more critical of the Muslim Brotherhood exclusionary rule. At the same time, strict background checks on new recruits were intensified to prevent the penetration of Islamist ideologies into the armed forces.

In the following months, Morsi's ability to work out differences with the opposition and even with Islamist partners faltered. The Muslim Brotherhood, which enjoyed hegemonic power over the presidency, the prime minister's office, the Shura Council, and the constitution-writing committee, adopted unilateral decision-making practices that alienated significant segments of the country's political landscape and increased society's polarization. In November 2012, only a few weeks before a vote on the newly drafted constitution, Morsi issued a constitutional declaration giving himself broad powers and removing judicial oversight over his decrees. The move created a strong public backlash against Morsi, especially as it came only a few days after he had held closed meetings with prominent political leaders who had led the opposition against Mubarak and supported Morsi's presidential bid against Mubarak's disciple, Ahmed Shafiq. That Morsi did not disclose his intention to issue the declaration with any of the revolutionary comrades was received as sign of encroaching authoritarianism by the powerful Muslim Brotherhood. Levels of trust between the presidency and most political parties plummeted, such that the president's call for a "national dialogue" was shunned while the opposition welcomed a similar call by the military. In an attempt to contain the explosive situation, then minister of defense General Sisi called upon all parties to convene. The president, who first accepted, declined the general's invitation a day later. The contradicting statements issued by the presidential office negatively affected Morsi's public image and exposed the limits of his independence vis-à-vis other leaders within the Muslim Brotherhood, who objected to Sisi's initiative.[40] Wishing to limit the military's political role, the Muslim Brotherhood was not in favor of a military-brokered negotiation between the presidency and the opposition.[41] In the following weeks, the military grew more frustrated with the inability of the presidency and opposition to work out differences,[42] given the increasing need to attend to new security threats developing in Sinai and on the western Libyan border.[43]

The second half of Morsi's rule witnessed soaring tensions between the Muslim Brotherhood and the armed forces. Overestimating the movement's power at the ballot box and unable to take notice of the tactics of the new military leadership, the Muslim Brotherhood and its close allies adopted a policy of attack, albeit verbally, against the armed forces. In his weekly message, the general guide of the Muslim Brotherhood, Muhammad Badie, described Egyptian soldier as docile and called for their indoctrination.[44] A few months later, another prominent figure described the military's leadership as cowardly mice.[45] Perhaps the most serious attack came from the head of the Islamist al-Wasat Party and a close Morsi associate, Abul Ela Madi, who claimed that Egyptian generals were involved in criminal activities. Madi accused the General Intelligence Service of training an army of three hundred thousand thugs to bring havoc to Egyptian streets. In a public meeting, Madi stated that the information was relayed to him by then president Morsi.[46] The statement was most alarming to the military given its close association with the General Intelligence Service.[47] The allegation was substantiated by neither Madi nor Morsi and ran contrary to dynamics of domestic repression that characterized Mubarak's rule.[48] Just days after the allegations were made, a meeting between the SCAF and the president took place at the Ministry of Defense. Generals expressed grave concern over three main issues: what they saw as an orchestrated smear campaign directed at their institution,[49] the lack of consultation with the military regarding development projects in the Suez Canal and on the eastern border, and the president's ban on military actions against militant jihadist groups in Sinai. Morsi's acknowledgment of such concerns could not prevent the deterioration in the relationship between him and the military.[50]

In the following months, public discontent with Morsi's performance grew, in part due to the exclusionary policies of the Muslim Brotherhood, the presidency's stubbornness toward popular calls for change of cabinet, and his inability to forge cooperative relations with various groups within the state and society.[51] The Tamarrud Movement gained momentum as it collected signatures for a petition calling for early presidential elections. Mass protests erupted on June 30. Again, the military intervened to oust a president, bringing the second republic to an end.[52]

Back to the Military: Egypt's Third Republic

The ouster of the first democratically elected president was led by the Tamarrud Movement and supported by state institutions and social groups including the police force, a substantial part of the judiciary (represented by the Judges' Club), religious groups including those led by the grand sheikh of Al-Azhar and the Coptic pope, the non-Islamist opposition, and even the strong Salafi Nour Party.[53] Just as was the case in February 2011, these state and social groups would not have managed to displace the president had the military not provided protection and support. In a perfectly choreographed televised meeting that gathered representatives of all these forces, then minister of defense General Sisi announced the ouster of Morsi, the suspension of the 2012 constitution, and the appointment of Chief Justice Adly Mansour, head of the Supreme Constitutional Court, as interim president of the country. Egypt embarked upon a second transitional period, albeit under tighter control by the military.

Although the direct reintervention of the military received unprecedented domestic public support, the government's dispersal of Morsi supporters' sit-in and the killing of hundreds in Rabaa Square were heavily criticized, especially at the international level. The crackdown on the Muslim Brotherhood was met with strong condemnation from some Western and Middle Eastern capitals,[54] and resulted in deterioration in bilateral relations with the United States. To show its disapproval of Morsi's ouster, the Barack Obama administration suspended the joint exercises with the Egyptian military, delayed the transfer of fighter planes for almost two years, and threatened a revision of the $1.3 billion annual military aid to Egypt.[55] Only in 2015 did the United States authorize the delivery of the F-16 planes. It also revisited the aid terms, preventing the Egyptian military from future cash flow financing and putting more constraints on the kind of weapons to be sent to Egypt.[56] Betting on Egypt's geostrategic importance, Sisi capitalized on the tension between Cairo and Washington to push for the renewal of the historical military cooperation between Egypt and Russia while intensifying economic, military, and political cooperation between Egypt and the Gulf States.

Six months into the second transitional period, the military announced its support for General Sisi's presidential bid.[57] Even prior to Sisi's ascension to the presidency in June 2014, the military became the economic powerhouse of the country,[58] winning the major construction projects financed by the wealthy Gulf States.[59] The emergence of ultranationalist rhetoric in response to international criticisms of the post-Morsi transitional period has glorified the military as the guardian of the nation and supporter of the people's will. In this context, the Sisi regime has managed to either neutralize nonsupporters or coercively silence voices of contention, especially from youth movements, through legal measures that restricted demonstration rights. The rhetoric picked up steam of its own as Islamist militants waged terrorist attacks against state officials, including officers and judges, and against Egyptian society more broadly. A strong media machine has played a role in Sisi's efforts through self-censorship and by waging campaigns against regime critics, who were often labeled as supporters of terrorism. The military's execution of large state projects, such as the digging of the Suez Canal's second branch, promised material benefits for Egyptian society and enabled the military and the presidency to maintain a certain level of economic growth, thus fostering charismatic legitimation of authority.

Militaries, Presidents, and the Future of Democratic Transition

Since Nasser, Egypt has enjoyed two strong institutions of power: the presidency and the military. Up until 2011, Egyptian presidents had been able to work out issues of friction and avoid direct military intervention. Both Sadat and Mubarak managed to decouple the presidential seat from the military establishment while preserving the institutional interests of the military. Sadat's effort to extricate the military from missions of domestic control paralleled a desire by the officer corps to disengage from daily management of state affairs as it insulated them from political volatilities.[60] Mubarak removed the strong minister of defense Abd al-Haleem Abu Ghazala in 1989, yet continued to support the preservation of military interests, especially the army's control over its own budget and economic resources. He was able to maintain this balance by relying on the constitutional powers vested in the presidency[61] while devoting attention to the institutional interests of the officer corps.

Morsi assumed the presidency at a tumultuous time, facing strong state actors with entrenched interests, but lacked the political acumen to adopt confidence-building measures and manage compromises. There is no doubt that the SCAF's dissolution of the parliament and its last-minute constitutional addendum minimized the degree of trust between the political partners and sent mixed signals about the military's intentions to hand over real power to the future president. Trust ensues when institutions make it far less likely that one group will be able to capture the state and take advantage of the other.[62] However, the Muslim Brotherhood and President Morsi failed to diffuse crises, preempt challenges, and identify cooperative partners within the state. This has been in part due to the opportunistic behavior of the movement's leadership and its ill-advised political tactics.

On one level, the Muslim Brotherhood lacked a clear strategy on how to dismantle corruption and introduce reform, often pursuing the status quo while adopting a populist discourse that promised more than could be delivered.[63] This was most evident in its ambiguous policy that aimed at reforming the national police force. Proposals for reform by either police officers or human rights activists were ignored, and small-scale purges had limited effects given the lack of real attention to improving policing services.[64] As social and political disaffection with Morsi's performance grew, he sought the help of the unreformed Ministry of Interior and even praised the performance of its police force during the January 25 uprising.[65] The Muslim Brotherhood's security sector restructuring policy reflected an interest to infiltrate the state's armed actors rather than reform the administration of law and order.[66] The lack of direction was also manifested in the Muslim Brotherhood's hypocritical position vis-à-vis the military. Its leadership oscillated between courting the military and encouraging a campaign to undermine its public image and decrease its institutional coherence.

On another level, the Muslim Brotherhood also fostered an environment of distrust by choosing exclusionary policies that alienated weaker players and pushed societal groups to seek military intervention. Distrust can stimulate political involvement among those who feel politically efficacious.[67] The transitional period shows that the military has gained politically every time it distanced itself from an unpopular president. The Muslim Brotherhood treated civilian political actors as separate entities in a noniterating game. This shortsighted policy discounted future gains. The party's leadership failed to understand that making changes to decades-old political rules required more institutional bargaining with coplayers beyond the gains of the ballot box.[68] It also failed to grasp that the fluidity of the political scene had the effect of the communicating vessels law on political relationships, enabling political coalitions between groups with historical enmities.[69] The Muslim Brotherhood's appeasement of the military while shunning weaker civilian partners during the first transitional period revealed its opportunistic behavior and resulted in the loss of revolutionary zeal the movement had tried to appropriate.

The outbreak of mass protests and the fall of the Mubarak ruling elite in February 2011 have created a critical juncture in the military-presidency relationship. While the first transitional period inserted an unprepared military into the plight of daily governance, Morsi's presidency provided an opportunity for the military to reorganize its efforts and work to carve out a constitutionally privileged status for itself. Morsi's failure to lead the country through the transitional period and the military's ability to maintain public trust seem to have solidified a political culture in which military engagement in politics is accepted, if not sought after.

Military disengagement from politics is neither linear nor evolutionary; as a sociopolitical process it can be consolidated or reversed. The presence, or lack, of trust facilitates political groups' coalitions with state institutions, whose composition is neither democratic nor civil, over mistrusted civilian movements. Despite two popular mass uprisings and a number of democratic elections, the end result of Egypt's transition from authoritarian rule remains unclear. Egypt's political system has come full circle since the founding of the republic in the 1950s, with the military more entrenched now than before. Democratic models of civil-military relations stress the following features of a military-civilian division of power. In a democratic regime, external defense of the state is the primary mission of the military; the military budget and appointments are submitted to civilian control, the military's neutrality vis-à-vis political parties is maintained, and representation of ethnic, regional, religious, and tribal groups within the military is instituted.[70] Some of these features have been established components of the Egyptian Armed Forces' doctrine, but others may be stickier and hard to operationalize.[71] Moreover, two issues prevent officers' disengagement with political affairs in the near future: weakness of civilian social and political powers and a regional environment that is plagued with direct military threats from nonstate armed actors. Older political parties are fragmented and weak. Their

144 | Dina Rashed

inability to resolve sociopolitical conflicts or mobilize has led to extensive reliance on the military for protection and guidance. Nascent political parties and civil society groups in the post-Mubarak era are still in their formative years, and their ability to provide leadership for Egyptian society remains unclear.

Meanwhile, external threats and the political interests of donor countries may deepen the military's political role. The rising threat of nonstate armed actors and the mushrooming of cross-border terrorism, combined with state collapse in neighboring countries, are bound to consolidate military influence over domestic policies and even create substantial public support for it. Regional instability may also prompt democratic donor countries to limit calls for democratic reforms. In addition, Gulf donors such as Saudi Arabia, the United Arab Emirates, Kuwait, and Bahrain are most likely to continue their support for a military-backed government, given the instability of the region.

Notes

1. Eric A. Nordlinger, *Soldiers in Politics: Military Coups and Governments* (Englewood Cliffs, NJ: Prentice-Hall, 1977).

2. Alfred Stepan, *The Military in Politics: Changing Patterns in Brazil* (Princeton, NJ: Princeton University Press, 1971).

3. Samuel Edward Finer, *The Man on Horseback: The Role of the Military in Politics* (New Brunswick, NJ: Transaction, 2002); Samuel Huntington, *Political Order in Changing Societies* (New Haven, CT: Yale University Press, 1968).

4. Samuel Huntington, *The Soldier and the State: The Theory and Politics of Civil-Military Relations* (Cambridge: Belknap Press of Harvard University Press, 1957); Huntington, *Political Order*.

5. Morris Janowitz, *The Professional Soldier: A Social and Political Portrait* (Glencoe, IL: Free Press, 1960).

6. Stepan, *The Military in Politics*.

7. For the debate on professionalism and military intervention in politics or the civil-military problematique, see Peter D. Feaver, "The Civil-Military Problematique: Huntington, Janowitz, and the Question of Civilian Control," *Armed Forces and Society* 23, no. 2 (1996): 149–178.

8. Juan J. Linz and Alfred Stepan, *Problems of Democratic Transition and Consolidation: Southern Europe, South America, and Post-Communist Europe* (Baltimore: Johns Hopkins University Press, 1996); Richard H. Kohn, "How Democracies Control the Military," *Journal of Democracy* 8, no. 4 (1997): 140–153.

9. David Pion-Berlin, Diego Esparza, and Kevin Grisham, "Staying Quartered: Civilian Uprisings and Military Disobedience in the Twenty-First Century," *Comparative Political Studies* 47, no. 2 (2014): 230–259; Ozan O. Varol, "The Democratic Coup d'État," *Harvard International Law Journal* 53, no. 2 (2012).

10. The "ruling but not governing" argument posits that the military may delegate some of its powers with regard to the handling of the day-to-day governance to other institutions, yet continue to set the overarching policies behind closed doors. Constantine Danopolous, "Military Dictatorship in Retreat: Problems and Perspectives," in *The Decline of Military Regimes*, ed. Constantine Danopoulos, Westview Special Studies in Military Affairs (Boulder, CO: West-

view, 1988); Steven A. Cook, *Ruling but Not Governing: The Military and Political Development in Egypt, Algeria, and Turkey* (Baltimore: Johns Hopkins University Press, 2007).

11. Barbara Geddes, "What Do We Know about Democratization after Twenty Years?," *Annual Review of Political Science* 2, no. 1 (1999): 115–144.

12. Juan J. Linz and Alfred Stepan, *The Breakdown of Democratic Regimes* (Baltimore: Johns Hopkins University Press, 1978); Adam Przeworski, "Some Problems in the Study of the Transition to Democracy," in *Transitions from Authoritarian Rule: Comparative Perspectives*, ed. Guillermo O'Donnell, Philippe C. Schmitter, and Laurence Whitehead (Baltimore: Johns Hopkins University Press, 1986); Alfred Stepan, *Rethinking Military Politics: Brazil and the Southern Cone* (Princeton, NJ: Princeton University Press, 1988).

13. Michael Hoffman, "Military Extrication and Temporary Democracy: The Case of Pakistan," *Democratization* 18, no. 1 (2011): 75–99.

14. Disengaging the military from policies of domestic control does not necessarily mean the complete and total absence of militaries as institutions of force from domestic politics. Conditions may arise that prompt leaders to summon their militaries to carry out specific missions, as the events of the 1977 Bread Riots and 1986 Central Security Forces attest. Yet, as long as such missions remain isolated and temporary, the disengagement of militaries can be sustained.

15. The Ministry of Defense is the umbrella organization overseeing all branches of the Egyptian Armed Forces: the army, the navy, the air defense, and the air force. The minister of defense is the general commander of the armed forces. I use the terms *Ministry of Defense* and *the military* interchangeably in this chapter.

16. Mohamed Ali Pasha built the Egyptian military during the period from 1820 to 1830. For a detailed analysis on the establishment of the military as a state-building process, see Khaled Fahmy, *All the Pasha's men: Mehmed Ali, His Army and the Making of Modern Egypt*, vol. 8 (Cambridge: Cambridge University Press, 1997). The Ministry of Interior was founded in the 1880s under British colonialism. British officials designed the national police as a semi-militarized force to facilitate their rule. Professionalization of the police force under colonial rule meant the militarization of the force, with an emphasis on strict discipline over skillful detective work. For more on the relation between colonial rule and policing by coercion versus consent, see Harold Tollefson, *Policing Islam: The British Occupation of Egypt and the Anglo-Egyptian Struggle over Control of the Police, 1882–1914*, Contributions in Comparative Colonial Studies 38 (Westport, CT: Greenwood, 1999); Jill Crystal, "Criminal Justice in the Middle East," *Journal of Criminal Justice* 29, no. 6 (2001): 469–482.

17. Morris Janowitz, *Military Institutions and Coercion in the Developing Nations* (Chicago: University of Chicago Press, 1977).

18. Kirk J. Beattie, *Egypt during the Nasser Years* (Boulder, CO: Westview, 1994).

19. Risa Brooks, *Shaping Strategy: The Civil-Military Politics of Strategic Assessment* (Princeton, NJ: Princeton University Press, 2008).

20. Mohamad Al-Gawady, *Kadat al Shurta fi al Syasah al Masriyah: 1952–2000* [Police officers in Egyptian politics: 1952–2000] (Cairo: Egyptian Public Authority for Books, 2008). After 2011, this unit was renamed National Security.

21. The ban, which remains in effect, applies to active officers of all security institutions: the Ministries of Defense and Interior, and the General Intelligence Service.

22. The 1973 cabinet that oversaw the October War remains an exception, with more appointed officers compared to other cabinets formed under Sadat. However, it included fewer officers compared to those cabinets formed under Nasser. Mark N. Cooper, "The Demilitarization of the Egyptian Cabinet," *International Journal of Middle East Studies* 14, no. 2 (1982): 203–225.

23. The appointment of less ambitious and more loyal officers does not necessarily mean that they are professionally less qualified: there is no evidence to support the claim that

Mubarak's reshuffling of high-ranking officers has jeopardized the institutional professionalism or coherence of the military.

24. The military's engagement with the consumer goods industry was engineered by Field Marshal Abd al-Haleem Abu Ghazala, defense minister during the period from 1981 to 1989. The production of food items was justified by the need to ensure supplies for the Egyptian Armed Forces and minimize reliance on government resources during Egypt's debt crises of the early 1980s. Gradually, military-owned factories increased production and tapped into the domestic marketplace, offering food and other consumer products to the public. Over the 1990s and 2000s, the military expanded its economic projects and provided housing, chains of grocery stores, resort complexes, and sporting clubs, all geared toward the improvement of the living conditions of both officers and enlisted personnel. Timothy Mitchell, *Rule of Experts: Egypt, Techno-politics, Modernity* (Berkeley: University of California Press, 2002); Yezid Sayigh, *Above the State: The Officers' Republic in Egypt* (Washington, DC: Carnegie Endowment for International Peace, 2012).

25. The US-brokered peace agreement between Egypt and Israel, which culminated in the 1979 Camp David accords, brought financial dividends to the two warring states, making them recipients of the highest levels of US aid. Egypt has received an average of $1.3 billion in annual military aid. For more on US aid as a component of the peace agreement, see Jason Brownlee, *Democracy Prevention: The Politics of the US-Egyptian Alliance* (Cambridge: Cambridge University Press, 2012).

26. According to governmental statistics, in 1993/1994 the number of Ministry of Interior employees stood at 554,623. The number jumped to 693,600 in 2001/2002 and to about 715,000 in 2002/2003. Abd el-Khaleq Farouk, *The Roots of Administrative Corruption in Egypt* [*Jezzor al-Fassad al-Idary fi Misr*] (Cairo: Dar al-Shorouk, 2008).

27. In 2005 Mubarak amended Article 76 of the constitution to change the decades-old structure of presidential succession. Despite protests from opposition groups led by the Kefaya movement, the amendment was approved by the regime-controlled parliament, allowing for the first multicandidate presidential elections. Jason Brownlee, *Authoritarianism in an Age of Democratization* (New York: Cambridge University Press, 2007); and "The Heir Apparency of Gamal Mubarak," *Arab Studies Journal* (2008): 36–56.

28. Muhammad Abdul Aziz and Youssef Hussein, "The President, the Son, and the Military: The Question of Succession in Egypt," *Arab Studies Journal* 9/10, nos. 2/1 (2001): 73–88.

29. In 2007, Field Marshal Tantawi, then minister of defense and the general commander of the Egyptian Armed Forces, disclosed to fellow cabinet members his disapproval of Gamal Mubarak's economic policies, especially the privatization of state assets. For more on Tantawi's comments and their leak to opposition press, see Mostafa Bakri, *Al-Jayish wa al-Thawra: Quessat al-Ayam al-Akheera* [The military and the revolution: The story of the final day] (Cairo: Akhbar al-Youm, 2011).

30. Zeinab Abul-Magd, "The Egyptian Military in Politics and the Economy: Recent History and Current Transition Status," *CMI Insight* 2 (2013).

31. Amendments were put to a public vote and then followed by a constitutional declaration that was issued by the SCAF in March 2011. Hesham Sallam, "Reflections on Egypt after March 19," Jadaliyya.com, May 31, 2011, http://www.jadaliyya.com/pages/index/1728/reflections-on-egypt-after-march-19.

32. Quotb al-Arabi, a Muslim Brotherhood leader, acknowledged that the Muslim Brotherhood mobilized in objection to the SCAF only when setting election dates was an issue of concern, but was supportive of its policies otherwise. "A Qatar-Based Muslim Brotherhood Leader: alSisi Projected an Illusion about His Religiosity and His Fate is Black," CNN Arabic, http://arabic.cnn.com/middleeast/2014/03/10/qout-alarabi-interview.

33. Contrary to its record of disengaging from the repression of civilians under Sadat and Mubarak, the military police instituted repressive measures during the transitional period when faced with protesting civilians. For more details on the killing of civilian protesters during the 2011 Maspero events, see Ekram Ibrahim, "Justice Denied: Egypt's Maspero Massacre One Year On," Ahram Online, October 9, 2012, http://english.ahram.org.eg/News/54821.aspx.

34. Anne Alexander, "Brothers-in-Arms? The Egyptian Military, the Ikhwan and the Revolutions of 1952 and 2011," *Journal of North African Studies* 16, no. 4 (2011): 533–554.

35. In the final years of Mubarak's rule, opposition groups including the Muslim Brotherhood were much less threatened by the military, considering the Ministry of Interior and the police force the real repressive machine of the regime. One Muslim Brotherhood leader noted, "We have no problem with the armed forces; military men are respectable people. It is the police that have been crushing the opposition, especially with the advent of the NDP's Policies Secretariat." Personal interview with author, winter 2009.

36. Field Marshal Tantawi, then minister of defense during the first transitional period, repeatedly described the transfer of power from Mubarak to the SCAF as a ball of fire that was thrown at the military. He posited that the military was interested in transferring power as soon as politically possible to rid itself of the burden of governance. See Mostafa Bakri, *Al-Jayish wa al-Ikhwan: Asrar Khalf al-Sitar* [The military and the Ikhwan: Secrets behind the scene] (Cairo: Egyptian Lebanese House, 2013).

37. Prior to parliamentary elections, Field Marshal Tantawi estimated Islamists would win a 25–30 percent. Ibid., 79–80.

38. Enjoying house majority, Freedom and Justice Party members objected to the performance of the cabinet led by Prime Minister Kamal al-Ganzouri, which was appointed by the SCAF prior to parliamentary elections, and announced they would call for a no-confidence vote. The disagreement between the parliamentary majority and the SCAF revolved around which side has the right to form and dismiss the cabinet, given that the March 2011 constitutional declaration was still in effect and the SCAF was operating in its capacity as governor of the state. For more on the developments of the crisis see Bakri, *The Military and the Ikhwan*.

39. For details of the June 17, 2012, addendum, see "English Text of SCAF Amended Egypt Constitutional Declaration," Ahram Online, June 18, 2012, http://english.ahram.org .eg/NewsContent/1/64/45350/Egypt/Politics-/English-text-of-SCAF-amended-Egypt -Constitutional-.aspx.

40. The Muslim Brotherhood's leadership interfered with presidential decision making, often objecting to policy recommendations by President Morsi's close advisers. In several cases, the president was pushed by the movement to issue decrees that were legally faulty, against the advice of his legal team, including the constitutional declaration of November 2012. For more on the power struggle over decision making between Muslim Brotherhood leadership and Morsi's non–Muslim Brotherhood advisers, see the detailed letter of resignation of his legal adviser, Judge Mohamad Fouad Gaddallah, that was submitted in April 2013. "Gaddallah's Resignation: 'The Brotherhood Is Encroaching on Morsi and the Judiciary Is Being Assassinated,'" Al-Masry Al-Youm, April 23, 2013, http://www.almasryalyoum.com/news/details/307740.

41. For more details on the public statements issued by the presidency, the military, and the Muslim Brotherhood regarding the military's initiative, see Ahmad al-Bahnasawi and Ahmad Abd al'Azeem, "AlWatan Looks at the behind the Scenes Confusion in the Military's Invitation to Civilian Forces for Dialogue," *el Watan*, December 12, 2012, http://www.elwatannews .com/news/details/95069.

42. See the military's statement warning political groups of the consequences of internal disputes on the state, "A Statement by the Official Spokesperson of the Armed Forces," Facebook, December 8, 2012, https://ar-ar.facebook.com/Egy.Army.Spox/posts/236373153160341. Also see

the discussion of then defense minister Sisi's fears of state collapse, Maha Salem, "AlSisi: Continuation of Fighting among the Political Forces May Lead to the Collapse of the State," Ahram, January 29, 2013, http://gate.ahram.org.eg/News/301967.aspx.

43. Neven al'Aiadi and Mohamad Abd al-Gawad, "Sinai: Chronology of Violence in 21 Months," Al-Masry Al-Youm, November 11, 2012, http://www.almasryalyoum.com/News/details /240043.

44. In his weekly message on December 20, 2012, Badie praised the quiescence of Egyptian soldiers, arguing that they are in need of indoctrination and better military leadership. See the complete message, titled "Egyptian People Talk about Themselves" [Sha'ab Misr Yatahadath 'an Nafsouh], http://www.ikhwanwiki.com.

45. Mohie al-Deen al-Zaeit wrote a poem accusing the military of cowardice and mismanagement. The poem was publicly recited in a Mother's Day celebration in the Muslim Brotherhood's Freedom and Justice Party Cairo branch in early April 2013. Hani al-Wazeeri and Mahmoud Sha'aban Bayoumi, "What Is the Worth of a Military When Its Lead by a Mouse," April 7, 2013, http://elwatannews.com/news/details/160040.

46. See recorded statements by Madi on March 25, 2013, in the following link, http://www .youtube.com/watch?v=-KHACyy3LwI&feature=youtube_gdata_player&hd=1.

47. Though the General Intelligence Service employs officers of civilian and military background, traditionally, it has been headed by members of the military's intelligence. Appointed by Morsi in August 2012, Raafat Shehata, a career officer from within the apparatus, was the first chief spymaster of nonmilitary background.

48. Since Sadat's restructuring of the security sector in the early 1970s, the General Intelligence Service has focused its work on espionage activities. General Omar Suleiman, its former head under Mubarak, stated that the primary mission of the apparatus was to gather information to guide the political decision making in foreign policy. Its reports were submitted directly to the president. In the 1990s and 2000s, the apparatus maintained close cooperation with the United States and its allies in international antiterrorism efforts, and became responsible for coordinating the Israeli-Palestinian talks (Tewfick Aclimandos, "'Healing without Amputating?' Security Reform in Egypt," Arab Reform Initiative, September 2012). Although the General Intelligence Service has maintained some information-gathering roles domestically, its officers have refrained from involvement in dissent control or the repression of domestic opposition, which were missions of the Ministry of Interior. Author's interviews with Ministry of Interior officers and opposition activists in 2012–2013.

49. In the months prior to Madi's comments, it became noticeable that several Facebook pages close to the Muslim Brotherhood included verbal attacks on the military and other state institutions. For the Muslim Brotherhood's electronic campaigns, see Linda Herrera and Mark Lotfy, "E-Militias of the Muslim Brotherhood: How to Upload Ideology on Facebook," Jadaliyya, September 5, 2012, http://www.jadaliyya.com/pages/index/7212/e-militias-of-the-muslim-brotherhood_how-to-upload. For the presidential-military relationship and the production of political rumors, see Mona El-Kouedi, "From Morsi with Love," Sada: Middle East Analysis, Carnegie Endowment for International Peace, March 12, 2013, http://carnegieendowment.org/sada/?fa=51179.

50. For the military's grievances and President Morsi's response to them as discussed in the meeting, see "Morsi: We Are Capable of Securing our Homeland . . . Minister of Defense: The Armed Forces Do Not Betray Their People," Ahram, April 13, 2013, http://www.ahram.org.eg /NewsQ/204040.aspx.

51. For more on the details of Morsi's last few weeks in power and the unresponsiveness of his presidency to popular demands, see Hazem Kandil, "Sisi's Turn," *London Review of Books* 36, no. 4 (2014): 15–16.

52. David D. Kirkpatrick and Mayy El sheikh, "Morsi Spurned Deals, Seeing Military as Tamed," *New York Times*, July 6, 2007, http://www.nytimes.com/2013/07/07/world/middleeast /morsi-spurned-deals-to-the-end-seeing-the-military-as-tamed.html?pagewanted=2&_r=2 &smid=fb-share.

53. Some reports show that in addition to public support, some police officers have lent a hand to the Tamarrud Movement's efforts to gather petitions for early presidential elections. See Asma Alsharif and Yasmine Saleh, "The Real Force behind Egypt's 'Revolution,'" *Reuters*, October 10, 2014, http://www.reuters.com/article/us-egypt-interior-specialreport -idUSBRE99908D20131010.

54. Both Qatar and Turkey remain close allies of the Muslim Brotherhood, and have provided shelter and financial and logistical assistance to members of the movement who fled the country after the dispersal of the Rabaa sit-in.

55. On the development of the American position with regard to the ouster of Morsi before the crackdown on his supporters, see http://www.nytimes.com/2013/08/02/world/middleeast /egypt-warns-morsi-supporters-to-end-protests.html. For more on the details of the suspension of the United States' military aid after the crackdown on the Muslim Brotherhood, see https://www.washingtonpost.com/world/national-security/us-plans-to-curb-military-aid-to -egypt/2013/10/08/bab3b5a6-307f-11e3-9ccc-2252bdb14df5_story.html.

56. "Mixed Messages in Egypt's Military Aid," *New York Times*, April 1, 2015, http://www .nytimes.com/2015/04/01/opinion/mixed-messages-in-egypts-military-aid.html.

57. "Egypt Army Backs Sisi as Presidential Candidate," *BBC*, January 27, 2014, http://www .bbc.com/news/world-middle-east-25917452.

58. For how Sisi secured military interests while minister of defense, see Dina Rashed, "What Al-Sisi's Presidency Will Mean for Egyptian Politics," Muftah, March 2014, http://muftah .org/al-sisis-presidency-will-mean-egyptian-politics/.

59. Abigail Hauslohner, "Egypt's Military Expands Its Control of the Country's Economy," *Washington Post*, March 16, 2014, https://www.washingtonpost.com/world/middle_east /egyptian-military-expands-its-economic-control/2014/03/16/39508b52-a554-11e3-b865 -38b254d92063_story.html.

60. Steven A. Cook, *The Struggle for Egypt: From Nasser to Tahrir Square* (Oxford: Oxford University Press: 2011); Saad Al-Shazli, *Harb October: Mothakerat alFareeq Saad al-Shazly* [October War: Memoirs of General Saad al-Shazly] (Cairo: Roaya, 2011).

61. Though a new constitution was drafted at the behest of Sadat in 1971, it kept intact all powers awarded previously to the president. Amr Hashem Rabea, *Legislative Monitoring in Political Regimes: Study in the Experience of Egyptian People's Assembly* (Cairo: Ahram Center for Political and Strategic Studies, 2002).

62. Barry R. Weingast, "Constructing Trust: The Political and Economic Roots of Ethnic and Regional Conflict," *Institutions and Social Order* (1998): 163–200.

63. Ibrahim El Houdaiby, "From Prison to Palace: The Muslim Brotherhood's Challenges and Responses in Post-revolution Egypt," *Transitions and Geopolitics in the Arab World: Links and Implications for International Actors* 117 (2013): 1–13.

64. On several occasions, the presidency ignored calls by human rights activists—including from state affiliates—to work on improving the policing service, as Taquadom al-Khateeb's case shows. Khateeb, a university professor and then member of the government's National Council of Human Rights, was beaten publicly by a police officer. The first reaction of Morsi's presidential office was to ask Khateeb to rescind his official complaint and accept a verbal apology from the officer. The case caused public outcry, underscoring the piecemeal plans to reform the Ministry of Interior. *el Watan*, October 29, 2012, http://elwatannews.com/news/details /68452.

65. Attending a celebration at the campus of the Central Security Forces, Morsi praised the role of the police in the Egyptian uprising, saying that they have been at the heart of it. The statements enraged activists of all political standings. For more information, see "Strong Objections by the Khaled Saeed Movement to Morsi's Statements" [in Arabic], *al Masry al Youm*, March 15, 2013, http://www.almasryalyoum.com/news/details/295431.

66. The Muslim Brotherhood's initiative to reform the police force included suggestions to inject the force with university graduates to help with staffing. Such plans were viewed by police officers as efforts to infiltrate the police force rather than improve the policing service through the provision of better training and equipment for the existing staff. For more on efforts to reform the police force, see Dina Rashed, "Reforming the Egyptian Police," *Foreign Policy—Middle East Channel*, July 8, 2013, http://mideast.foreignpolicy.com/posts/2013/07/08/reforming_the_egyptian_police.

67. Margaret Levi and Laura Stoker, "Political Trust and Trustworthiness," *Annual Review of Political Science* 3, no. 1 (2000): 475–507.

68. Narcís Serra and Peter Bush, *The Military Transition: Democratic Reform of the Armed Forces* (Cambridge: Cambridge University Press, 2010).

69. This is evident in the alliance between the Wafd Party and Nasserites, and their collective support for a military intervention against the Islamist president in the summer of 2013.

70. For theories of democratic reform of armed forces see Narcis Serra, *The Military Transition: Democratic Reform of the Armed Forces* (Cambridge: Cambridge University Press, 2010); and for a practical guide, see Dennis Blair, *Military Engagement: Influencing Armed Forces Worldwide to Support Democratic Transitions* (Washington, D.C.: Brookings Institution, 2013).

71. All Egyptian constitutions, including those of 1971, 2012, and 2014, have described the Egyptian Armed Forces as owned by the Egyptian people.

9 Policing Egypt during Revolutionary Times

Hesham Genidy and Justine Salam

In MODERN EGYPTIAN history, the national police force has played a considerably large role in stoking Egyptian resentment against each consecutive governing regime. Since the 1952 coup, such feelings of hostility toward the police have continued to be exacerbated, even more so over the last ten years of Hosni Mubarak's rule, culminating in the events of January 2011. This resentment was most telling, considering that political activists chose Egypt's Police Day holiday to hold their popular uprising against the Mubarak regime.[1] Salwa Ismail describes this move as "turn[ing] the day into an occasion to indict the institution in charge of policing—in a sense, putting it under public trial."[2]

Police authority in Egypt has been the preferred state tool for the preservation of security and order. Police work necessitates the imposition of some restrictions on individual rights and the acceptance of these restrictions by the public. Such limitations or restrictions can often be unwelcomed or challenged by citizens, and can contribute to a tense relationship between the public and the police. A tense public-police relationship is not unusual throughout the world, and can be found in developing and developed countries alike. As a hallmark of sociopolitical development, the general public should follow the rules and laws of the land and understand the nature and necessity of police work. Ideally, the public would recognize that a strong police force serves their best interests. In turn, a nationally respected police force also heeds best practices in police transparency, ethical conduct, and enforcement of laws, and should assist in crime prevention and build positive community relationships.

The situation in Egypt is, however, far removed from these ideal best practices. Police behavior and actions in the country's recent history have led to public resentment of what is widely perceived as selective justice, and provoked enmity against the institution. The Egyptian public has a tendency to vent their wrath against police authorities in wider public and community disputes, even in instances where the latter have little control over the outcome of events. Enforcement officers, for instance, are often blamed for erroneous court rulings resulting from corruption in judicial processes and court systems. In fact,

Egypt's police (mis)conduct is part of a broader problem with the Egyptian "securitocracy."

Inside Egypt's Securitocracy

Juha Mäkelä defines securitocracy as "a system of security elites (intelligence and security services, military and police forces) that, at the executive level, use either direct or indirect political power and influence in matters related to a state's foreign and security policy, internal security, and even in the finance and economic sectors."[3] In the case of Egypt, the country has been under continuous emergency law since 1981, when Mubarak's regime took power following the assassination of President Anwar Sadat. The Emergency Law permitted detention without charge and prohibited gatherings of five or more people without prior authorization from the Ministry of Interior (MoI). Under Egypt's Emergency Law, the president and, by extension, the prime minister and the minister of interior have gained tremendous power. In the name of preventing terrorism and suppressing political dissidence, the Emergency Law gave the executive branch a free hand to "restrain the movement of individuals, search persons or places without warrants, tap telephones, monitor and ban publications, forbid meetings, and intern suspects without trial."[4]

The State Security Investigation Service (SSIS) is the most infamous organ of the intelligence community. Founded during the 1920s with British officials' help, the SSIS's primary goal was the collection of security intelligence. Under the Mubarak regime, the SSIS gained increasing power and extended its activity to include the intense surveillance of Egyptian citizens. The SSIS was not only put in charge of counterterrorism and counterintelligence, but came in immediate contact with ordinary people by monitoring a wide spectrum of groups in Egyptian society, including political opposition groups and activists, religious extremists, Christian missionaries, judges, and foreign nationals living in Egypt.[5] In effect, the SSIS was Mubarak's extended arm in the streets. Under emergency law, the SSIS revived techniques that some accused of amounting to torture to extract information and punish suspected political activists. As a result of the widespread use of these techniques, people have been known to have "disappeared" for days or weeks at a time.[6] The police thus evolved in the context of the Emergency Law and the constant human rights violations and abuses by the SSIS, irremediably adopting some of their worst practices to ensure "stability" in the streets. That said, Christopher Schneider reminds us that the "police are a unique group with special powers that[, under Mubarak, included] the authorized use of deadly force."[7] Authorized or not, their use of force has been demonstrably excessive.

Unfortunately, as the Mubarak regime increasingly chose security-based solutions in the face of numerous social and political phenomena, the regime drew on police authority alone to deal with matters such as terrorism. As is the case in many nondemocratic—or even some democratic—countries, the war on terrorism was also a pretext for many political extrajudicial practices. This eventually led to the normalization of the state of emergency in Egypt. The ruling regime used the police as a formidable shield to quell threats to its power, while police were left to encounter the wrath and disdain of the people.

Inside the Egyptian Police Force

According to the Police Corps Act, the police are a "civilian disciplinary authority . . . composed of various officers and agents as well as police officers."[8] There are two main categories of officers: the first are officers with higher levels of education; second are police warrant officers, agents, privates, and patrolmen, as well as staff officers and policemen. This latter is the largest category in Egypt's MoI, and often the hardest to control; they are—in the opinion of one of the authors, who worked in the MoI—notorious for being the most corrupt group in the police force. The members are recruited from the wider community, usually from vulnerable socioeconomic groups and communities that have been repeatedly victimized by the Egyptian regime. The corruption of this police force is manifested in the case of Khaled Said, who, now an icon of the Egyptian revolution, was beaten to death by two warrant officers, Mahmoud Salah and Awad Suleiman.

The police force is part of the MoI. The most important criterion for the selection of ministry leaders is loyalty. Consequently, blind obedience to ministry orders, regardless of conformity to laws, morals, or customs, has been paramount. Under Mubarak, the ministry spent lavishly on officials who filled top positions, be they security managers, department heads, or chiefs of administrations. Managers usually earned salaries more than five times the salaries of their peers of the same rank, not to mention material privileges that often involved assigned cars, drivers, and recruits. These privileges are vital to understanding excesses perpetrated by MoI leaders.

Article 47 of the Police Corps Act stipulates that "any officer who violates the duties stipulated in this law or in decisions issued by the Minister of Interior, or transgresses proprieties in a job or behaves or appears in a manner that dishonors the job is disciplinarily punished." The article is so flexible that it gave a free hand to the MoI regarding the punishment of accused suspects. Moreover, to protect the state regime, many senior police promotions, transfers, rewards, and penalties have been highly politicized. Thus, police corruption cannot be understood outside the broader institutional context of Egypt's security state and the leadership at the helm of this institution.

The desire of police leaders to keep their positions and privileges has negatively affected the performance of the MoI at large, and has been largely responsible for the internal corruption that has plagued the ministry. Police frustrations with the system and resulting feelings of disloyalty to the badge drove some officers to perform only a minimum amount of work. This phenomenon—described as "working only to the extent of warding off blame"—has been markedly detrimental to the ministry's performance and internal morale. David Carter identified the factors that cause police corruption and induce greed. These include personal motivation (such as ego, sex, or the lust for power), cultural intolerance, socialization from peers or the organization, poor selection of officers, inadequate supervision and monitoring of behavior, a lack of clear accountability for police officers' behavior, and the lack of a real threat of discipline or sanctions for transgressions.[9] In Egypt, location placements that indirectly offer material privileges are distributed on the basis of cronyism or favoritism. In turn, internal police corruption has contributed to a state of frustration and indifference among officers, who have witnessed little justice or retribution for internal corruption.

Moreover, a prevailing feeling among Egyptian citizens is that no interaction with the police can happen without bribery or cronyism. In the case of Egypt, the United Nations Office on Drugs and Crime has reported, "When asked whether any government official, for instance a customs officer, police officer, traffic officer, court official, pensions officer or building inspector, had either asked for or expected to be paid a bribe for his/her services, 17.7 per cent of the survey respondents answered yes. Such requests for bribes most frequently involved police officers (31 per cent of cases) and municipal/local government officials (23 per cent)."[10]

The same reports highlights that while 71.4 percent of car thefts are brought to the attention of the police, only 1.3 percent of corruption cases are reported to the police, showing that the police is trusted with recovering stolen cars but not with solving corruption issues. Police misbehavior toward people is manifested in two ways: corruption and excessive use of force. Police corruption is often found in nine specific areas: meals and services, commissions, accidental theft, preplanned theft, blackmailing, offering a cover-up for criminal activities, manipulation of evidence in the interest of the suspect, providing private security services, and cronyism. The wide-ranging legal powers granted to police officers leave open the door for opportunities to engage in corruption.

In this regard, three main theories explain the persistence of police corruption: the society-at-large theory, the structural-affiliation theory, and the rotten apple theory.[11] The first of the three proposes that corruption occurs among officers within the larger framework of their relationship with citizens, especially relationships involving the acceptance of gifts or the overlooking of minor offenses like traffic violations in return for pay. According to this theory, the whole community bears the brunt for corruption on the part of the police, since police corruption is the result of community corruption. The structural-affiliation theory is an extension of the general community theory: corruption starts when the officer believes that criminal behavior is not limited to criminals, but can also be committed by citizens or by officers in their own departments. Finally, the rotten apple theory posits that corruption arises among a few deviant officers who spread criminal activity among the rest of the officers. It would be fair to point out that corruption has prevailed in all state departments, not just among the police. Too often, Egyptians offer bribes to public officials or draw on personal connections and networks to receive public goods and services. Finally, although police corruption in Egypt has had destructive consequences for the wider community, the real problem lies in the normalization and legalization of corruption, grounded in the idea that police misconduct is justified because, in an inherently corrupt system, it achieves a public good.

Hence, it has been the general view among the wider Egyptian public that justice is selectively administered. This has undermined the relationship between the people and the police, and further undermined the rule of law, its enforcement, and just prosecutions. For example, taxi drivers often bear the brunt of the selective law enforcement policies conducted by the police. Unlike army officers, parliament members, and athletes, who are granted special treatment for traffic violations, taxi drivers are selectively chosen for punishment, to enforce common and widespread traffic violations. These inequities have fed feelings of oppression and escalated enmity toward police authority.[12] It should also be noted that the large degree of the state's dependence on the police to carry out security functions and enforce laws negatively reflects on the regime's legitimacy. Likewise, the more that corruption erodes the regime's legitimacy and, by extension, its ability to quell protests and anger directed at the political system, the more the police lose their capacity to enforce law and order. This has perpetrated a persistent cycle of poor governance and the erosion of legitimacy.

The omnipresence and extended jurisdiction of the Egyptian police, combined with abuses of citizens, have led to fierce civilian discontent. The Egyptian police's omnipresence in people's everyday lives was justified by the need to conduct surveillance of public spaces. However, abuses of police authority and humiliation of the citizenry eventually became the institution's modus operandi. Encounters between the police and citizens were thus frequently marked by verbal threats and physical violence, eventually leading to public spectacles of humiliation.[13] Ann Lesch emphasizes that due to Egyptians' desire to avoid constant police harassment in the streets, officers receive bribes from shop owners and free food from street vendors, who see this as the cost of business in their anxiety to contain the risk of being brought to the police station.[14]

Furthermore, the police have felt immune to prosecution because of the Mubarak government's heavy reliance on the police force as a governance mechanism. Indeed, police jurisdiction under Mubarak included (and this is by no means an exhaustive list) surveillance of markets, transport, roads, food supply, public utilities, public morality, taxation, public security, national security, surveillance of political activists, and the rigging of elections.[15] In turn, police impunity negatively impacted citizens' ability to file official complaints against abuses by police officials. Relying on the police as the sole source of evidence in complaint cases made citizen reports nearly impossible. Human Rights Watch (HRW) reported the conflict of interest arising from "placing the responsibility to monitor detention facilities, order forensic exams, and investigate and prosecute abuses by law enforcement officials within the same office that is responsible for ordering arrests, obtaining confessions, and prosecuting criminal suspects."[16]

Moreover, the interior minister was permitted under the Police Law to act at his or her discretion in placing offending officers back in their previous positions after serving their sentences.[17] This obviously has disastrous consequences for the Egyptian people's trust in the government's ability to punish offenses fairly and perpetuates police officers' "unconcerned"[18] attitude toward the potential consequences of their abuses. HRW also reported that according to the Egyptian government's statistics, "Egyptian criminal courts convicted and issued final sentences to only six officers between 2006 and 2009."[19] This statistic clearly reveals the extent of the lack of accountability and broader impunity of the Egyptian police under Mubarak's regime.

The Deteriorating Police-Public Relations

To understand the relationship between the Egyptian people on one hand and their government and its representatives on the other, we need to look back at least three decades. Prior to the 1980s, Egypt's public sector had been the main provider of jobs in the country. The Egyptian state not only provided its citizens with a profession, but also protected people under a strong social welfare system. With Mubarak's rise to power, however, Egypt opened up to neoliberal economic policies, shifting a large proportion of citizens from the public sector to the private sector. As Ismail puts it, "Larger segments of the population ceased to be clients of the state and were no longer bound by the social contract of earlier days whereby political quietism was exchanged for social goods."[20] This shift in government-citizen social relations resulted in a growing distance between the former and latter and spurred the government to develop its securitocracy regime. Simply put, Mubarak increased police presence to challenge the growing number of regime opponents.

More than three decades later, the evolving frustration of people with the institutions of the state erupted in the Kefaya movement. Often considered to have prepared the ground for the January 2011 protests,[21] Kefaya—meaning "enough" in Arabic—was a group of intellectuals and community activists from all political backgrounds who denounced corruption, the country's perpetual state of emergency, Mubarak's fifth term, and "dynastic succession,"[22] which alluded to Mubarak's intention to have his son Gamal succeed him. Throughout 2004 and 2005, the Kefaya movement held several protests across the country. The police reaction was immediate. Attacks against the demonstrators, including infamous stick-wielding assaults on female protesters, were all part of the government's covert attempt to stop the spread of the Kefaya movement. Police brutality marked the minds of Egyptians.

Despite the worsening situation, the Egyptian people continued to harbor hope. Like Tunisia's Mohammed Bouazizi, Egypt's Said, mentioned in the previous section, fueled the January 2011 protests. During the summer of 2010, thirty-two-year old Said was arrested by the police, dragged out of a café, and beaten to death in front of eyewitnesses. The same night, young men and women gathered in front of the police station, demanding justice for Said's death. The government covered up the story, infuriating many Egyptians. The protests went on throughout Egypt during the summer of 2010 as people gathered for silent marches or demonstrations. The death of Said became a symbol of police brutality and received intense and widespread scrutiny. The famous Facebook page "We are all Khaled Said"[23] reflected broad Egyptian sentiments. The stubbornness of the protesters eventually forced the Egyptian government to reopen the case and file a lawsuit against the two police officers responsible for Said's death.[24]

The January 2011 Protests

By starting the protest on the national Police Day, the Egyptian people clearly expressed their criticism and contempt for the police forces. For many Egyptians, joining in the protest and protesting against the police was as much in opposition of the police and its abuses of civilians as it later became in opposition to the Mubarak regime responsible for police deviance. In particular, people protested against Minister of Interior Habib al-Adli, whose ministry had been responsible for countless citizens' abuses over fourteen years.[25] Thousands participated in the march toward Tahrir Square, encouraged by activists who appealed to all segments of the population.

In districts such as Bulaq al-Dakrur in the poorer Giza governorate where people had suffered for many years from police abuses and heavy unemployment, locals were quickly convinced to join in.[26] Egyptians from different backgrounds and classes were so united once they were in Tahrir Square, they outnumbered the police, which desperately attempted, with water cannons and tear gas, to stop the distraught crowd from reaching the parliament building. As Lesch puts it, "A protest seeking limited reforms swiftly transformed into a revolutionary uprising. In three days, people were calling not only to end police brutality and remove the minister of interior, but also for President Hosni Mubarak to leave."[27]

During the protest in Tahrir Square, tensions between the police and the people escalated. Following the interior minister's warning to the demonstrators to cease their protests, a large part of the protesters were violently dispersed overnight by police forces. Yet, protesters gathered again in the square to denounce the government and voice their demands. As the head of the Egyptian Organization for Human Rights, Hafez Abu Saeda, declared months prior to the protest, "The humiliation of the simple citizen has become so widespread that the people are fed up."[28] If there is but one positive outcome of police abuses, it is that it united many individuals under a unique banner: the removal of Mubarak and his regime of brutality.

The police also became a target. The January protests caused the majority of the police to be gathered in the protest areas, which left police stations with fewer personnel than usual. Residents of districts where abuses of police powers had been particularly harsh over the years took that opportunity to express their discontent. Ismail reports that "in the first days of the uprising, 99 police stations were burned down and many detention cells were opened and detainees let out."[29] These attacks on police stations were met with mixed feelings. On the one hand, many were appalled by the attacks and saw them as added lawlessness, while others viewed the measures as necessary to keep the protests unfettered by police forces.[30]

Some scholars have also underlined the collaboration of the police and the people. Khadidja El Alaoui describes some situations in which witnesses reported that many officers showed hesitation to follow their official orders during the protest and even attempted to protect the protesters from violence coming from their ranks. She reports, "Officer Naji, [for example,] . . . famously threatened to shoot himself, if his superiors kept the order of non-intervention to defend the unarmed protestors when they were being murdered."[31] She also reminds us of the "ethics of the square: if the enemy is family, he is a son, a father, a cousin and then nonviolence becomes the only acceptable way of dealing with such a violent relative";[32] in other words, some police officers considered themselves Egyptian first and police second. Finally, she highlights that it was not uncommon for the protesters to protect their oppressors by escorting the tired and hungry ones out of the square, with some young people even bringing refreshments to some police officers on duty.[33]

The militarization of the Egyptian police has been the focus of most scholars interested in the Egyptian case. Scholarly interest peaked as militarization was exacerbated in the aftermath of the January protests. The four decades of Mubarak's rule had made the police an intrusive and semi-military body allowed to practice paramilitary violence.[34] Moreover, under the Emergency Law, civilians were increasingly trialed in front of specialized security courts, and sometimes in front of military courts, even when their accusation amounted to demonstrating for more labor equality.[35] Often in these civilian cases, "officers served as judges and there was no judicial appeal process."[36] In the aftermath of the uprising, the situation got worse: twelve thousand civilians were brought before military courts between January 29 and September 1, 2011, more than the total in the previous thirty years of Mubarak's regime. Joe Stork notes that "the majority . . . were not political, not street protesters, but people accused of ordinary crimes like theft."[37] The police were nursed by the military, which was omnipresent in the everyday duties of police officers: "At street level, a policeman could be seen guiding traffic; beside him a military police man was watching over his work."[38]

Thus, historical tensions culminated with the citizens' revolutionary call for the toppling of police authority, yet it was equated with calls for the collapse of the regime. This led some police officers to refrain from performing their duties throughout the revolutionary period, fearing potentially false accusations. During the revolutionary period, police absenteeism meant safety and security were lost in the streets and police were accused of provoking further violence. An attempt to preserve or defend the need for police authority was often met with further charges that the police were just Mubarak-regime cronies. In addition, the death or injury of hundreds of protesters had a profound impact on the people, who rejected police authority and further demanded the prosecution of police officers on charges of treachery and the abandonment of their line of duty. The situation worsened under the interim government of the Supreme Council of the Armed Forces (scaf), and then deteriorated even further under the Muslim Brotherhood (mb).

Media Impact on Police-Community Relationship

Egyptian media has typically portrayed police officers in a negative light. The ruling regime's control over the cinematic industry and media in general perpetuated the negative image of the police, furthering the deep enmity between the institution and the people. It is notable that under Gamal Abdel Nasser, Anwar Sadat, and then Mubarak, each regime supported and encouraged filmmakers to address the violations of its predecessor, at times in an exaggerated manner. Moreover, several Egyptian cinematic works have tarnished the image of security bodies even during the Mubarak era. Movies were used as a tool to denounce Mubarak's brutality as subtly as possible.[39] These films criticized security practices under Nasser's regime to expose its flaws. The most important and most famous of these films, which are also most influential in the Egyptian community, is *Al-Karnak*.[40] This film depicts the state of political dictatorship embraced by Nasser's regime. It also portrays the enormous violations committed by security forces in a systematic manner.

At the beginning of the third millennium, the Mubarak regime adopted a new policy to uphold the regime, allowing freedom of expression in an unprecedented manner in Egypt. It also allowed writers, journalists, and opposition parties to extensively criticize the government and expose its flaws and errors, as an outlet for venting political tension and frustration. The changes were put in effect on the condition that the president and his family were not mentioned: an untouchable red line. Therefore, writers blatantly criticized the police, producing movies such as *Heena Maysarah* (Till things get better),[41] *ʿImarat Yaʿqubian* (The Yacoubian Building)[42] and *Hiyya Fawda* (This is chaos).[43] Undoubtedly, the cinematic industry sheds light on already existing social realities experienced in Egyptian communities. Yet, police corruption should not overshadow the corruption in other government bodies.

The MoI often ignored recurring instances of police corruption, selectively issuing statements dispelling potential accusations of corruption. This led the media to doubt the sincerity of the ministry's intentions. The MoI has also consistently defended its own role in corruption cases to avert responsibility, claiming that incidents of corruption have nothing to do with its general policy, instead of admitting its mistakes and working toward rectifying the problem. Thus, within the police force, officers believed that the media had been deceived by a consistent Egyptian government cover-up of the most controversial cases.[44]

During the events of January 25, Egyptian media consistently highlighted police officers' violations against peaceful protesters, without distinguishing between peaceful protesters in public squares and criminals who broke into various police stations or public offices. Egyptian media often portrayed the police as criminals, while police officers who shot at those attempting to break into police stations believed that they were practicing their legal right of self-defense, ensured by Articles 245 to 251 of the Egyptian Penal Code. Moreover, Article 102 of the Police Corps Act allows police officers to use force in measures necessary to perform their duties.

However, with the rise of social media, police brutality could not go officially unnoticed. User-generated content produced by the recording, uploading, and sharing of videos online, available for all to see, has made abuses harder to conceal, challenging police control and authority.[45] The Battle of the Camel on February 2, 2011, for example, displayed striking proof of police brutality; yet, state media reported that the protest was "a seditious plot hatched by the unlikely alliance of Israel, Iran, Hezbollah, and the United States."[46] Both camps thus used media to assert their positions. But Mubarak had power to shape the dialogue surrounding these events and to shape public opinion to a great degree. As Lesch points out, "Legislation passed in 2006 made thirty-five offenses punishable by prison sentences for up to five years, such as publishing 'fake' news, undermining 'national security,' and defaming a domestic or international figure, public servant, or head of state."[47] The government also ensured its grip on the internet by requiring internet cafés and mobile phone companies to register each customer for tracking purposes.[48] Infiltration of communication by the police was a daily reality for the Egyptian people.

Deterioration of Police-Government Relations after January 25

From the perspective of observers and employees of the MoI, just as police often fabricated charges against innocent citizens, the revolutionaries also accused the police of crimes it did not commit. For example, the bombing of Alexandria's Al-Qiddisayn (Two Saints) Church in December 2011 was falsely blamed on a special unit within the MoI.[49] Despite falsified evidence, this accusation gained currency among various political movements and media outlets trying to hold the MoI responsible for its past mistakes and violations. Again, the view from within the MoI was that honest police officers were at times charged with crimes they did not commit and that, moreover, military authorities would appease revolutionary forces by willingly forsaking police legitimacy. This loss of police legitimacy was exacerbated by continued nonenforcement of court rulings against convicted persons with ties to the Mubarak regime.

The situation did not change under the rule of the SCAF, as a lack of training and modern policing techniques resulted in accidents such as the Port Said Stadium massacre,[50] in which seventy-two people were killed and police forces were blamed. While it was the police's responsibility to secure the event, the lack of necessary modern policing tools and methods, combined with a lack of accountability on the part of police leadership, worsened the situation.

Under the MB, police grew disenchanted and angry when, on multiple occasions, information available to security services regarding the presence of terrorists was ignored and President Mohammed Morsi restrained MoI officials from taking action. Allegedly, the MB released jihadist prisoners, granting them Egyptian nationality as per President Morsi's orders. This endangered Egyptian national security and entrenched the breech of the rule of law under the MB government,[51] exacerbating the tense relationship between the police force and the government.

Furthermore, the executive branch did not pay attention to police reform. Rather, the president focused on securing police loyalty to himself and the regime, even at the cost of continuing malpractice. In fact, Morsi appeared to give both the police and the MoI a green light to commit abuses in exchange for ensuring the security and stability of the regime, as was done during Mubarak's era.[52] Unfortunately, after the popular coup, widely supported by the majority of Egyptians, removed Morsi, the police did not change their practices, nor did they adopt modern policing techniques.

The new equation of power changed in favor of the police, as most non-Islamist citizens supported the police forces and the new regime rather than the MB. As a result, MB members occupied Rabaa and Nahda Squares in Cairo, initiating a peaceful protest. Things degenerated when roads were blocked, preventing pedestrians and locals from accessing their homes and businesses. Eventually a political decision was made to disperse the gathering: demonstrators were given time to leave and provided safe passage.[53] The choice to employ harsh tactics to quell the violence and the massive citizen death toll that resulted perpetuated a vicious cycle of violence. The MB responded with violence and terrorist attacks on police, judges, and state officials, eventually reaching ordinary people as they moved on to target utility facilities, hospitals, and transportation stations. The police now had justification for an even more brutal crackdown on dissent and civil rights.

Egyptians turned their hatred toward the MB and acquiesced to these violations, seeing them as an emergency measure to combat terrorism. In addition, with the wide public support of President Abdul Fatah el-Sisi and his regime, and the absence of the parliament as a legislative check on his power, the president took the opportunity to issue laws that gave the police a free hand in fighting terrorism. The El-Nadeem Center for Human Rights reported forty-eight deaths as a result of medical negligence in prisons in 2014 and 2015, as well as 289 cases of torture, and twenty-seven cases of group torture.[54] Finally, some officers viewed this war against terror as a justification to exact revenge for the 2011 uprising. Few acts of brutality and rights violations connected to the ruling regime were reported in state-controlled or private, state-connected media.

Practical Steps for Police Reform in Egypt

The state of insecurity in Egypt negatively affected all segments of society. The economy, including the invaluable tourism sector, was near complete paralysis. The security situation in Egypt was grave; the crime rate rose sharply and new types of violent crimes emerged.

In light of the January 25, 2011, protests, the actions of the SCAF, the MB's brief rule, and the gravity of the security situation, a number of practical steps can be taken to reform Egypt's police forces. First, police officers should be deployed to locations where they are most qualified. Former interior minister Adli effectively put in place rules for staff mobility, increased police salaries, and improved the general appearance of police officers. Second, the four-year police academy training system needs to be reviewed and shortened. The main focus needs to shift from law courses to courses that teach specifically designed policing techniques and provide field training. Furthermore, student boarding should not be mandatory since it separates the police from the citizenry and entrenches a military-like socialization incompatible with the civil nature of a police corps. A quota for graduating officers should be determined for each governorate on the basis of its population, allowing the governorate to request an increase in its quota as long as it bears the extra costs for students beyond the government-assigned quota.

Gradually canceling the practice of annexing conscript soldiers to the Central Security Forces, and replacing them with volunteers would also be a positive step forward. Hundreds of thousands of military conscripts without educational qualifications are often recruited to join the Central Security Forces for a three-year period. They are trained and accommodated under extremely harsh living conditions and are given very modest salaries. These conscripts are then sent to the MoI to carry out policing duties without adequate support. Unfortunately, the MoI heavily relies on those conscripts for cheap labor. They live where they work and get a one-week vacation a month. It is also worth noting that the Central Security Forces are quasi-military forces, and their main purpose is to preserve internal order during disturbances. This sector generally incorporates riot police and SWAT teams. Thus, the MoI relies on police officers without genuine training in modern methods of riot dispersal.

Another helpful reform would be to establish a union to protect the rights of these lower-ranking recruits. This is not a new concept. A precedent has already been set with the establishment of the Police Club, which has an elected board of directors, as a first step in defending officers' rights. Yet, the representative body is not an independent union and has not met the officers' needs so far. A totally independent union should be formed to represent the social and economic interests of its members.

On a broader scale, HRW has made several recommendations with regard to allegations of torture. It approached the Egyptian government with a request for the amendment of the definition of torture in Article 126 of the penal code to align it with Article 1 of the Convention against Torture and emphasized the need to make penalties proportionate to the seriousness of the offenses.[55] Regarding the Office of the Public Prosecutor, HRW advised that it is crucial to increase the speed and impartiality of all investigations, including those of superiors.[56] And regarding the MoI, it demanded the suspension of any law enforcement official directly or indirectly involved in acts of torture or the ill treatment of suspects.[57]

The government needs to set a higher standard for police conduct. As Richard Ericson points out, "Crime control is an impossible task for the police alone. They are expected to handle a phenomenon caused by social, political, economic, and cultural forces beyond their control and have to give the *appearance* that things are (more or less) under control" (italics added).[58] Reform and dialogue between the government, the police forces, and citizens are necessary; there also needs to be recognition of the responsibilities and limitations of the police in order to improve laws and procedures.[59] After decades of repression and brutality, the Mubarak regime squandered its only chance to make peace with the Egyptian people: it shattered the reputation of one of the key national security organs and started a vicious cycle of a love-hate relationship between the police and the people, fueled by political instability and a demand for regime change.

Notes

1. Laila Amin Morsy, "American Support for the 1952 Egyptian Coup: Why?," *Middle Eastern Studies* 31, no. 2 (1995): 307–316.

2. Salwa Ismail, "The Egyptian Revolution against the Police," *Social Research: An International Quarterly* 79, no. 2 (2012): 435.

3. Juha P. Mäkelä, "The Arab Spring's Impact on Egypt Securitocracy," *International Journal of Intelligence and Counterintelligence* 27, no. 2 (2014): 218.

4. Human Rights Watch (HRW), "Work on Him until He Confesses: Impunity for Torture in Egypt," January 2011, 1–95, http://www.hrw.org/sites/default/files/reports/egypt0111webwcover_0.pdf.

5. Mäkelä, "The Arab Spring's Impact on Egypt Securitocracy," 222.

6. Joe Stork, "Egypt: Human Rights in Transition," *Social Research: An International Quarterly* 79, no. 2 (2012): 466.

7. Christopher J. Schneider, "Police 'Image Work' in an Era of Social Media: YouTube and the 2007 Montebello Summit Protest," in *Social Media, Politics and the State: Protests, Revolutions, Riots, Crime and Policing in the Age of Facebook, Twitter and YouTube*, ed. Daniel Trottier and Christian Fuchs (London: Routledge, 2015), 228.

8. Egyptian Const. of 1971, law no. 109.

9. Nabil Abu shawl, Nasser al-Sharqawi, "Referral of the Policemen Accused of Killing Khaled Said to the Criminal Court," *Egypt Independent March 7, 2010*, http://www.almasryalyoum.com/news/details/782.

10. United Nations Office on Drugs and Crime, "Victimization in Egypt," October 2009, 3–4, http://www.unodc.org/documents/data-and-analysis/dfa/Egypt_victimization_exsum.pdf.

11. Lawrence F. Travis, *Introduction to Criminal Justice* (London: Routledge, 2010).

12. Almasry Alyoum, "Invitation on Facebook to Demonstrate on January 25th under the Slogan 'Tunis Did It,'" *Egypt Independent*, January 20, 2011, http://www.almasryalyoum.com/news/details/109928.

13. Ismail, "The Egyptian Revolution against the Police," 438.

14. Ann M. Lesch, "Concentrated Power Breeds Corruption, Repression, and Resistance," in *Arab Spring in Egypt: Revolution and Beyond*, ed. Bahgat Korany and Rabab El Mahdi (Cairo: American University in Cairo Press, 2012), 19.

15. Ismail, "The Egyptian Revolution against the Police," 435–436.

16. HRW, "Work on Him until He Confesses," 61–62.

17. Ibid., 3.

18. Lesch, "Concentrated Power Breeds Corruption," 20.

19. HRW, "Work on Him until He Confesses," 2.

20. Ismail, "The Egyptian Revolution against the Police," 437.

21. Lesch, "Concentrated Power Breeds Corruption," 37.

22. Rabab El Mahdi and Philip Marfleet, *Egypt: The Moment of Change* (London: Zed Books, 2009).

23. Wael Ghonim, *Revolution 2.0: The Power of the People Is Greater Than the People in Power: A Memoir* (New York: Houghton Mifflin Harcourt, 2012) is cited in Stork, "Egypt," 464.

24. Stork, "Egypt," 464.

25. Ismail, "The Egyptian Revolution against the Police," 435

26. Lesch, "Concentrated Power Breeds Corruption," 17.

27. Ibid., 18.

28. Quoted in Ibid., 38.

29. Ismail, "The Egyptian Revolution against the Police," 445.

30. Ibid., 446.

31. Khadidja El Alaoui, "The Ethics of Tahreer Square," *Peace Review: A Journal of Social Justice* 26 (2014): 80.

32. Ibid., 81

33. Ibid.

34. Ismail, "The Egyptian Revolution against the Police," 436.

35. Stork, "Egypt," 468.

36. Lesch, "Concentrated Power Breeds Corruption," 19.

37. Stork, "Egypt," 412.

38. Mäkelä, "The Arab Spring's Impact on Egypt Securitocracy," 223–224.

39. Lesch, "Concentrated Power Breeds Corruption," 32.

40. *Al-Karnak*, Aly Badrakhan (Egypt: Gamal El Leithy Films, 1975).

41. *Heena Maysara* [Till things get better], Khaled Youssef Cairo: Albatrous film production and distribution - Kamel Abo Ali, 2007.

42. *The Yacoubian Building* (Marwan Hamed, 2006).

43. *Hiyya Fawda* [This is chaos], Youssef Chahine and Khaled Youssef (Egypt: Misr International Films & 3B Productions, 2007).

44. Stork, "Egypt," 464.

45. Schneider, "Police 'Image Work,'" 228.

46. Stork, "Egypt," 471.

47. Lesch, "Concentrated Power Breeds Corruption," 25.

48. Ibid.

49. "Habib al-Adli Plan Details of the Bombing of the Saints Church in Alexandria," The Seventh Day, March 3, 2011, http://goo.gl/Dl37aV.

50. "Egypt Football Violence Leaves Many Dead in Port Said," BBC, February 12, 2012, http://www.bbc.com/news/world-middle-east-16845841.

51. "Mohamed Morsi | The Counter Jihad Report," Counter Jihad Report, The Fiction of Political Islam, September 2, 2015, http://counterjihadreport.com/tag/mohamed-morsi/.

52. "Report: Police Performance Is the Same under Morsi's Rule," *Aswat Masriya*, November 11, 2012, http://aswatmasriya.com/news/view.aspx?id=a083f973-a0ba-4176-b2b9-0d1b8d6a00dc.

53. Nour Egypt, "Video lelmamar alaamn lfad e'tesam Rabaa'" [Exclusive video displays the safe zone during dispersal of Rabaa sit-in], YouTube, May 2, 2014, https://www.youtube.com/watch?v=4EAJxARVDow.

54. Nadeem Center, "Violation of Citizens' Rights in the Name of the War on Terrorism," *People Newspaper*, February 23, 2014, http://alnadeem.org/ar/node/448.

55. HRW, "Work on Him until He Confesses," 8.

56. Ibid.

57. Ibid., 9.

58. Richard V. Ericson, *Reproducing Order: A Study of Police Patrol Work* (Toronto: University of Toronto Press, 1982), 11.

59. Herman Goldstein, "Police Discretion: The Ideal versus the Real," *Public Administration Review* 23, no. 3 (1963): 148.

Conclusion

Moving beyond Tahrir

Ismail Alexandrani and Isaac Friesen

THE CONTRASTING PERSPECTIVES provided in this volume help capture the complex debates that have dominated Egyptian public discourse throughout the revolutionary period. These accounts look beyond the headlines of Tahrir for a more nuanced understanding of the recent political upheaval. But what precisely does "beyond Tahrir" mean? Above all else, the authors show this phrase to denote the incredible intricacy found in the fabric of Egyptian society, which can be lost in cursory narratives of the Egyptian revolution. This is no simple story of heroes and villains. By illuminating overlapping dynamics that are not mutually exclusive, we learn of the interplay between activists, intellectuals, journalists, police officers, religious groups, and the military. There remains, however, one key angle of the revolution beyond Tahrir left unexamined: Egypt's geographic periphery. As Sahar Aziz mentions in chapter 3, Cairo is *the* Egyptian metropolis for the rich and privileged. The capital's national predominance in politics, media, and economy is undeniable. It is not surprising, then, that this volume's authors center their analyses on Cairo. At the same time, there are certain privileges to the perspectives offered in this book that sometimes marginalize the many subaltern narratives that fall out of earshot of Cairo elites and Western academic institutions. Before closing with a reflection on the current state of the Arab Spring, this conclusion joins the other chapters in problematizing broader reductionist narratives of the Egyptian revolution. We investigate the trajectory of the revolution for those Egyptians who were not demonstrating in the capital. In other words, what does Tahrir mean for the majority of Egyptians, and what might it mean for the foreseeable future?[1]

Centralization and Marginalization Narrative

In contrast to the secretive and carefully executed Free Officers' Movement, which rose to power in 1952, the January 25 revolution was a massive popular mobilization that occurred spontaneously across Egypt. Despite the unprecedented scale of the more recent uprising, there has been a tendency to confine discussion of the revolution to the events in Tahrir Square. Indeed, in Egypt it is customary to conflate the political, economic, and social capital of Cairo with the rest of the country, so much so that Egyptians living outside Cairo call their capital city "Masr" (Egypt)—as if they are living outside the country. Such oversimplifications were apparent even at the beginning of the uprising, when Western commentators dubbed Hosni Mubarak's overthrow the "Facebook Revolution"—thereby relegating the real achievements of ordinary Egyptians to cyberspace. Many other Western observers have interpreted highly complex sociopolitical phenomena as simply the result of Egypt's young generation of Web 2.0 users, despite the fact that the illiteracy rate in Egypt is over 40 percent. Equally astonishing is the fact that five years have passed since the revolution, and yet it has not been sufficient time for scholars, journalists, and filmmakers to uncover the marginalized narratives hidden from the media and political spotlights.

No attention has been paid to Egypt's revolutions since January 2011, except for a few researchers who have tried to study the diverse manifestations of political activism and social movements. This neglect is caused by what Mohamad Hamas Elmasry and Mohammed El-Nawawy describe in chapter 7 as the media's ties and subservience to the Egyptian state. In spite of select researchers' efforts, there is a salient paucity in documentation, and therefore analysis, of the uprisings witnessed outside Cairo. A clear example of this is the large difference in coverage between Cairo and Egypt's second city, Alexandria. While the former has seen much media coverage and academic study (such as the chapters in this volume), the latter has enjoyed much less. Alexandria's demonstrations were distinct from Cairo's in part due to the fact that in Tahrir protesters came from all over the country, while in Alexandria demonstrators were almost entirely from the Mediterranean city. Hence, while it is true that Alexandria received some coverage in international media and scholarship, it was of a much smaller scale than the coverage of Cairo. In turn, Cairo came to symbolize the entire nation of Egypt. Ultimately, the imbalance in media and scholarship on the revolution in the rest of Egypt has consolidated the belief that the 2011 uprising was the Tahrir Square revolution. We need to recognize that this is untrue.

Perhaps the reason that the April 2006 incident in the delta city of Mahalla, when demonstrators tore down a poster of Mubarak and hit it with shoes, is celebrated as the first such occurrence of protest is because it had the good fortune of being captured on video. However, the first protests for Mubarak's ouster were not in the Nile valley or in the delta at all. Rather, they occurred two years prior, after the first calls for Mubarak's fall by the Syndicate of Journalists, and saw their nascent manifestation in the first small protests held by the Kefaya movement. In December 2004, families of detained Egyptians in North Sinai took to the streets, calling for the fall of the regime. This alienation was a result of the expanded crackdown imposed on the border region in Shaykh Zuwaid and Rafah after the unprecedented terrorist attacks by Gamaat il-Twaheed we il-Jihad in 2004, 2005, and 2006.

Revolutions and Violence in Sinai

Years later, in 2011, it is ironic that longtime activists of the Kefaya movement were working only for the limited goals of socioeconomic reform and an end to police torture—avoiding direct calls for Mubarak's ouster. Yet these very activists were quickly forced to change strategies and keep pace with the general public, spontaneously cheering for the fall of the regime. In fact, the first calls for the fall of the regime were in North Sinai, where the Ministry of Interior launched its aforementioned campaign against terrorism, distinguishing little between security threats and ordinary citizens there and applying a policy of collective punishment. Reports indicate that the number of Egyptians detained following the Taba, Sharm el-Sheikh, and Dahab resort bombings exceeded four thousand—this in an area with a population of under fifty thousand people. Speaking in interviews, victims and their relatives, including elders, women, and children, have chronicled the violations they experienced while in custody, and expressed their desire for revenge against the police.

In his book *Sinai Where I Am: Years of Wandering*, a collection of blog entries written over several years, writer Ashraf al-Anani details the hardship and turmoil that unfolded during the 2011 uprising in a North Sinai region that had witnessed political unrest, burned tires, and road blocks since 2005. Anani calls January 25, 2011, an ordinary day in Sinai. Corroborating the police brutality described in chapter 9 by Hesham Genidy and Justine Salam, people in the border region often refer to the Shaykh Zuwaid police department as "Guantanamo Sinai," describing it as a huge torture- and slaughterhouse. Those who entered it were seen as "the fallen," while those who were released were termed "newborn." A graduating college student and native of Shaykh Zuwaid, Ayman Mohsen, began to film and document protests. The result of his research was the documentary film *Ticking Bomb* (Al-qunbela al-mawquta), which examined the populations of Shaykh Zuwaid and Rafah, recording their suffering over basic rights like water supply, education, health care, and employment. Most notably, the film captured scenes of armed revolution, images that mostly stood in contrast to the relatively peaceful uprising in other parts of Egypt, including the North Sinai governorate capital of el-Arish, only thirty kilometers west of Shaykh Zuwaid.

Initially opposition forces in al-Arish participated in peaceful protests during the 2011 uprising. The Bedouins in Shaykh Zuwaid and Rafah did the same in the face of arbitrary detention, torture, and sentences in absentia. Yet the patience of North Sinai Bedouins could only go so far. As soon as the first peaceful protester (Mohammed Atef) was shot dead by security forces on January 26, peaceful protests turned into armed revolution. Banners and leaflets were traded in for Kalashnikov rifles and RPGs—the latter of which targeted the security headquarters in Rafah. As the situation spiraled out of control, the political activists who led the peaceful uprising lost the ability to direct the broader opposition. All the fighting ended in a crushing defeat for the police and the major deployment of heavy army units in the region for the first time since Egypt's 1967 defeat, after which the security annex of the peace treaty between Egypt and Israel was amended. This was the birth of the revolutionary Sinai that was ignored by the media, politicians, and activists alike in Cairo. The marginalization of Sinai in popular awareness and political discourse resulted in the gradual crystallization of armed groups such as Ansar Bayt al-Moqadis, which had been loyal to al-Qaeda before shifting its allegiance to ISIS (the Islamic State) and renaming itself Wilayat al-Sina (Province of Sinai) in November 2014. Problems in North Sinai only began to come to the forefront with the bombing of gas lines that lead to Israel and Jordan, and later with deadly attacks on Egyptian soldiers. Lost in all these reports was the marked contrast between the Bedouins of the border region and the sophisticated social activists in al-Arish, the latter of whom possessed far more political wisdom and experience than the naively idealistic revolutionary youth in Cairo discussed in chapter 2 by Mohammad Fadel. Of course, national and international media missed all of this, focusing solely on the aforementioned militant groups instead.

Environmental Activism in Aswan

In this context, another of the most important and successful social movements unfolded in the southern city of Aswan. In contrast to North Sinai's focus on torture and armed struggle, Aswan's activists engaged issues of health and the environment. There, accompanying the construction of the Nile valley estuary was the outright criminal spread of industrial pollution by way of a bank held primarily to protect the city from risk of flooding and to direct excess water to the Nile River. It conducted hundreds of tons of industrial toxins to the Nile each day. Legal and human rights movements emerged from one of the most famous and oldest human rights centers in Egypt, the Hisham Mubarak Legal Center, which had achieved several victories in Egyptian courts since the end of the 1990s. However, none of the court rulings were implemented. With the 2011 revolution, hopes were aroused that public pressure might be able to extract these long-sought-after rights.

Aswan played a small role in the 2011 uprising, similar to the participation witnessed by other cities of similar size such as Luxor, Nag Hammadi, and other towns in Upper Egypt. The people in these Upper Egyptian provinces had a keen sense of marginalization and a resulting belief in the centrality of Cairo. This peripheral outlook led many to travel to the Egyptian capital to participate in the Tahrir Square protests. Data from interviews with activists reveals an initial optimism and sense of urgency to network across the country in order to expand their revolutionary base; however, this nascent cross-country mobilization disappeared gradually in conjunction with the rise of the counterrevolution. In the first two years after the revolution, the people of the Aswan village of Abu el-Riesh witnessed the unprecedented activism occurring around the country. This manifested in new revolutionary demands by them for environmental reform for the Nile water, which supplies the faucets and fields of Egypt's eighty-six million people.

Abu el-Riesh is located north of Aswan on the east bank of the Nile, less than five kilometers from the stream famously known as Kima Canal—named for the chemical plant that unofficially belongs to the Egyptian army. This village is most affected by poisoning by industrial and agricultural waste, as well as by waste disposal from a number of hospitals and security bases. The high rate of kidney failure, hepatitis, and cancer led to a popular reaction among the families of those infected. These ordinary citizens organized protests against the government's refusal to implement court rulings that would stop the poisoning of the Nile. Working as an investigative journalist, one of the authors of this chapter succeeded in bringing this account to light in December 2014 in a two-part story of subaltern activism, which he came across only by chance while investigating the poisoning of the Nile. The case of Abu el-Riesh reveals a great amount of self- and collective awareness on the part of activists in Aswan who organized peaceful mobilizations of opposition to the government without much contention among the leadership of the movement. This led to formal negotiations and the government's acceptance, in principle, of a fair resolution. The movement's leadership subsequently formed committees for this task, and registered their concerns in the official records of government meetings. In spite of these tentative gains and the massive social implications regarding the health of tens of millions of Egyptians, Aswan's environmental rights social movement now faces substantial adversity accompanying the rise of the military-led counterrevolution. As will be discussed later, President Abdul Fatah el-Sisi's government has closed the public domain almost completely. Yet, despite the best efforts of the state, public pressure in the Egyptian periphery has not disappeared since the summer of 2013.

Sinai Struggles after July 3, 2013

Immediately following the ouster of President Mohammed Morsi, Islamists formed a sit-in in el-Arish that threatened Sisi—Egypt's defense minister at the time—with a new stage in the Sinai insurgency. On July 5, 2013, Salafi jihadist groups held a massive armed rally in Shaykh Zuwaid, calling for the Muslim Brotherhood (who likely have no presence in the border zone) to join them in their armed struggle. Attending representatives of the brotherhood, however, could not condone the violent language of the jihadists, and withdrew after less than ten minutes. This was the last joint event the two Islamist groups held. Time will tell if the brotherhood's ability to adapt in the face of change, as discussed in chapter 5 by Dalia Fahmy, will facilitate its survival in an increasingly bloody era. It is important to note that at this time, violent clashes between the jihadists and the army have not yet occurred, and the political distrust and hysteria have above all else surfaced in response to the removal of the democratically elected president Morsi and the return of the police state. Police were expelled from the border area on January 28, 2011, and have yet to return, with all subsequent attempts to rebuild the Rafah police station ending in failure. The military demolished entire residential areas of the region in order to create a buffer zone between Sinai and Gaza in late 2014, acting against the "threat of militant Islam"—a security discourse akin to that discussed in chapter 6 by Mai Mogib Mosad.

The 2011 revolution did not resolve the deep tension and distrust between the police and the people in the border region, and the groups did little to reconcile, compensate, or even apologize for past violence and rights violations. Moreover, the Muslim Brotherhood, which North Sinai militants regarded as being too soft in its implementation of Sharia, was on the receiving end of a brutal crackdown. In this context, what could the stigmatized people of the border region in general, and the hardened militant groups in particular, expect in their dealings with the new government? Thus, conditions in Sinai deteriorated from bad to worse through the self-fulfilling terrorism-security narrative pursued by both parties. By September 2013, the brutal open warfare had devolved so much that locals longed for the days of the "merciful" Habib al-Adli, Mubarak's longtime minister of interior who imposed the very abuses on Sinai residents that fomented their armed revolt in January 2011. The people of North Sinai might not have imagined a scenario worse than that created by Adli, but the winter of 2013 turned out to be an especially painful one. Residents suddenly faced forced displacement, aerial bombardment, tanks and artillery, the uprooting of orchards and crops, and the bulldozing of houses. Communications were cut, ambulances were stopped, and schools and hospitals were sabotaged. Dozens of women and children were killed in the harsh repression—a collective punishment without parallel in the entire history of the Sinai Peninsula. Much as Shereen Abouelnaga and Belal Fadl and Maissaa Almustafa argue in their respective chapters, the root causes of discontent in Sinai not only remain, but are also being exacerbated. Interestingly, it is the military in the region that faces a precarious position in service of the government—not the police, as discussed in Genidy and Salam's chapter.

The Rise of Nubian Activism

In sharp contrast to the deterioration of security in North Sinai, southern Egypt has witnessed stabilization since the July 3 counterrevolution or coup. This is due in part to the unique ethnic, linguistic, and cultural diversity in Egypt's south, and is reflected in the social and popular ambiguity of the region since 2013. The Nubian people are composed of two branches: the Fadjiicka and the Matocka (Kenuz). This diversity necessitates a multidimensional engagement with political issues like cultural and linguistic discrimination and calls for the countering of stereotyping along color and professional lines. All of this is compounded by, and ultimately centers on, the question of compensation for the largest forced displacement in the history of the African continent, which accompanied the mid-twentieth-century construction of the Aswan High Dam. Despite the great social cohesion among Nubians and their Cairo-based migrants, the ethnic group's grievances have not translated into organized social and legal movements aiming to make political demands on issues in Aswan. Interviews with Nubians in Cairo, Alexandria, and Aswan reveal a general lack of political mobilization.

The 2011 revolution brought some change to the Nubian public domain, where Nubian activist groups became more active in pursuing political, socioeconomic, and educational initiatives. Sometimes the extent of Nubian diversity was a problem, and internal conflicts did result. And yet, reminiscent of the cosmetic political change embraced by the military, discussed in Rashed's and Fadel's articles, little initially changed following Mubarak's fall. For instance, although Field Marshal Mohamed Tantawi, who ruled Egypt until Morsi's 2012 election, is Fadjiicka Nubian (from the village of Abu Simbel), his ethnicity brought few improvements for the livelihoods of Egypt's Nubians. Moreover, during the time of Morsi's presidency, the constitutional committee rejected a proposed document recognizing the ethnic diversity of Egypt and refused to schedule the right of return for Nubians to the shores of Lake Nasser. As a result, the Nubian member of the constitutional committee resigned in protest.

However, during President Adly Mansour's 2013/2014 administration, the Nubian writer Hagag Oddoul successfully led a push for ethnic pluralism in Egypt's new constitution. In turn, the July 3 regime was able to contain the Nubian issue that had troubled previous administrations. Oddoul's sole priority during the revolutionary period was to gain recognition for Nubian rights. The Nubian activist was indifferent to the 2013 coup, demonstrating little interest in the uprising's broader national issues of democracy and social justice. Instead he seized a unique moment in Egyptian center-periphery relations to achieve the historic progress that marginalized Nubians had long dreamed of. The place of Nubians in Egypt reached wider exposure in the media in April 2014, when clashes broke out between members of the Arab Banu Hilal tribe and the Nubian Daboud tribe, leaving twenty-five dead. At that time, it became clearer that many army, police, and intelligence officers had Nubian origins. This shone a light on how the state was able to contain the Nubian struggle and mobilization in the past. While the Egyptian state's interests centered on its political legitimacy and stability, the Nubians saw their national exposure as a chance to reaffirm constitutional rights that stood against the proposed plan to draw new administrative borders between governorates, splitting the Nubian lands. It was a symbolic victory for the Nubians, and it opened the door to future dialogue and negotiation to secure their newly acquired rights.

The Cairo-centric narrative of a narrowly interpreted Tahrir revolution inadequately captures the great diversity among Egyptian people, parties, and social movements. Such an oversimplified view is reductionist to the extreme, and it insufficiently captures the aspirations, struggles, and actions of communities around the country. The greatest challenge to the ongoing revolution is that the ascendant counterrevolution continues to appreciate the grassroots networks that reinforce the legitimacy of the Egyptian state, and accordingly strives to network the local communities, as the deep state is known to do. The counterrevolutionary Sisi government leveraged its knowledge of the fragmented, marginalized society to besiege the centralized revolution in Tahrir and then to push it out of the public sphere altogether. At the same time, the revolution outside Cairo is far from decided, and as such we must take the *longue durée* view, as numerous authors in this volume suggest.

Whither the Arab Spring?

There is no question that Egypt still possesses a special sort of influence that far exceeds its financial and economic resources. While Tunisia played the role of first domino in the winter of 2010–2011, it was only when Egyptians rose up en masse that the Arab world's concatenation was truly unleashed.[2] Egypt remains a key marker for the Arab Spring today. Nowhere is this clearer than in the interests and actions of other regional powers. Wealthy Gulf states such as the United Arab Emirates, Qatar, and Saudi Arabia spent much of the past few years engaged in a high-stakes proxy contest of diplomacy and dollars. Recently released documents confirm that the United Arab Emirates acted as a major supporter of the June 30 protests that ended Morsi's rule. Other leaked files illuminate Saudi reservations about the Shia presence in Egypt during the Muslim Brotherhood's rule, and exhibit the Riyadh government's fear that the revolution opened a space for Iranian influence in the country. The Saudi regime also supported Sisi's ascension to power and Egypt's vocal opposition to Iranian interference in the country. That they have provided similar support in Syria, Yemen, Bahrain, and elsewhere indicates that the Saudis are enjoying a good return on their investment.[3] How Egypt will use all this Gulf money remains to be seen, but there is troublingly little indication that the necessary reforms are being undertaken to make resource-poor Egypt the manufacturing hub that its growing labor force requires.

Aside from their tricky involvement in the ongoing Syrian and Libyan conflicts, Turkey and Qatar's fortunes in foreign policy have largely run parallel with those of the Muslim Brotherhood. Their resulting relations with Egypt (and its

Saudi and Emirati supporters) are today marked by tension. The Qatari-Egyptian struggle over Al Jazeera reporters Baher Mohamed and Mohamed Fahmy drags on into its third year, and diplomatic relations between Ankara and Cairo have been all but severed amid the hurling of insults and accusations. Indeed, the region's pro-brotherhood axis has been on the defensive since Egypt's hot summer of 2013.

Unlike Misrata or Aleppo, where the chants of peaceful demonstrators have been muted by mortar and machine-gun fire, Egypt remains relatively stable. But while the Nile valley has thankfully been spared large-scale violence, Sisi's critics argue that earlier calls for democracy, dignity, and social justice have gone largely unanswered and the old order has effectively returned. Opposition figures highlight the rise in forced disappearances of political activists, and the small protests that do break out often turn deadly, as the state continues to brook no opposition. The media and entertainment sectors in Egypt seem similarly besieged, and the numerous journalists killed during the revolutionary period partially explains why the press appeared unready for the independent, oppositional role recommended by Elmasry and Nawawy. While news editors have formally agreed to curtail their criticism of the military and government, Muslim Brotherhood sympathizers decry the government's ban on the Islamist group's newspapers, satellite channels, and radio stations. Bassem Youssef, a star critic during Morsi's presidency, is now off the air, and other comedians in Egypt are too afraid to poke fun at the political establishment. Echoing the argument of Abouelnaga's chapter, we can conclude that subservience to the state is a near necessity for Egyptian artists, journalists, and intellectuals. Similar waves of repression can be found in other Arab states.[4]

Supporters of the Sisi regime defend recent crackdowns as necessary steps in Egypt's escalating war on terror. The enormous Egyptian military and security apparatuses strain as they struggle to contain threats coming from its western border with Libya, the North Sinai militants discussed earlier in this chapter, and a growing number of attacks in the Nile valley. Hence, with barely faded memories of the Upper Egyptian insurgency of the 1990s, Egyptians are again becoming accustomed to sporadic outbreaks of political violence. Although respect for and confidence in the Egyptian military remains high among many Egyptians, the challenge of how the armed forces will deal with the increasingly bold ISIS affiliate Province of Sinai is a perplexing one. Indeed, Egypt's new enemies have brought it into "uncharted territory."[5]

Yet Sisi's critics argue that this fight is precisely what gives the current regime its raison d'être, and some political scientists go so far as to argue that the reverse is simultaneously true as well, framing Egypt's government as a "gift to the Islamic State."[6] Robert Fisk articulates Egypt's choice as one between "a megalomaniac president [and] the madness of ISIS"—hardly the two options Tahrir demonstrators dreamed of in 2011. The "new" dynamic, however, is in fact not new at all, and echoes Asef Bayat's critique of the old authoritarian-Islamist binary.[7] More troublingly, there is evidence that the post-2013 repression of the Muslim Brotherhood has driven elements within the Islamist organization to reconsider their disavowal of political violence.[8] This is especially clear on brotherhood social media platforms, and hints at a generational divide that has been apparent since the earliest days of the uprising. Ironically analogous to how Fadel criticizes young activists for not being pragmatic enough, some young brotherhood members now denounce their leadership as being *too* pragmatic.

It would be misleading, however, to portray Sisi's government purely in terms of national security, repression, and terrorism. Many Egyptians support the Sisi regime for reasons other than stability. Egyptian secularists, liberals, and Christians nervously celebrate the apparent recession of Islamism in the country, even as they have mixed feelings about aspects of the Sisi regime, as Mosad suggests. Moreover, Egyptians of various political stripes view the state's new economic projects with favor. The military has invested heavily in a General Electric power generation plan, a one-million-unit housing project with the Emirati urban developer Arabtec, and the New Suez Canal. Some observers, affirming the view expressed in Rashed's chapter, consider these expenditures as proof that Egyptians now enjoy a less corrupt, more accountable government after the revolution. The result could be sustainable, long-term economic growth. Conversely, others question the source of the military's income in the first place, claiming that the projects are costly ploys akin to Mubarak's disastrous Toshka land-reclamation project.[9] Time will tell, and Egypt's citizenry (half of whom are under the age of twenty-five) wait uneasily amid ongoing unemployment and worsening inflation.

Ultimately, the postrevolutionary persistence of Egypt's political and socioeconomic problems forces us to ask what the Arab Spring has really accomplished. The Middle East's other revolutionary states are also largely in disarray. Tunisia, the most lasting success story of the uprisings, has been rocked in 2015 by two terrorist attacks on Westerners that have frightened away vital tourism dollars and renewed calls for the surveillance and repression of Islamists. Beyond Tunisia, the specter of ISIS looms essentially everywhere in the region. In the cases of Libya (where Egypt now intervenes militarily), Iraq, Yemen, and Syria, the chaos of civil war reigns, and one wonders if the continued decline of these countries will leave them fractured and destitute like the failed state in Somalia.

With these concerns in mind, how can the fateful uprising best be conceptualized today? Was it a revolution, a coup, a rebellion, or a moment? Was it really an Arab Spring, or did an Islamist or Authoritarian Winter dictate events more forcefully?[10] Judging by the diverse perspectives found in this volume, answers vary depending on one's disciplinary or political perspective. What can be agreed on is the fact that the ripples caused by Egypt's revolution affected developments well beyond Cairo and the country's borders. For a younger generation, the revolution was a time of hope and change that will not be soon forgotten. Yet the uprising also brought its own threats and anxieties. Surveying the region today, trepidation abounds: civil war, state repression, democracy, terrorism, economic crisis; the possibilities and perils of Tahrir extend out into a most uncertain future.

Notes

1. The views expressed in this chapter do not represent those of the other authors in this volume, and are not indicative of a consensus among contributors.

2. Perry Anderson, "On the Concatenation in the Arab World," *New Left Review* 68 (March–April 2011).

3. Mohamed Hamama and Shady Zalat, "Wikileaks: Saudi Arabia and Azhar on the 'Shia Encroachment' in Egypt," *Mada Masr*, July 9, 2015, http://www.madamasr.com/sections/politics/wikileaks-saudi-arabia-and-azhar-shia-encroachment-egypt; Mostafa Mohie and Hossam Bahgat, "Exclusive Wikileaks Cables Trace Ebb and Flow of Egypt-UAE Relations," *Mada Masr*, July 26, 2015, http://www.madamasr.com/sections/politics/exclusive-wikileaks-cables-trace-ebb-and-flow-egypt-uae-relations.

4. Dana Priest, Diedre Phillips, and Katy June-Friesen, "After Arab Spring, Journalism Briefly Flowered and Then Withered," *Washington Post*, July 26, 2015, http://www.washingtonpost.com/investigations/after-arab-spring-journalism-briefly-flowered-and-then-withered/2015/07/25/cb4c43fe-1c2a-11e5-ab92-c75ae6ab94b5_story.html.

5. Ellis Goldberg, "Sinai: War in a Distant Province," *Jadaliyya*, July 30, 2015, http://www.jadaliyya.com/pages/index/22303/sinai_war-in-a-distant-province; Steven A. Cook, "Egypt's Coming Chaos," *Foreign Policy*, July 3, 2015, http://foreignpolicy.com/2015/07/03/egypts-coming-chaos-isis-terrorism-sisi/.

6. Shadi Hamid, "Sisi's Regime Is a Gift to the Islamic State," *Foreign Policy*, August 6, 2015, http://foreignpolicy.com/2015/08/06/sisi-is-the-best-gift-the-islamic-state-ever-got/.

7. Robert Fisk, "What a Choice for Egypt—A Megalomaniac President or the Madness of ISIS," *Independent*, July 20, 2015, http://www.independent.co.uk/voices/comment/what-a-choice-for-egypt—a-megalomaniac-president-or-the-madness-of-isis-10400354.html; Asef Bayat, *Life as Politics: How Ordinary People Change the Middle East*, 2nd ed. (Palo Alto, CA: Stanford University Press, 2013).

8. Abdelrahman Ayyash, "The Brotherhood's Post-pacifist Approach," *Sada*, July 9, 2015, http://carnegieendowment.org/sada/2015/07/09/brotherhood-s-post-pacifist-approach/id6y.

9. Abdel-Fattah Barayez, "More than Money on Their Minds: The Generals and the Economy in Egypt Revisited," *Jadaliyya*, July 2, 2015, http://www.jadaliyya.com/pages/index/22023/more-than-money-on-their-minds_the-generals-and-th; Safiaa Mounir, "Critics Say Suez Canal Project Falls Short of Expectations," *al-Monitor*, July 30, 2015, http://www.al-monitor.com/pulse/originals/2015/07/egypt-suez-canal-corridor-project-development.html#.

10. Marc Lynch, "Obama's 'Arab Spring'?," *Foreign Policy*, January 6, 2011, http://foreignpolicy.com/2011/01/06/obamas-arab-spring/. Some scholars, such as Joseph Massad, disparage these terms as a form of Western imperialism: Joseph Massad, "The 'Arab Spring' and Other American Seasons," *Al Jazeera*, August 29, 2012, http://www.aljazeera.com/indepth/opinion/2012/08/201282972539153865.html.

Contributors

SHEREEN ABOUELNAGA is a professor of English and comparative literature at Cairo University. She has published extensively in Arabic and English, with a special focus on gender. Her Arabic books include *A Passion of Difference: Readings in Selected Feminist Texts*, *Feminist or Women's?*, *Nation in the Narration of Arab Women Writers*, and *Intellectuals in the Transitional Phase*. Forthcoming in English is *Women in Revolutionary Egypt*.

ISMAIL ALEXANDRANI is a sociopolitical researcher, investigative journalist, award-winning writer, and human rights activist. In addition to his expertise in Egypt's extremities and Sinai affairs, he studies social and youth mobility, Islamist movements, and state-religion relations in Muslim-majority societies.

MAISSAA ALMUSTAFA is a doctoral candidate in the Global Governance Program at the Balsillie School of International Affairs, Waterloo, Ontario. Her broad research interests include refugee journeys in search of protection as a response to failing national and international protection policies.

SAHAR AZIZ is an associate professor at Texas A&M University School of Law. She serves on the board of the Egyptian American Rule of Law Association. Her scholarship focuses on the intersection of national security, civil rights, and American Muslims.

MOHAMAD HAMAS ELMASRY is an associate professor in the Media and Cultural Studies Program at the Doha Institute for Graduate Studies. He has published extensively on the Egyptian press system and is a political and media analyst, appearing regularly on international television news networks.

MOHAMMAD FADEL is an associate professor and Canada Research Chair for the Law and Economics of Islamic Law at the Faculty of Law of the University of Toronto, which he joined in January 2006. Professor Fadel was admitted to the New York State Bar Association in 2000 and practiced law with the firm of Sullivan and Cromwell in New York City, where he worked on a wide variety of corporate finance transactions and securities-related regulatory investigations. Professor Fadel has published numerous articles in Islamic legal history, Islam and liberalism, and post–January 25 Egypt.

BELAL FADL is a screenplay writer, journalist, and column writer at *Al-Shorouk* and *Almasry Alyoum*. Fadl is one of the few local journalists who participated in and supported the 2011 Egyptian revolution.

DALIA FAHMY is an assistant professor of political science at Long Island University and a member of the Egyptian Rule of Law Association. She has published several articles in academic journals focusing on democratization and most recently on the effects of Islamophobia on US foreign policy. Dr. Fahmy's current research examines the intellectual and political development of modern Islamist movements. She has been interviewed by various media outlets including MSNBC, CNN, and *Huffington Post*, and appears regularly on Al Jazeera.

ISAAC FRIESEN is a PhD student in the Near and Middle Eastern Civilizations Department at the University of Toronto. His research examines the politics of religion, sectarianism, and state-society relations in Egypt since the 1970s.

HESHAM GENIDY is currently a candidate for the doctor of juridical science at Indiana University Maurer School of Law. His research interests are focused on the intersection of law and political science, and his dissertation is about democracy and the rule of law in Egypt.

EID MOHAMED is an assistant professor in the Comparative Literature Program at Doha Institute for Graduate Studies and an adjunct assistant professor in the History Department at the University of Guelph. He is the author of *Arab Occidentalism: Images of America in the Middle East* (2015). His research focuses on the interplay of religion, culture, and politics in shaping relations between America and the Middle East.

BESSMA MOMANI is Professor in the Department of Political Science at the University of Waterloo and the Balsillie School of International Affairs in Canada. She is senior fellow at the Centre for International Governance and Innovation (CIGI), Brookings Institution in Doha, and 2015 Fellow of the Pierre Elliott Trudeau Foundation. She is author of *Arab Dawn: Arab Youth and the Demographic Dividend They Will Bring* (2015).

MAI MOGIB MOSAD is an assistant professor of political science at Cairo University. Her research focuses on state-religion relations, ethnic studies, and minorities in the Middle East. She is the author of *Copts between Inclusion and Exclusion* (2012) and coauthor of *The State Return: The Egyptian Political System after 2013* (2015).

MOHAMMED EL-NAWAWY is Charles A. Dana Professor of International Communication and Middle Eastern Studies in the Department of Political Science and Sociology at Queens University of Charlotte and Visiting Scholar in the Media and Cultural Studies Program at the Doha Institute for Graduate Studies.

DINA RASHED is a PhD candidate in the Political Science Department at the University of Chicago. Her research focuses on civil-military relations, state violence, policing, authoritarian regimes, and Middle East politics.

JUSTINE SALAM is a PhD candidate in the Global Governance Program at the Balsillie School of International Affairs, University of Waterloo, Ontario. She is interested in many aspects of Middle East politics, especially energy governance, federalism, and Kurdistan.

Index

Morsi, Mohammed (*cont.*)
33–34, 139; criticism of, 35, 139; overthrow of, 43, 91, 141, 171, 173; election of, 54, 88–89, 106, 122; military and, 54, 133, 137–140, 141, 142, 143; speech of, 73; SCAF and, 90; media and, 90, 118, 122–124, 174; Coptic Christians and, 105, 106, 107–108; police and, 161
Moyo, Dumisani, 126
Mubarak, Gamal, 50, 51, 157; military and, 51, 137
Mubarak, Hosni, 1, 4, 7, 8, 9, 10, 11, 12, 14, 23, 25, 41, 43, 47, 49, 50, 51, 53, 82, 92, 96, 104, 109, 113, 121, 139, 161; Coptic Christians and, 11, 95, 100–102, 112; resignation of, 28, 37, 76, 83, 84, 102, 165, 172; military and, 42–43, 133, 135, 136, 137, 138, 141, 142, 143; media and, 46, 80, 118, 119–120, 123, 124, 160; censorship by, 68; State Security Investigation Service and, 151; police and, 152–153, 155–156, 157, 158, 159, 160, 161, 163
Musa, Amr, 91
Muslim Brotherhood, 2–3, 7, 9, 10, 11, 12, 24, 26, 49, 76, 104, 109, 111, 162, 173, 174; protests against, 4; failings of, 23–25; 1948 ban of, 24; military and, 35, 137–140, 142–143; death penalties and, 39; arrests of, 39, 82; police and, 56, 159, 161, 162; intellectuals and, 65–66; and culture, 66–67, 68; political alliances, 77, 78; criticism of government, 78; earthquake of 1992 and, 78; elections and, 79–80, 86, 92, 122; committee participation and, 80–81; platform of, 82; the revolution and, 83; SCAF and, 84–89, 137; youth and, 85, 86; Islamic street movement and, 101; Coptic Christians and, 104, 105, 108, 113; suppression of, 175

El-Nadeem Center for Human Rights, 162
Nag Hammadi, 169
Nahda Party, 85
Nahda Square, 56, 161
Al Najjar, Abdul Wahab, 23
Nasser, Gamal Abdel, 42, 55, 119, 120, 133, 135, 136, 137, 141, 159
National Democratic Party, 44, 49, 50, 79, 80, 81
national identity. *See* identity
National Radio and Television Commission, 127
Nazif, Ahmed, 51
NDP. *See* National Democratic Party
New Woman's Foundation, the, 47
Nile: bombings in valley, 38, 167; river, 169–170; valley, 174
non-governmental organizations, 46–47

nongovernment professional associations, 46
Nour, Ayman, 91
Nour Party, 2, 86, 87, 90, 140
Nubian, 14, 172, 173; Nubian activists, 14, 171–173
Al Nukrashi, Mahmoud: assassination of, 24

Obama, Barack, 87, 141
Oddoul, Hagag, 172
O'Donnell, Guillermo, 110
Orabi, Ahmed, 18–19
Orabi Revolt, 18–19
Orfy marriages, 46

parliamentary elections. *See* elections
People's Assembly, 2, 78, 79, 82; dissolution of, 2; Mubarak and, 49
pluralism: political, 30–31, 85; ethnic, 172
police: violence and, 13, 45, 50, 55–56, 153, 154–155, 157, 160, 161, 162, 168; reform of, 14, 161, 162–163; authority of, 50–51, 151, 152; Muslim Brotherhood and, 56, 159, 161, 162
Police Club, 163
Police Day, 151, 157
Police Law, 156
political liberalism: implications of, 29
Port Said Stadium massacre, 161
presidential elections. *See* elections
protest: law, 37. *See also* January 25 Revolution

Al-Qaeda, 169
Qatar, 173, 174
Al-Qiddisayn Church, 161
Al-qunbela al-mawquta, 168

Rabaa Square, 161; killings in, 4, 141
Rafah, 167, 168, 169
Al Rafie, Abdul Rahman, 18
Raunig, Gerald: transversality and, 72
Rawls, John, 31, 34
referendum: constitutional, 3, 37, 52, 108; March 19, 30
Revolutionary legitimacy, 29
Rushdie, Salman, 67

Sadat, Anwar, 42, 77, 90, 113, 120; assassination of, 76, 119, 152; Coptic Christians and, 110; military and, 133, 135, 136, 142; police and, 159
Saeda, Hafez Abu, 158
Said, Edward, 64

www.ingramcontent.com/pod-product-compliance
Lightning Source LLC
Chambersburg PA
CBHW030843270326
41928CB00007B/1199